Praise for *The Long Crisis*

Rene E. Ofreneo, Ph.D.
Professor, University of the Philippines

The Long Crisis: Gloria Macapagal Arroyo and Philippine Underdevelopment, provides a masterful and vivid summation of the numerous corruption scandals that characterized Arroyo's Presidency. Fuller, a retired British trade unionist turned historian in his adopted Philippine homeland, has produced a seamless blow-by-blow recounting of how the culture of corruption literally flourished under the Arroyos' noses—in the bureaucracy, military establishment and even the Church.

...Fuller takes pains in providing the readers a short history course on Philippine underdevelopment and its root causes. Foremost among these is the absence of a nationalist development blueprint aimed at modernizing the economy in an inclusive and sustainable manner, on one hand, and the continuing efforts of external forces and neo-liberalizers to thwart such a program of national development, on the other.

...The beauty of Fuller's book is that it shows, clearly and unerringly, that the nation's struggle for growth and development cannot be reduced to a narrow anti-corruption drive focused on changing personalities without changing or altering a socio-economic system that perpetuates poverty, inequality, foreign domination and underdevelopment.

Rinaldo Francesca,
Liberation (UK)

The broader picture we are offered a glimpse of in Fuller's book, far from being an exercise in pointing the finger at yet another corrupt country in the developing world, is in fact a sad look at the inevitable consequences of colonialism—old and new—where a sovereign nation and its people are subordinate to the interests of a dominating superpower.

In fact, given the Philippines' history of foreign domination and exploitation by the US empire, the logical conclusion one can see underlying *The Long Crisis* is that, in a country where economic affairs are directed by foreign interests, such levels of corruption tend to inevitably become the natural order of things "like typhoons or landslides," in Fuller's words, ultimately blocking the political leadership from even considering a nationalist stance aimed at putting the interests of the Filipino people before all else.

Kenny Coyle,
Morning Star (UK)

The Long Crisis shows that the GMA years were the by-product of the continued failure to follow a path of national development and political independence. For anyone interested in the contemporary Philippines or the more general themes of imperialism and under-development in Southeast Asia this book is essential reading.

The Long Crisis

The Long Crisis

Gloria Macapagal Arroyo and
Philippine Underdevelopment

Ken Fuller

The Long Crisis: Gloria Macapagal Arroyo and Philippine Underdevelopment was first published as an e-book in 2013 by Flipside Publishing, Quezon City, Philippines.

CONTENTS

Preface to the Second Edition   1
Preface to the First Edition   3
1 Limited Patriotism   7
2 "Something will happen"   21
3 "Everything is for sale"   39
4 "More obedience to God"   71
5 "Insufficient in substance"   95
6 "A state of panic?"   105
7 "The cry of the people"   119
8 "A very well developed democracy"   143
9 "We are open to other arrangements"   173
10 "A step that cannot be bypassed   201
11 National development, truth and
    reconciliation   239
    Bibliography   265
    About the author   277

ABBREVIATIONS

AFP	Armed Forces of the Philippines
AHI	Amsterdam Holdings Inc.
APEC	Asia-Pacific Economic Cooperation
ARMM	Autonomous Region in Muslim Mindanao
ASEAN	Association of Southeast Asian Nations
BAYAN	Bagong Alyansang Makabayan (New Patriotic Alliance)
BIR	Bureau of Internal Revenue
BJE	Bangsamoro Juridical Entity
BMP	Bukluran ng Manggagawang Pilipino, or Struggle of Filipino Workers
CBA	Collective bargaining agreement
CBCP	Catholic Bishops' Conference of the Philippines
CHA-CHA	Charter change
CHR	Commission on Human Rights
CIA	Central Intelligence Agency
CoC	Certificate of canvass
Comelec	Commission on Elections
CPP	Communist Party of the Philippines
DILG	Department of the Interior and Local Government
DOLE	Department of Labor and Employment
DPWH	Department of Public Works and Highways
EDSA	Epifanio de los Angeles Avenue
EFF	Extended Fund Facility
EPIRA	Electrical Power Industry Reform Act
EPZ	Export Processing Zone
FPJM	Freedom, Peace and Justice Movement
FTA	Fair Trade Alliance
	Free trade agreement
GDP	Gross Domestic Product
GNP	Gross National Product
GO	Genuine Opposition
Hukbalahap	Hukbong Bayan Laban sa Hapon (People's Anti-Japanese Army)
IMF	International Monetary Fund
IMPSA	Industrias Metallurgicas Perscarmona Sociedad Anonimo
JPEPA	Japan-Philippines Economic Partnership Agreement
JUSMAG	Joint US Military Assistance Group
KAMPI	Kabalikat ng Malayang Pilipino (Partner of the Free Filipino)

KMP	Kilusang Magbubukid ng Pilipinas (Peasant Movement of the Philippines)
KMU	Kilusang Mayo Union (May First Movement)
KNP	Koalisyon ng Nagkakaisang Pilipino (Coalition of United Filipinos)
Lakas-CMD	Lakas ng Tao [People Power]-Christian Muslim Democrats
LDP	Laban ng Demokratikong Pilipino (Struggle of the Democratic Filipino)
LFS	Labor Force Survey
LTA	Lourdes Tuazon Arroyo
MAN	Movement for the Advancement of Nationalism
Meralco	Manila Electric Company
MILF	Moro Islamic Liberation Front
MKP	Makabansang Kawal ng Pilipinas (Patriotic Army of the Philippines)
MSLA	Mutual logistics and support agreement
MWSS	Metropolitan Waterworks and Sewerage System
NAMFREL	National Movement for Free Elections, later National Citizens Movement for Free Elections
NBI	National Bureau of Investigation
NBN	National Broadband Network
NBP	New Bilibid Prison
NDF	National Democratic Front
NEDA	National Economic Development Authority
NPA	New Peoples Army
NSCB	National Statistical Coordination Board
OFW	Overseas Filipino worker
PC	Philippine Constabulary
PCCI	Philippine Chamber of Commerce and Industry
PCGG	Presidential Commission on Good Government
PCIJ	Philippine Center for Investigative Journalism
PKP	Partido Komunista ng Pilipinas (Philippine Communist Party)
PNP	Philippine National Police
RAM	Reform the Armed Forces Movement
SWS	Social Weather Stations
TUCP	Trade Union Congress of the Philippines
TNC	Transnational corporation
TU	Team Unity
USAID	US Agency for International Development
VFA	Visiting Forces Agreement
WTO	World Trade Organization
YOU	Young Officers' Union
YOUNG	Young Officers' Union of the New Generation
ZTE	Zhongxing Telecommunication Equipment

PREFACE TO THE SECOND EDITION

The publication history of *The Long Crisis* has not been problem-free. In 2012, I submitted the manuscript to Flipside Publishing, the e-publisher based in Quezon City, and was greatly cheered by the enthusiastic reception it received. The company found "its narrativization and analysis of the social ills exemplified by the Arroyo regime insightful and thoroughly engaging, and [we] like the way it's written: scholarly but not stodgy, political but not preachy. To wit: we are very enthusiastic about publishing this work."

Wow.

However…

The e-book was duly published in April 2013 and immediately faced two problems. First of all, there were few reviews in the Philippines (and, indeed, few Philippine publications—least of all newspapers—have regular book review pages); and, secondly, the e-book market in the Philippines appears to be pitifully small.

Indeed, Flipside Publishing itself seemed to arrive at this very conclusion, as in 2016 it advised its authors that it was waving the white flag. All was not lost, however, as the parent company, Flipside Digital Content (FDC), would assume responsibility for the existing catalogue. That lasted until May 2019, when FDC advised authors that it, too, was withdrawing from the business.

Since *The Long Crisis* first appeared, a number of potential readers have asked me whether there were plans to publish the book in print form. At one stage, I tried to interest University of the Philippine Press, which was then two-thirds of the way through its publication of my three-volume history of the Philippine left, but its reviewers decided not to recommend publication due to the book's reliance on secondary sources and the absence of any interviews with the Arroyos. In other words, while Flipside Publishing had found the book "scholarly but not stodgy," UP Press thought that it was not academic enough. Well, guys, it was never intended to be that kind of book. Which is why, I suppose, it was a mistake to submit it to UP Press.

Apart from contacting F. Sionil Jose, who advised that his Solidaridad company now only publishes his own output, I took no further step towards print publication. But now, with the e-book no longer available, it seems that the time has come. So here it is.

Since the initial publication of the e-book, of course, there have been two presidential elections in the Philippines. Benigno "Noynoy" Aquino III has come and gone, and we are now halfway through the term of Rodrigo Duterte. The obvious question presented itself: should *The Long Crisis* be updated for print publication? I decided against this for two reasons: the book is, after all, very largely an account of the presidency of Gloria Macapagal Arroyo; it also demonstrates that the crises and scandals which occurred during her presidency had their roots in a dysfunctional economy and a failure to break decisively with the colonial past. These latter problems have still not been tackled in a determined fashion and thus, it seems to me, the analysis put forward in *The Long Crisis* is still valid.

Ken Fuller,
July, 2019.

PREFACE TO THE FIRST EDITION

The following book, which focuses on the presidency of Gloria Macapagal Arroyo (2001-2010), has not had a straightforward gestation. The first draft, completed as early as 2004, intended to tell the story of a leader who, having ascended to the Philippine presidency by dubious means, thereafter attracted numerous allegations of corruption and electoral malpractice and was, as a result, rejected at the polls in that very year. But Mrs. Arroyo survived the 2004 elections—by, once again, questionable means. The book was therefore expanded and might have been terminated at any of several points in the following six years—as Arroyo was swept aside by a tidal wave of national outrage as further evidence of electoral malpractice emerged in 2005; as she was convicted by an impeachment court in that or any of the next three years; as rebel members of the military joined with civilians to oust her from office. But Mrs. Arroyo survived all these threats and simply bowed out at the end of her term in 2010. Clearly, the book would not have the fall of a president as its denouement.

Of course, Mrs. Arroyo did not "simply bow out" in 2010, but got herself elected as a member of Congress in her home province of Pampanga. And a fall, of a kind, is still a possibility, as at the time of writing a number of charges have been filed against her and her husband (something not possible until now except by impeachment, due to her presidential immunity), and after being released on bail concerning the charge that she intervened in the senatorial elections of 2007 she is now, having been charged with plunder, under hospital arrest once more.

In a sense, Mrs. Arroyo's alleged wrongdoings and the attempts to dislodge her were a distraction. Her presidency must be seen (at least in part) as a product rather than the cause of the fundamental problems confronting the Philippines, and during those nine-and-a-half years people and parties who had earlier declared their commitment to fundamental change found themselves concentrating on their attempts to overthrow a president to such an extent that the task of laying the groundwork for that change was almost totally neglected. Where were the attempts to build an understanding of the nature of imperialism in the popular consciousness? What efforts were made to forge a broad nationalist movement during these years? As, at the end of the day, the president in question was *not* toppled, it might not be too harsh to say that a decade had been wasted.

My original intentions for this book may be said to have suffered from the same problem, and therefore the volume you have before you is rather different from that originally intended, focusing now not merely on the headline-grabbing events of those years—which, no matter how much of a distraction they may have been, certainly cannot be ignored—but also on their deeper causes and the path required to overcome them.

*

The first two, relatively brief, chapters of this book provide the background from which the Arroyo presidency emerged, the first providing a short sketch of Philippine history to the late twentieth century, emphasizing the role of the USA both during and after its colonial regime, the second dealing with the abbreviated presidency of Joseph Estrada.

The long crisis of the Arroyo years has value in that it provides illustrations of the symptoms of the deeper sickness. The following six chapters therefore discuss corruption, the alleged malpractices during the 2004 presidential election, Mrs. Arroyo's survival of annual attempts to impeach her, the failed attempt by military rebels to dislodge her and the brief state of emergency to which this led in 2006, the outrageously dishonest attempts to change the Constitution in order to protect Mrs. Arroyo from civil prosecution, and, as an example of the extent to which the political culture has degenerated, the midterm elections of 2007.

These were the issues which screamed from the headlines for much of the Arroyo decade, monopolizing the attention of politicians and activists. The two elephants in the room were perfectly happy that this should be so. The much longer and more fundamental crisis which afflicts the Philippines has its roots in the suffocating colonial and neo-colonial influence of the USA, and a dysfunctional economic model that has denied the country the fruits of development. True, the US elephant was not totally ignored, as we will see in chapter 9, but outside of the left the basic relationship (as opposed to elements of it, like the Visiting Forces Agreement) went unchallenged. The economic elephant, on the other hand, was hardly ever submitted to examination, the increasing flow of remittances from overseas Filipino workers serving to conceal the fact that this was a very sick animal, and thus chapter 10 deals with this in some detail.

The final chapter further develops some of the points discussed earlier in the book, relating them to this "real long crisis" and discussing how the legacy of the past might be overcome by the development of a broad nationalist movement determined to take the country down the path of genuine development.

Some of the material in this book has previously appeared in a somewhat different form in my commentaries for *BusinessWorld* and my *Daily Tribune* column in Manila, and articles for the *Morning Star* and *Tribune* in London.

Thanks are due to Roger Posadas at the University of the Philippines for taking the time to read and comment upon the book's final chapter. As always, any unintentional errors of fact or interpretation must be laid at my door.

Ken Fuller,
October 2012.

1 LIMITED PATRIOTISM

There was a time, of course, when the word "Philippines" (or, in the Spanish, "Filipinas") was unknown. Then, the archipelago was a scattering of communities and language groups with few common bonds apart from Islam (which had spread throughout the south and was beginning to make its way northwards) and the trade, good fellowship and occasional raiding party often found with close neighbors. The first European contact was not a happy one. The Portuguese Ferdinand Magellan, employed by Spain, "discovered" the archipelago in 1521, but when, traveling through the Visayas, he sought to lord it over the people of Mactan, he was killed by the chieftain Lapulapu and his men put to flight.

Having given the archipelago the name of a Spanish prince in 1542, it was 1565 before the Spanish returned in earnest, this time under the command of Miguel Lopez de Legazpi, thus commencing over 300 years of Spanish rule. The most determined resistance to the invaders came in the southern island of Mindanao and the Sulu archipelago, due to the unifying effect of Islam. Elsewhere, sword in one hand and Bible in the other, the Spanish conquered, following which they ruled by taking advantage of the islanders' low level of cultural cohesion to inscribe Christian "values" on their minds: obedience and diligence earned rewards in the hereafter, while rebellion invited hellfire and eternal damnation. And, despite the consequent depredations of the friars and the isolated rebellions to which these gave rise, the locals believed it, and so for much of their three-century rule the Spanish were able to maintain order with priests rather than soldiers, the former usually outnumbering the latter until the Revolution of 1896. The Spanish introduced feudal practices that survive in modified form to this day. As just one of numerous examples, many positions in the colonial administration were simply sold to the highest bidder, thus ensuring they went to Spaniards of limited ability and vision, whose priority was to recoup their initial investments and then make handsome profits. Bureaucratic accumulation is of colonial parentage.

The opening of the Suez Canal in the 19th century greatly shortened the journey time between east and west, and this, along with the Spanish decision to relax restrictions on foreign trade and investment, opened the islands to new influences. At the same time, the more rapid development of communications between the various parts of the archipelago made it possible to think on a country-wide scale, and for the people to conceive of themselves as Filipinos rather than, for example, Tagalogs, Cebuanos, Ilocanos or Pampangos. This budding national consciousness was articulated by the ilustrados ("enlightened ones"), sons of the local elite educated in Europe, where they had been exposed to a host of new ideas. Most ilustrados were, however, not revolutionaries. While their further development, individually and as a class, required concessions from Spain, they were not so much anti-Spanish as desirous of being considered Spanish themselves. For them, a degree of local autonomy and representation in the Spanish Cortes would have been — for a time, anyway — sufficient. Foolishly, from its own point of view, Spain refused to concede this.

Thus it was that the more proletarian Andres Bonifacio[1] found himself at the helm of the Revolution of 1896, the aim of which was independence. When it appeared that the Revolution had a following, ilustrado elements joined its ranks, and it was in their interest that Bonifacio was murdered and Emilio Aguinaldo installed as leader. After initial successes, the revolutionary forces were stalemated, leading to the conclusion of a peace agreement and Aguinaldo's brief exile in Hong Kong.

*

Meanwhile, the USA was looking for new sources of trade and investment, and the possessions of Spain, Europe's weakest colonial power, looked easy pickings. The Spanish-American War ensued. When the Americans offered to assist Aguinaldo in achieving independence, he entered an alliance with them, and on May 1, 1898, the fleet of Commodore George Dewey (promotion to the rank of Rear Admiral came nine days later) put paid to Spanish naval power in Manila Bay, following which Manila was besieged. However, while the revived Philippine Revolution threw off Spanish rule in the rest of the country, the Americans, stalling until the arrival of reinforcements, agreed with the Spanish governor-general that Filipino troops would not enter the capital, and that it would be the US forces that accepted the Spanish surrender after a token battle. Following negotiations in Paris between the two main belligerents, the USA agreed to pay Spain $20 million for the Philippines, which was seen as a springboard to market opportunities in China. However, the graduation of the USA to the status of colonial power required the consent of its Congress, and this was far from guaranteed. An "incident" between US and Filipino troops was therefore contrived, leading to the outbreak of the Philippine-American War. As a few more congressmen rallied to the flag, the motion to acquire the Philippines scraped through.

Directly and indirectly, the war caused the deaths of almost 600,000 on the northern island of Luzon alone.[2] Methods previously used in the "Indian wars" at home were now used in the Philippines (several of the same generals were involved), along with techniques later employed in Vietnam.

Thereafter, however, the USA proved to be a more astute colonizer than Spain, co-opting the local elite and holding out the prospect of eventual independence. As the revolution had appeared to be on the brink of success, the ilustrados had climbed aboard, but with the outbreak of war with the Americans, they disembarked again, preferring lives and careers of privilege under a new colonizer to taking their chances in a regime led by rough revolutionary veterans. They provided the personnel for the colonial administration and, of course, the business leaders among them took advantage of the opportunities brought by the American regime. Where Spain had used Catholicism for the purposes of social control, the USA used education. Except for the children of the elite, Spain had hardly made provision for education at all, but now the first batch of teachers arrived from the USA aboard the USS Thomas to inscribe American values on the consciousness of the young. Henceforth, the language of tuition and the civil service would be English. The political institutions were, when allowed, modeled on those pertaining in Washington, DC—and this, after the Marcos interregnum, remains so. American enlightenment did not, however, extend to the economy: after a ten-year period during which Spain retained trade privileges, the Philippines would export raw materials to the USA and receive in return American manufactured goods—an arrangement that effectively prevented any Philippine attempt at industrialization.

While officially the US regime combated corruption, in reality its officials and policemen often contributed to it, and by declaring the numbers game jueteng (along with opium and prostitution) illegal the colonial government in effect laid the basis for the development of a large criminal underground and police corruption, and thereby facilitating the buying of elections. In 1930, two years after Mariano Pidal Arroyo had been elected governor of Iloilo, a judge found that he had been receiving illegal gambling payoffs in order to "cover anticipated election expenses." Arroyo was dismissed by the governor-general, whereupon the family sank into political obscurity until Arroyo's grand-nephew married Gloria Macapagal in 1968.[3]

In the mid-1930s, the advent of "Commonwealth" status gave the Philippines internal self-government (i.e. defense and foreign relations excepted), with the promise of independence ten years later. The Japanese wartime regime, while it attempted (very largely unsuccessfully) to wean Filipinos away from American influences, at the same time was intent upon the country becoming a part of its "Greater East Asia Co-Prosperity Sphere," effectively as a colony. Just as had been the case at the end of the 19th century, the USA, under the leadership of General Douglas MacArthur (who, like many members of his staff, had a long association with, and business interests in, the Philippines) ensured that "liberation" would be delivered by US forces rather than by Filipinos, thus ensuring that the country remained a haven for US investment and a bastion of anti-communism.

*

The US period left the Philippines with an economy that was heavily dependent upon the former colonial power. In a paradox more apparent than real, after "independence" in 1946 this dependence was strengthened by a treaty giving US investors "parity rights." The USA continued to dictate economic and foreign policy, although in the 1960s the former task was outsourced to the International Monetary Fund and the World Bank, the "Bretton Woods twins" — which were, of course, dominated by the USA. The new republic was further tied to Washington by military treaties, including the Military Bases Agreement which allocated vast areas to US military control. While in 1991 the Philippine Senate ensured that the bases agreement came to an end, other agreements such as the Mutual Defense Treaty remain.

The Bretton Woods prescription has given the Philippines an economy that to a very large extent has absolutely nothing to do with the needs of the Philippine people. The needs served are those of transnational corporations (TNCs) which, accommodated in export processing zones (EPZs or "ecozones"), are provided with tax-breaks and an abundance of cheap labor. This is sometimes referred to as "enclave development," as the EPZs have little connection either to each other or to the real Philippine economy. For decades now, the focus has been on "export-orientation" (largely the manufacture or assembly of electronics and garments), although the very nature of the model means that the Philippines only rarely achieves a balance of trade surplus: components are imported, the amount of local value-added is low, and profits are expatriated. Some TNCs do not even bring money into the country in the first place, raising the funds for their "investment" on the local market and, thus, crowding out local business borrowers at the same time. Since the Philippines joined the World Trade Organization during the presidency of Fidel Ramos (1992-1998), cheap imports have clobbered local industry. Programs by the IMF, World Bank and the Asian Development Bank are dependent upon foreign debt, and while the level of that debt was one of the major criticisms of the regime of Ferdinand Marcos (1966-86), it has since more than doubled.

*

Successive leaders of the "independent" Philippines have faced a common dilemma. As the economic affairs of the country have been directed by foreign interests, one of the few levers of influence available to them has been that of patronage, and so the persistence of graft and corruption should not, perhaps, surprise us. Quite possibly, many political leaders in the past six decades have come to view the subaltern role of the Philippines and many of the evils flowing therefrom as unalterable if unfortunate facts of life, like typhoons or landslides. For them to consider taking a nationalist stance, putting the interests of the Filipino people before all else, would be to think the unthinkable, almost like challenging the natural order. The few who have contemplated mounting a challenge to the status quo have been only too aware of the consequences—not only the prospect of firm opposition from Washington, but also the realization that, to be successful, such a challenge must entail the mobilization of popular support and (horrors!) participation, and many modern-day ilustrados still share the apprehension of the masa which limited the patriotism of their forebears. This being the case, how can we be surprised if many have chosen to coast along, never seeking to change that which appears unchangeable and, if the interests of the population appear impossible to satisfy, looking after their own?

Manuel Roxas, widely suspected of having been a leading collaborator during the Japanese occupation, was General Douglas MacArthur's candidate for president. It was his regime which launched an offensive against the Hukbalahap (the former wartime guerrillas led by the Partido Komunista ng Pilipinas, or PKP) in Central Luzon, leading to what became known as the "Huk Rebellion," a conflict lasting until the mid-1950s. He also ensured the adoption of the Bell Trade Act and the constitutional amendment required to allow its grant of "parity rights" to US investors.

When Roxas died of a heart attack (ironically while visiting a US military base), he was succeeded by Elpidio Quirino, whose administration was plagued with allegations of corruption. No less than the president's own nephew Carlos Quirino would later record a discussion during which Senate president Jose Avelino, harried by investigations into corruption, blurted out to the president: "If you cannot permit abuses, you must at least tolerate them. What are we in power for? We are not hypocrites. Why should we pretend to be saints when in reality we are not?"[4] To his credit, however, it was the Quirino administration that, in combating a balance of payments crisis, imposed exchange controls in 1949 (a move tolerated by Washington on the understanding that this was a temporary arrangement and that US companies setting up shop in the Philippines would also be protected by the high tariffs).[5]

By this time, the USA (and in particular CIA officer Col. Edward Lansdale, whose plan was to turn the Philippines into a "showcase for democracy" which could intervene in Asia on behalf of US policy objectives), had begun to groom Ramon Magsaysay as a future leader, first ensuring he was installed as defense secretary then, on the basis of his prosecution of the anti-Huk campaign and his strong stand against corruption, boosting his popularity to an extent that there could be no doubt that Magsaysay was the "American boy."[6] He defeated Quirino at the polls in 1953, assisted by US money and the National Movement for Free Elections, established in 1951 by the CIA (which also, according to Ralph G. Lovett, chief of its Manila station, drugged Quirino before he was due to deliver a campaign speech[7]). Moreover, the anti-corruption drive was intended as little more than a psy-war device[8] in the campaign against the Huk rebels, the implication being that once the rebellion was defeated it could be allowed to run down.

When Magsaysay died in an air crash in 1957, he was succeeded by Carlos P. Garcia, who, with his "Filipino First" campaign, proved to be something of a nationalist. This was not to the liking of Washington, which was also concerned by the significant influence of the strongly nationalist Claro M. Recto within the Garcia administration. Furthermore, the USA demanded that exchange controls now be lifted, as, in the words of its National Security Council, "The Philippines is increasingly utilizing exchange controls for protection of local manufacturers as its industrialization program progresses...The obligation under the Revised Trade Agreement for the Philippines to consult with the US prior to the institution of trade restrictions has so far been disregarded, despite our formal protests..."[9] Garcia's offer to institute gradual decontrol being deemed insufficient, Washington supported Diosdado Macapagal in the 1961 elections, in which the main issue was ostensibly Garcia's corruption (although in fact he lived quite modestly). The "new coalition we started working on after November 1959," a self-satisfied Joseph B. Smith of the CIA would later write, "swept the elections."[10]

Aside from fathering the child who would later become Gloria Macapagal Arroyo, Macapagal is noteworthy for the fact that it was he who in 1962 lifted exchange controls and entered into the Philippines' first agreement with the International Monetary Fund, thereby effectively scuppering the country's modest attempts at industrialization. For decades hence, Philippine economic policy would be decided by the Bretton Woods twins and Filipino "technocrats" trained at the IMF and World Bank Institutes in Washington. Paradoxically, early in his presidency, Macapagal also flirted with left and nationalist forces, declaring his commitment to the "unfinished revolution" of 1896. While Washington found it easy enough to dissuade him from such a course, he had demonstrated his unreliability, and therefore in the elections of 1965 its support was given to Ferdinand Marcos.

If, with the possible exception of Garcia, the foregoing sequence of presidents is seen as a smooth continuum in which each administration acted out its role as directed by Washington, providing a secure location for US investments at the expense of the Philippines' own economic development, and faithfully supporting US foreign policy, we hit a sizeable bump when we get to Marcos. In his first term, he seemed to conform to type, sending troops to Vietnam (albeit engineers, which he withdrew after popular protests) and hosting a summit conference on the conflict in that country at which President Lyndon Johnson memorably referred to him as "my boy."[11]

Late in his first term, however, Marcos caused dismay in imperialist circles by discussing the possibility of relations with the socialist countries and criticizing the manner in which US corporations raised their finances on the local market rather than importing their own capital. Then again, in 1969 he signed into law House Joint Resolution No. 2, the "Magna Carta for Social Justice and Economic Freedom" which, prominent nationalist Alejandro Lichauco would recall, "embraced the entire range of the nation's political economy, including its foreign relations; it demanded an end of parity, the Filipinization of the economy and called for an independent foreign policy."[12] In an episode that neatly summarized the conundrum that was Ferdinand Marcos, the Magna Carta fell victim to his own profligacy, as he bought his way to victory in the 1969 elections to such an extent that the peso was rendered vulnerable, forcing him to concede the World Bank demand for devaluation and therefore for all practical purposes sinking the nationalist blueprint.[13]

Marcos was not, as is often alleged, merely a compliant puppet. Amid rumors of an assassination plot in 1971, for example, he insisted that the entire CIA team be recalled. In his state of the nation address that same year, he spoke in terms of a "democratic revolution" (his thoughts on this subject appeared as a book that year[14]) and proposed several reforms of a nationalist, interventionist nature.

By this stage, a Maoist insurgency was underway, led by the Communist Party of the

Philippines (CPP), a 1968 breakaway from the PKP, and in September 1972 Marcos, using inflated estimates of the strength of the New People's Army (NPA), the CPP's armed wing, declared martial law.

It was obviously the case that the martial law regime curtailed civil liberties and led to a significant number of deaths, particularly of those thought to be Maoists or sympathetic to the Maoist cause, and a fierce war was waged against Moro National Liberation Movement insurgents in Mindanao.[15] But Marcos also took a number of initiatives indicative of a desire for a greater degree of independence than any of his predecessors had enjoyed. Relations with the Soviet Union, China and the other socialist countries were established, and foreign policy no longer slavishly tailed that of the USA. For all its shortcomings, the Marcos agrarian reform was more thoroughgoing than its predecessors. From time to time, he would speak of bold plans for industrialization, for example announcing eleven projects in 1979 which, had they all been implemented, would have constituted a significant step in genuine development.

But the World Bank not only torpedoed most of the industrialization projects but undertook a stealthy operation to effectively bypass Marcos[16] and enlist the Philippines as a guinea pig for one of its first structural adjustment programs, further reorienting the economy toward exports; effectively placing the economy at the service of transnational corporations this, as elsewhere in the Third World, proved disastrous. By this time, corruption had mushroomed and it was this issue that, as critics and opponents at home and abroad took aim at the "crony capitalists" surrounding Marcos, was used to undermine his credibility. Some who utilized this issue were in fact motivated by other concerns—foreign capital by the inroads the cronies were making into industries the former considered its own domain, the Catholic Church by Marcos's occasional expressions of interest in taxing some of its activities, for example.

If Marcos was sincerely interested in using his "New Society" regime (martial law was formally lifted in January 1981, although aspects of it were retained) to usher in genuine development, he failed due to the fact that he too readily submitted to the prescriptions issued by the Bretton Woods twins and, more fundamentally, did not popularize his vision and mobilize significant sections of the population behind it. Thus, when his opponent Benigno Aquino Jr. was assassinated in August 1983—an act for which responsibility has still not been conclusively established—Marcos found himself isolated, as opposition not only developed but took to the streets. When he called a "snap" election for February 1986, Aquino's widow ran against him and, with both camps claiming victory, a combination of a limited military rebellion, a "people power" demonstration organized by the church, and the withdrawal of support by Washington resulted in Marcos being helicoptered from the presidential palace and then flown to Hawaii.

Corazon Aquino's accession to the presidency amounted to a restoration of sorts, and the Philippines saw a return of the elite democracy which had held sway before the declaration of martial law. Mrs. Aquino swiftly abandoned many of the progressive policies she had promised to introduce before the election. Having initially said that the US military bases treaty would not be renewed, she first adopted a "wait and see" attitude and then, towards the end of her presidency, was reduced to campaigning to undermine the Senate decision to close the bases.

Rather than embarking upon the nationalist economic strategy indicated in the document adopted by the political grouping of which she had been a member in December 1984, Mrs. Aquino let loose the Bretton Woods twin upon the economy, adopting their prescriptions unquestioningly. The task of formulating a new agrarian reform program was handed to the new Congress, where the landlords ensured that it would be less than the situation demanded—and her own family's vast Hacienda Luisita was allowed to adopt a "stock distribution" scheme instead of dividing the land among the farmers. Having initially favored the legalization of the CPP, within a year or so of taking office Mrs. Aquino was giving encouragement to anti-communist vigilantes.

The Aquino regime was plagued with a series of coup attempts, sometimes by Marcos loyalists, sometimes by the Reform the Armed Forces Movement which had staged the mutiny against Marcos in February 1986 and, in December 1989, by both tendencies combined. Having been acting head of the armed forces under Marcos and then Aquino's defense secretary, her successor would not have that problem.

Fidel V. Ramos was the great globalizer. It was during his tenure that the World Trade Organization (WTO) came into being and the Philippines, promised prosperity and a rate of job creation never before seen, signed up to it. Whereas Marcos had occasionally dragged his feet over the implementation of IMF and World Bank programs, particularly when national or particular interests were threatened, and Aquino had simply allowed the Twins free rein, Ramos took their prescriptions, assembled them into a program which was ostensibly his own, and called it Philippines 2000—the latter year being the point at which the Philippines would achieve the status, it was promised, of newly-industrialized nationhood.

Not only did WTO liberalizing requirements hold no terrors for Ramos, but he was ahead of the game, reducing tariffs more than was strictly required. While lip service was paid to the pioneering efforts of the "Asian tigers," Ramos and his economic team lost sight of the fact that those countries had developed by conferring sweeping interventionist powers on the state in order to build integrated industries. To become newly-industrialized countries, in other words, *they had industrialized.* There were no such plans in the Philippines, merely the expansion of the "enclave development" serving the interests of TNCs. The loss of revenue occasioned by the lower-than-necessary tariffs and reduction of the tax-base resulting from the elimination or shrinking of domestic firms by cheap imports was compensated during Ramos's term by the proceeds from aggressive privatization. But when there was little left to privatize budget deficits would become the order of the day, leading to more foreign borrowing. And the Asian financial crisis of 1997 revealed the fragility of the whole structure.

Only the presidency of Joseph Estrada separates those of Ramos and Gloria Macapagal Arroyo. As the Arroyo years cannot be fully understood without a brief consideration of the two-and-half years that preceded her entry into Malacañang palace, the Estrada period deserves its own chapter.

NOTES

1. Doubts have been thrown on the class origins of the "Great Plebeian," as Bonifacio is
   called. For example, Jonathan Fast and Jim Richardson argue that he "occupied a
   position closer to the center of the social pyramid than to its base, closer to the petty
   bourgeoisie than the proletariat." See *Roots of Dependency* (Quezon City: Foundation
   for Nationalist Studies, 1987), 70. Although his father had been a tailor and held public
   office for a time in Tondo, a working class area of Manila, Bonifacio himself was a

maker of canes and fans, a messenger, a salesman and a warehouseman, a progression which would seem to the current writer to place him in the ranks of the emerging working class.

2. This was the estimate of none other than General Franklin Bell. See William Pomeroy, *American neo-colonialism: Its Emergence in the Philippines and Asia*, (New York, International Publishers, 1970), 96.

3. Alfred W. McCoy, *Policing America's Empire: The United States, the Philippines, and the Rise of the Surveillance State* (Quezon City: Ateneo de Manila University Press, 2011), 352-354

4. Carlos Quirino, *Apo Lakay* (Makati: Total Book World, 1987), 119-120, quoted in Lewis E. Gleeck Jr., *The Third Philippine Republic, 1946-1972* (Quezon City: New Day, 1993), 88.

5. Temario C. Rivera, *Landlords & Capitalists: Class, Family, and State in Philippine Manufacturing*, Quezon City, 1994, p. 114, citing Sylvia Maxfield and James H. Nolt, "Protectionism and the Internationalisation of Capital: US Sponsorship of Import-Substitution Industrialisation in the Philippines, Turkey and Argentina", *International Studies Quarterly*, No. 34, 1990, 49-81.

6. According to one source, Lansdale and his subordinate Charles Bohannon "characterized Magsaysay as a superstitious, malleable pawn of their own creation." Michael McLintock, *Instruments of Statecraft: US Guerrilla Warfare, Counterinsurgency and Counterterrorism, 1940-1990* (New York: Pantheon Books, 1992), Chapter 4. The whole text is available on www.statecraft.org.

7. Ibid.

8. Uldarico S. Baclagon, *Lessons from the Huk Campaign in the Philippines*, (Manila: M. Colcol & Company, 1960), 180.

9. NSC Operations Coordinating Board, August 21, 1957, in Nick Culather (ed.), *Managing Nationalism: United States National Security Council Documents on the Philippines, 1953-1960* (Quezon City: New Day Publishers, 1992), 100.

10. Joseph B. Smith, *Portrait of a Cold Warrior* (Quezon City: Plaridel Books, 1987), 320.

11. *Manila Daily Bulletin*, October 28, 1966, quoted in Hernando J. Abaya, *The Untold*

Philippine Story, Quezon City, 1967, 314.

12. A. Lichauco, "The International Economic Order and the Philippine Experience," Vivencio R. Jose, ed., *Mortgaging the Future: The World Bank and IMF in the Philippines*, (Quezon City: Foundation for Nationalist Studies, 1982), 44.

13. When the first edition of this book was published, the full text of the Magna Carta was available on www.sundalo.bravehost.com/Magna Carta of Social Justice and Economic Freedom.htm, but the site no longer exists. In "The Ideology of Joint Resolution No. 2" which precedes this, Emmanuel Q. Yap claims that Marcos came under heavy pressure to let the document gather dust, and that its champion, Jose B. Laurel Jr., was toppled as House Speaker due to his continuing commitment to its implementation.

14. Ferdinand E. Marcos: *Today's Revolution: Democracy* (Manila: n.p., 1971). While the thoughts may have been Marcos's, the writing was Adrian Cristobal's. See Francisco Tatad, "Remembering Adrian Cristobal (February 20, 1932-December 22, 2007)," franciscotatad.blogspot.com, December 28, 2007.

15. In September 2011, Walden Bello and Kaka Bag-ao of Akbayan filed a resolution in the House of Representatives condemning the Marcos atrocities. They say that his martial-law regime was "responsible for 3,257 murders, 35,000 torture cases and 70,000 incarcerations." (*Manila Times*, September 23, 2011.) This may be compared to the toll in Chile where, at US instigation, the coup of General Augusto Pinochet launched a year after Marcos's declaration of martial law, resulted in 30,000 deaths.

16. For a fascinating account of how this was achieved, see Robin Broad, *Unequal Alliance, 1979-1986: The World Bank, the International Monetary Fund, and the Philippines* (Quezon City: Ateneo de Manila Press, 1988).

2 "SOMETHING WILL HAPPEN"

Gloria Macapagal Arroyo was the second Philippine president to achieve office by the toppling of a predecessor. Many Filipinos regard the ousting of Ferdinand Marcos in 1986 as legitimate for, even leaving aside the dictatorial aspects of Marcos's rule, it was said (and a large proportion of the population believed it, although it was never conclusively proven) that he had cheated in the "snap" election of February 1986 and that Corazon Aquino had won. Such was not the case in January 2001, when substantially the same forces were mobilized to eject a president who had been elected with the largest majority in Philippine electoral history less than three years earlier, and who had neither resigned nor been convicted by an impeachment court. Regardless of what the Supreme Court might say, the ouster of Estrada was widely perceived as illegitimate and significant forces within the country demanded redress. Unlike Marcos, Estrada remained in the Philippines and, although under house arrest during his marathon plunder trial, his presence was a constant factor in Philippine political life throughout the Arroyo presidency.

*

In August 1998, just weeks after Estrada had taken office, Pedro "Ka Pete" Baguisa, general secretary of the Partido Komunista ng Pilipinas (PKP-1930), was asked about the prospects of the "pro-poor" president. He thought for a moment and then said: "Something will happen."[1]

21

Joseph Estrada, president of the Philippines from June 30, 1998 to January 20, 2001, was a former movie star. He had been in politics for three decades, having been the mayor of San Juan, Metro Manila for many years, then senator and vice-president, but his many critics chose to concentrate on the earlier phase of his career-path. How could a mere action hero be president of Asia's first republic? Also held against him was the fact that he was close to the family of the late President Ferdinand Marcos and businessmen who, like Eduardo "Danding" Cojuangco, had been members of the economic grouping around Marcos (the label "cronies" captures only one aspect of the phenomenon). He was, in addition, known to be partial to a drink and to be an unashamed womanizer, having publicly acknowledged several long-time mistresses and supported his children by them. He was one of the boys, his nickname "Erap" (said to have been coined by his friend and fellow movie idol Fernando Poe Jr.) being a reversal of *pare*, meaning "buddy." Criticized for his allegedly poor command of English, he convulsed election meetings by joking in Tagalog that he had met the leaders of Japan and South Korea and—surprise, surprise!—they spoke even less English than he did. (There was more than mere flippancy here: Estrada was tickling a nationalist nerve in people upon whom the English language had been imposed at school.) The masses idolized him, and theirs was the audience to which he played in the presidential campaign with his pro-poor platform under the slogan "Erap para sa Mahirap!" ("Erap for the Poor!"). They rewarded him with a landslide victory.

Even before polling day, the elite bared its fangs and savaged him. "Anyone but Erap!" snapped Cardinal Jaime Sin, Archbishop of Manila, and the *Philippine Daily Inquirer* ran the words as its headline. Once he was in office, there was one accusation after another. How much was being spent on the refurbishment of the kitchen in the guesthouse of Malacañang, the presidential palace? Estrada invited reporters to see the kitchen. How much was being wasted on refurbishing the presidential yacht? Estrada explained that his friends were meeting the cost.

There was, in all of this, a distinctly Philippine factor at work among the elite sections of the opposition. Estrada didn't just trumpet his concern for the poor: he was *in touch* with them. They responded to him. This was dangerous. For many in the elite, the poor were regarded with a fear and loathing that was second nature to them. Such had been the case since the Spanish regime, when revolts by the poor had threatened the privileges of the principalia. Such was the case during the Philippine Revolution of 1896, when the interests of the better off were served by the murder of Andres Bonifacio, the proletarian leader of the Katipunan, the revolutionary organization he founded. Such was the case in the Philippine-American War that followed, when most of the foreign-educated elite opted for a new colonizer rather than take their chances in a country governed by Katipunan veterans. And such was the case now as this former movie star articulated the concerns of the poor, inspiring their devotion. It had been acceptable when, in the 1950s, President Ramon Magsaysay had done much the same, because the elite had known that he had been acting out a role written for him by the American intelligence officer, Col. Edward Lansdale, who had created him in the first place.[2] Estrada was different. He was his own creation and, thus, not subject to elite control. This was the man who, as senator, had voted against the new US bases treaty in 1991. In a sense, the fact that he had no consistent ideology made him more dangerous, as it meant he was unpredictable. Who could say, in a crisis situation, what actions his much-professed love for the poor might lead him to take, which floodgates might be irresponsibly flung open?

What the elite eventually did to Estrada in the Philippines was precisely what their counterparts in Venezuela would attempt to do to President Hugo Chavez.

One problem, however, was that although he used plenty of pro-poor rhetoric, Estrada had, apart from some ameliorative measures (cheap rice and pork sold in "Erap" stores in poor neighborhoods, for example), no pro-poor policies. He was no Hugo Chavez. This is not to single him out: no Philippine president has had a decisive influence on economic policy at the strategic level, because after nominal independence in 1946 this was first of all formulated by the USA and then, after President Diosdado Macapagal accepted the first IMF loan in 1962, taken over by the World Bank and the International Monetary Fund. In the absence of any ideological moorings of his own, Estrada simply drifted along with the current orthodoxy, whereas any claim to greatness in a Philippine presidency could only be based upon a determined challenge to that orthodoxy. That is something that could not be achieved merely by the will of a president, as it required the determination of a mobilized and united people.

That condition was not present in the Philippines.

The left was splintered. In chronological order of their foundation, there was the PKP-

1930, lately given that appellation in order to distinguish it from the breakaway Communist Party of the Philippines (CPP), which, formed by the expelled Jose Maria Sison in 1968-69, embraced the Maoist path of armed struggle. In the early 1990s, several groups had, in turn, split from the CPP, leading to the formation of an alternative organization in Manila-Rizal and a second based on the island of Negros. A third found its way into a new center-left electoral party called Akbayan. There would be others, as split followed split.

Like the left, the labor movement was disunited, being divided between a host of labor centers: the Trade Union Congress of the Philippines (TUCP, conservative), the Kilusang Mayo Uno (KMU, or May First Movement, influenced by the CPP), Katipunan (influenced by the PKP), Bukluran ng Manggagawang Pilipino (BMP, or Struggle of Filipino Workers, led by the Manila-Rizal group), and a clutch of others. Many divisions were ideological, but they were also based on what might be termed a "militant individualism," a disabling condition infecting many sectors of society.

The mainstream political parties were no exceptions, acting as electoral vehicles with no real life outside elections other than as caucuses, and standing for little except the ambitions of their leaders. With little if any difference between one party and another, office-holders had—if it meant the difference between winning and losing, sharing in the spoils of office or being frozen out—for decades switched parties with no apparent sense of shame. Although the economy was dominated by foreign capital, the local capitalists, while they might exert pressure on the government on single issues, looked to safeguard their individual rather than collective interests (and this often meant entering joint ventures with TNCs), developing no consistently nationalist approach.

Paradoxically, in this society riddled with formal religion, leaders of all stripes and in all sectors found it difficult to subjugate the interests of the self to those of the greater good.

*

The nationalist pressure on Estrada was, therefore, while able to prevent him doing further injury to the national patrimony by removing constitutional safeguards limiting the extent of foreign ownership, was insufficient to push him into challenging the TNCs or their policemen, the World Bank-IMF and the World Trade Organization (WTO). His friendships caused concern among the elite, as he was particularly close to an aggressive group of mainly Filipino-Chinese businessmen, some of them previously members of the Marcos group. His name was constantly linked with those of Eduardo Cojuangco (San Miguel Corporation and much more besides), Lucio Tan (Asia Brewery, Fortune Tobacco, Allied Bank, Philippine Airlines), Dante Tan (BW Resources), Mark Jimenez (wanted in the USA for illegal donations to the Democratic Party) and others. Although he launched a vociferous anti-corruption campaign and many cases were brought against public officials, it was not long before it was alleged that the president himself was corrupt (that, for example, he was a beneficiary of insider trading at BW Resources).

As protests against Estrada, largely led by the church, the political opposition and business, grew, they were joined by a left seemingly oblivious of the probable consequences of its actions.

On November 22, 1999 a US intelligence firm called Stratfor (Strategic Forecasting) predicted that Estrada would be unable to finish his term and that he could well be impeached for allowing corruption and the return of cronyism. Estrada accused Stratfor of having links with the opposition. On December 7, Stratfor claimed that its original prediction had been "accurate—perhaps even more so than we thought."[3] Why this talk of impeachment in December 1999, when there had not been the hint of a formal charge? Nevertheless, a couple of weeks later Amando Doronila, in his "Analysis" column in the *Philippine Daily Inquirer*, picked up the theme and ran with it. Estrada, he pointed out, needed to retain "control of Congress by his…coalition to discourage any move to remove him from office by impeachment…"

While impeachment seems to be a remote possibility, given the dim prospects of the opposition parties capturing control of Congress, there's widespread talk about removal of the President through "extra-legal means"—not necessarily meaning a coup.[4]

This passage could well have been inspired by the Stratfor report, which had said that even without a coup it was difficult to see how Estrada could survive. It is also remarkable that, although Doronila's column discussed impeachment, there was not a single mention of specific law-breaking by the president. Instead, the focus was on the balance of forces in Congress, giving the impression that the "widespread talk" was really about nothing more than a struggle for political power.

But it seemed that it would only be a matter of time before charges were brought against Estrada.

Apart from the allegation that he had interfered in an investigation of alleged insider trading at BW Resources, there were now the findings of the Philippine Center for Investigative Journalism (PCIJ), which had examined the records of 66 companies in which Estrada or members of his family were board members or incorporators, and in which they had shares amounting to P121.5 million. Eleven of the companies had been established in the short time he had been president, while 31 had begun life during his term as vice-president. Not all of these assets had been declared. Moreover, his mistresses lived in swank houses and his "wives and children" drove expensive imported vehicles.[5] This unexplained wealth would feature in the impeachment proceedings in the following December and January.

There were signs, however, that the opposition campaign was beginning to run out of steam, and an anti-Estrada rally on September 21, 2000 was able to muster only 10,000 according to reports in the *Philippine Daily Inquirer* (or 4,000 according to the TV station ABS-CBN). The campaign needed a boost. It got it a few weeks later, when Ilocos Sur Governor Luis "Chavit" Singson, a former member of Estrada's circle, alleged that between November 1998 and August 2000 he had handed the president a total of P414 million in protection payoffs from the overlords of jueteng, the illegal numbers game. Estrada countered that the allegations were "black propaganda and a smear campaign."[6]

The balance of congressional forces to which Amando Doronila had drawn attention was important, because in the impeachment process the House of Representatives had first to agree that the president should be impeached, in which case it would act as prosecutor, with the Senate sitting in judgement. It was therefore essential for the opposition to improve its strength in the House. The initial tactic it adopted, though, was to call for Estrada's immediate resignation, therefore avoiding the need for impeachment. Thus, Cardinal Jaime Sin and the 75-strong Presbyteral Council of the Diocese of Manila issued such a call less than a week after Singson had made his allegations. In this, they were soon joined by the Philippine Independent Church (established during the Philippine-American War) and the United Church of Christ in the Philippines (the largest Protestant denomination, of which former president Fidel Ramos was a member). Organized labor in the form of the Labor Solidarity Movement, a grouping of mostly moderate trade union organizations such as the TUCP and the Federation of Free Workers, issued both a resignation call and a warning that it would be organizing strike action.

*

Stratfor re-entered the scene in mid-October 2000, stressing the all-important balance of forces. It also expressed the view that "the United States may well be on the cusp of a new strategic relationship with the Philippines." Vice-President Gloria Macapagal Arroyo, the daughter of former president Diosdado Macapagal, had been educated at Georgetown, where she had been a classmate of Bill Clinton. Stratfor noted approvingly that she viewed China as a greater threat than the USA and "was one of two Philippine senators to visit Taiwan on its national day in 1994, a symbolic move that provoked protest from Beijing." Therefore, "[w]ith Arroyo in office, the military relationship between Manila and Washington may intensify."[7] (Events would demonstrate that this projection, which seemed to pay little regard to the role played by opportunism in Philippine politics, was a little wide of the mark, for when Mrs. Arroyo withdrew the Philippines' small contingent of troops from Iraq after kidnappers threatened to murder a civilian Filipino hostage in 2004, she incurred Washington's ire, and therefore moved into a very close relationship with China.)

As a means of beginning to shift the balance of power, Arroyo had started the ball rolling on October 12 by resigning her cabinet post as social welfare secretary, following which Representative Roilo Golez and Senator Ramon Magsaysay Jr. both resigned from Estrada's coalition. The USA's hands were not entirely clean, an opposition leader in the House of Representatives claiming that it had expressed concern over the political situation and had proposed a meeting with opposition leaders and Vice-President Arroyo. Later, Arroyo admitted having met US charge d'affaires Michael Malinowski, but said that he had advised her that the USA did not intend to intervene.[8] Malinowski himself admitted that the meeting had taken place, but claimed that it had been "routine." According to *Philippine Daily Inquirer* sources, however, the purpose of the meeting had been to discuss the opposition's role in the political crisis. "The sources said," reported the *Inquirer*, "the formation of a united front against Mr. Estrada was among the requisites laid out by Washington before it [would] support the opposition."[9] One week later, Mrs. Arroyo announced the formation of the "Unified Opposition," having met with opposition parties Reporma (led by former defense secretary Renato de Villa) and Promdi (the party of former presidential adviser Lito Osmeña), announcing an alliance between these and Lakas (formed as Fidel Ramos's electoral vehicle in 1992) and Kampi (her own vehicle). They were joined a short time later by Raul Roco's Aksyon Demokratiko. The Unified Opposition was launched on October 28, at which time Mrs. Arroyo announced that she had created six task forces to draw up a 100-day plan of action to be implemented in the event that Estrada resigned. On November 4, she revealed that she had prepared her cabinet. And all this before the impeachment trial had commenced.

Now the resignations began to come thick and fast. Trade and industry secretary Manuel Roxas II resigned, followed by a clutch of resignations from the ruling coalition in the House of Representatives and Senate. Even so, the Estrada coalition was left with nine members in the upper chamber—enough to throw out an impeachment complaint. Moreover, later in the month Teofisto Guingona Jr., who had originally brought Singson's allegations to the Senate, was defeated 13 to 6 by Aquilino Pimentel Jr. in the election for Senate president. It was clear by now, however, that the House would vote to commence the impeachment process, although some Estrada supporters were also in favor of this, arguing that a public trial was the only way the president could demonstrate his innocence. That the House was not overwhelmingly anti-Estrada was demonstrated by the fact that, after he forced through the impeachment vote, Speaker Manuel Villar was deposed.

Throughout all of this, the demonstrations and the calls for Estrada's immediate resignation continued. In late October, squatters and protesters led by Sanlakas, the mass organization affiliated with the Manila-Rizal breakaway from the CPP, attacked a "luxury mansion" allegedly owned by Estrada. A rally in Makati on October 18 had, according to *Time*, only attracted "about 10,000." The same journal noted: "Many of the loudest voices demanding Estrada's resignation come from the country's business elite, who admire Arroyo's economic credentials and lineage, while despising Estrada's fumbling of the economy."[10]

Surveys by the Makati Business Club and the Management Association of the Philippines indicated that between 80 and 90 percent of respondents were in favor of Estrada's resignation. Thus, as Herbert Docena was to write, by November "key sections of the elites were having private meetings in their mansions, eventually reaching a decision to actively lead the campaign for Estrada's ouster."[11] On November 4, some 50,000 attended an anti-Estrada rally. Four days later, Reuters reported a demonstration with distinct echoes of Chile prior to the Pinochet coup: "Thousands of women beating pots, pans and drums marched in Manila's Makati financial district to demand Estrada quit…Schoolgirls, nuns, slum-dwellers and well-dressed women walked through the pouring rain…"[12] On November 8, gays and lesbians marched in Baguio City, somewhat bizarrely blaming the economic crisis on Estrada's "womanizing culture."[13] On November 14, a strike was held and 15,000 protesters gathered near Malacañang, the presidential palace. It was questionable to what extent this was a genuine strike, for although it was true that trade union organizations like the TUCP and the KMU had called the action, the BBC reported that "[m]any offices and shops closed to allow employees to join the rallies."[14]

Inevitably, there were rumors that this or that group was planning a military coup. Unofficial military organizations called for Estrada's resignation less than a week after Singson made his allegations. On November 10, national police chief and Estrada ally Panfilo Lacson named five active and retired police and military officers who were among those recruiting colleagues to move against Estrada.

Just as the opposition had taken to the streets, so Estrada's supporters were mobilized, with the president sharpening his counter-attack at his public appearances. On October 24, 2000, some 20,000 supporters from urban poor organizations and NGOs, together with the People's Movement Against Poverty (PMAP, said to be an Estrada creation), gathered at Don Chino Roces Bridge (formerly Mendiola Bridge and the site of several, often violent, confrontations since the days of Marcos). The same day, Estrada addressed an audience of urban poor at Caloocan High School, where he charged that rich newspaper owners in Makati, and in particular those who owned the *Philippine Daily Inquirer*, were ganging up on him, and that the rich were behind the calls for his resignation. The owners of the *Inquirer*, said Estrada in a reference to earlier divisions in Philippine society, were peninsulares and insulares (of Spanish birth or antecedents). An urban poor leader responded: "Beloved President, we are warning those who want you out, we the poor are prepared to shed blood in the streets for you."[15] The following day, at a "national renewal rally" in Cebu City, 60,000 turned up to hear Estrada attack the "peninsulares, oligarchs and elitists who could not accept me as the duly elected president from the beginning."[16] On November 11, Estrada drew some 1.5 million (a police estimate) to a "national day of prayer" at Luneta Park supported by Christian sects El Shaddai, the Iglesia ni Kristo, the Jesus Miracle Crusade and various Muslim leaders.[17]

The developing crisis was, however, having a deleterious effect on the economy, with the peso declining against the dollar and investment slowing. By the end of October, Bangko Sentral Governor Rafael Buenaventura was warning that unless the crisis was resolved the Philippines could see a recession in 2001. The worrying economic news, more than the activity of the opposition itself, seemed to take its toll on Estrada, and at the end of October he made a televised address to the nation in which he stressed that if the political crisis continued it would result in a further fall in the value of the peso, factory closures and "economic misery and social unrest." With a view to securing a measure of national reconciliation, he therefore gave assurances regarding his conduct, authorized interior secretary Alfredo Lim to investigate his alleged acquisition of the "mansions" to which the media had linked him, and announced that a meeting of the national security council would be convened immediately, with invitations being extended to former presidents Aquino and Ramos and Vice-President Gloria Macapagal Arroyo.

Undoubtedly, this was a retreat by Estrada. But the opposition wanted capitulation, so the olive branch extended in this package, particularly to Arroyo, served no purpose. Within days of the broadcast, the resignations from his coalition began in earnest. It would be a fight to the death.

*

The impeachment trial began on December 7, and from 2 p.m. every weekday, as Filipinos in homes and offices all over the country sat on the edge of their seats before what was at times riveting television, the opposition attempted to prove that President Estrada had accepted jueteng payoffs as protection money, along with P170 million skimmed off tobacco excise tax from Ilocos Sur, the province of Governor Luis "Chavit" Singson, and that he held bank accounts in the name of "Jose Velarde." In the first two weeks, though, the prosecution did little to prove Estrada's link to jueteng money, apart from the testimony of Singson. At a press conference on December 22, Senator Blas Ople observed: "All that has been achieved so far is to give the public a good seminar on deposit and withdrawal practices. The education value to the public cannot be doubted, but its value to the prosecution appears to be negligible."[18] That afternoon, the prosecution announced that it had a "surprise witness." Clarissa Ocampo, a senior vice-president and trust officer of Equitable PCI Bank, was to drop a bombshell.

Ocampo told the court that one evening in February 2000 she had been at a cocktail party when George Go, her bank's president, had introduced her to lawyer Fernando Chua, who told her that he had a client who wished to lend P500 million to the Wellex Group, Inc. Go told her to approve the investment within 18 hours, necessitating a visit to the presidential palace the following day. Here, she had counter-signed three copies of an investment management agreement. Sitting next to her, a foot away, was President Estrada, who signed the documents as

"Jose Velarde." Estrada, the prosecution pointed out, had declared assets of P35 million. How could he explain this P500 million? On this note, the case was adjourned for the Christmas break.

Scanning the lengthy interview with Mrs. Arroyo carried by one of the *Inquirer* supplements on Christmas Eve, the casual reader from abroad might have assumed that she had just won an election. The Filipino keen to welcome the prospect of a government committed to a course independent of either transnational capital or the Catholic Church, however, would have been profoundly disappointed. Her national agenda embraced "the economic philosophy of the 21st century, so, recognizing that it's a world of competition, what do our entrepreneurs need in order to compete?" She would address poverty and inequity by means of "structural reforms, safety nets for sectors affected by globalization and safeguards for our environment." She responded to a question on jueteng: "Well, I have always taken the church's stand on anything, including gambling, whether legal or illegal, abortion, death penalty, divorce..." [19]

The interview with the vice-president was in keeping with the spirit of the period, for despite the Estrada camp's attempts to fight back, the whole country now had several days in which to digest Clarissa Ocampo's testimony. It soon became apparent that in putting her in the witness box immediately before the Christmas break the prosecution had played a masterstroke. Prior to this, there had been no direct link between the Velarde accounts and Estrada. It had still been possible for those who did not wish to believe in his guilt to suspect that a perfectly plausible explanation would emerge in due course, revealing the claims of his accusers to be wild fabrications. But now...

As the trial resumed on January 2, the tables were well and truly turned. Back in December, the prosecution had appeared bumbling and unprofessional, while the defense team had exuded self-assurance. Now it was the defense team that appeared amateurish and slipshod. The peso fell to 52 to the dollar before settling at 51.

Lonnie Kelly, acting director at the US Embassy's Public Affairs office, issued an assurance that the USA "will not interfere in the political developments" in the Philippines. However, the Bush team (George W. had yet to be inaugurated) had sent a posse to Manila a fortnight earlier to meet anti-Estrada leaders. A Bush foreign policy adviser now warned that the president-elect "would never recognize any government [installed] in the Philippines through the barrel of a gun."[20] The implication, of course, was that a government installed by "people power" might expect a warmer reception.

Cardinal Sin issued a statement in which he called upon his flock to continue the mass actions if Estrada failed to resign. On January 12, as it began to look as if the prosecution would be unable to muster the Senate votes for a conviction, Sin's spokesman warned that a "revolt" would be called if the president was acquitted. The watershed came on January 16, when the prosecution attempted to introduce into evidence the records of bank accounts that were, it was claimed, the property of Joseph Estrada. After the defense argued that, as the accounts had not been specified in the articles of impeachment, the court really had no business scrutinizing them, by a vote of 11 to 10 the Senator-judges voted against admitting them into evidence. "I thank the Lord," said Estrada in premature relief, "for giving us this initial favorable vote—which is the first major vote in the many more major votes to be cast."[21]

He was wrong. The senators had played right into the hands of his enemies. The prosecution team now resigned, Representative Joker Arroyo claiming that the accounts would have shown that Estrada had, using four aliases, piled up a fortune of $63.5 million in bribes and kickbacks. Without a prosecution team, Chief Justice Hilario Davide adjourned the trial.

*

The opposition forces now argued that, as it was impossible to remove Estrada by using the law, other methods must be employed. Demonstrations were immediately organized (one cannot say "broke out," as these events were hardly spontaneous). Corazon Aquino and Gloria Macapagal Arroyo, the once and future presidents, led the protest at the shrine at EDSA (Epifanio de los Santos Avenue, site of the "people power revolt" that had toppled Marcos), and the Catholic Church ensured the numbers were enhanced by cancelling classes in its schools.

Although the Estrada camp still thought its man could tough it out, the opposition began to wheel out its big guns. Former president Fidel V. Ramos marched through Villamor and Bonifacio military bases, where he was joined by residents, most of them dependents of military personnel. Upon his arrival at EDSA, he was joined by retired Brig. Gen. Edgardo Abenina and retired Navy Commodore Domingo Calajate, leaders of the unofficial military organization that had mutinied against Marcos. Felipe Medalla, head of the national economic development authority, tended to dismiss threats by big business to join the demonstration, but they would do so. Pressure began to build against Estrada and his supporters. While Mrs. Arroyo warned of a plot to install a civilian-military junta (events would shortly demonstrate this to be patently false), the media published details of the "Jose Velarde" account, which had been opened with a single peso in late August 1999 and had amassed P3.23 billion by July 2000.[22] A further wave of government resignations commenced.

On the evening of the January 18, Estrada consulted his lawyers, asking them to request that details of the Equitable PCI bank account now be revealed, despite the Senate ruling that the prosecution could not force their disclosure. That night, the number of demonstrators at the EDSA shrine was calculated to be 100,000, stretching six miles to downtown Makati.[23] "The crowd at EDSA," the Manila Times would report, "was a gathering of strange bedfellows: warring leftist groups and the traditional politicians, lawmakers taking a respite from legislative intramurals, housewives and powerful Makati executives, out of school youth and mestizo students from elite schools."[24] Inevitably, the phenomenon was given a name tag—two, in fact: "EDSA Dos," and "People Power II."

But information coming to light just a few days later would demonstrate that it was not "people power" that toppled Joseph Estrada but the threat of a military coup. On January 19, Executive Secretary Edgardo Angara called together the members of an ad hoc committee hastily assembled to deal with the burgeoning demonstrations. All were present except finance secretary Pardo and armed forces chief of staff Gen. Angelo Reyes. Angara would later recall:

Discussions on the state of security followed. "The military is 100 percent secure," reassured Orly [defense secretary Orlando Mercado]. I did not know that moments earlier he had told Macel [Ma. Celia Fernandez, head of the presidential management staff] that government had to act fast, because in the next few days the military would move. I also did not know that Orly's vehicle that day contained at least 20 high-powered firearms.[25]

Later that day, Mercado and Reyes were seen at the EDSA demonstration. According to a senior military officer quoted in the *Washington Post*, there "were [military] groups ready to take offensive action" against Estrada, and the armed forces top brass "recognized that if they didn't side with the opposition, the military would fracture and they could have a very violent situation on their hands."[26] With the army clearly gone, police chief Panfilo Lacson now undertook to check on the loyalty of his own men. Having met his fellow directors (and, according to the *Washington Post* version of the story, 50 armed officers who "stormed into his office"[27]), Lacson telephoned Angara to say that the police had withdrawn its support from the president.

By this time, the demonstration at EDSA was reported to be 250,000-strong[28] and the pressure continued to build. Negotiations were conducted sporadically throughout the evening and into the early hours of the morning, and for a while it looked as though Estrada would be given five days to vacate the palace with some dignity. But then it emerged that the opposition camp intended to have Arroyo sworn in as president at noon. Around 7.30 a.m., the two sides exchanged drafts of an agreement on the transfer of power, with the opposition team insisting on an unequivocal letter of resignation. Estrada, however, had already signed his own letter in which, rather than resigning, he had said that he was unable to discharge the powers and duties of the presidency and that the vice-president should therefore take over in an acting capacity.

After the Supreme Court justices had sworn in Arroyo at the EDSA shrine, Joseph Ejercito Estrada and his family left Malacañang by barge at 2.30 that afternoon, travelling to his home in San Juan.

The first foreign government to recognize the newly installed president was that of the USA where, by a remarkable coincidence, and in similarly controversial circumstances,[29] George W. Bush was sworn in as president on the very same date as the ceremony on EDSA.

NOTES

1. Pedro Baguisa, interviewed by the author, Antipolo, Rizal, August 1998.

2. See, for example, Joseph B. Smith, *Portrait of a Cold Warrior* (Quezon City: Plaridel Books, 1976) and Michael McLintock, *Instruments of Statecraft: US Guerrilla Warfare, Counter-insurgency and Counterterrorism, 1940-1990* (New York: Pantheon Books, 1992).

3. *Philippine Daily Inquirer*, December 8, 1999.

4. Amando Doronila, "Analysis," *Philippine Daily Inquirer*, December 20, 1999. Over two years later, the *Daily Tribune* (April 7, 2002) would report that, according to its sources, former national security adviser Jose Almonte and Fidel Ramos "were in the thick of providing Stratfor with the information predicting the fall of then President Estrada…"

5 Yvonne T. Chua, Sheila S. Coronel and Vinia Datinguinoo, "The State of the President's Finances: Can Estrada Explain His Wealth?", Philippine Center For Investigative Journalism (www.pcij.org), 2000.

6. Reuters, October 6, 2000.

7. Stratfor Global Intelligence Update, "Impeachment May Spark US-Philippine Alliance," October 17, 2000.

8. *Philippine Daily Inquirer*, November 5, 2000.

9. Ibid., November 9, 2000.

10. *Time Asia*, October 30, 2000.

11. Herbert Docena, "Corruption and Poverty: Barking Up the Wrong Tree?", in Walden Bello, Herbert Docena, Marissa de Guzman and Marylou Malig, *The Anti-Development State: The Political Economy of Permanent Crisis in the Philippines*, (Quezon City: Department of Sociology, University of the Philippines, 2004), 287.

12. Reuters, November 8, 2000.

13. *Philippine Daily Inquirer*, November 9, 2000.

14. BBC News, November 14, 2000.

15. *Philippine Daily Inquirer*, October 25, 2000.

16. *Manila Bulletin*, October 26, 2000.

17. *Manila Times*, November 12, 2000.

18. *Philippine Star*, December 23, 2000.

19. *Philippine Daily Inquirer*, December 24, 2000.

20. *Philippine Star*, January 3, 2001.

21. Agence France Presse, January 17, 2001.

22. See, for example, *Philippine Daily Inquirer*, January 18, 2001.

23. Agence France Presse, January 19, 2001.

24. *Manila Times*, January 20, 2001. Docena ("Corruption and Poverty…" in *The Anti-Development State…*, 287, 288) estimates that "as many as one in every five rallyers in EDSA came from the perfumed set", i.e., the elite, and that "almost 60 percent" of the demonstrators were middle-class.

25. Edgardo Angara, "Estrada's final hours told," *Philippine Daily Inquirer*, February 4, 2001.

26. *Washington Post*, January 22, 2001.

27. Ibid.

28. Agence France Presse, January 19, 2001.

29. Democrat Al Gore received a majority of the popular vote. However, in Florida (where Bush's brother was governor) votes were excluded from the electoral register and it was this state which gave Bush a majority in the electoral college.

3 "EVERYTHING IS FOR SALE"

It is true that, to a certain extent, corruption[1] is a "cultural" problem in the Philippines, in that the practice was inculcated during centuries of colonialism, first Spanish, then American. In addition, the persistence of low-paid officials eager to augment their salaries and citizens willing to sell their votes are almost inevitable features of the dysfunctional economy (itself fashioned by a combination of colonialism, neocolonialism and "globalization").

An example of the "cultural" variant of illegality and the accompanying corruption would be jueteng, the outlawed numbers game. Mrs. Arroyo and her family were, following the election of 2004, accused of using pay-offs from jueteng to fund electoral irregularities. Thereafter, a great show was made of ordering the police to eradicate the game, and this exercise revealed the complexity of the jueteng issue. Joseph Estrada had always taken the view that the game should be legalized, thereby giving security to the tens of thousands of poor people who made a living from it, and providing the government with a further source of income. Mrs. Arroyo, less attuned to the needs of the poor, seemed not to realize that to simply remove jueteng without providing an alternative would create dislocation and heighten the desperation of those displaced. Soon, there were reports that former collectors were, seeing no other means of putting food on the table, gravitating to other forms of crime. Those charged with eradicating the game were also feeling the pinch, as rank and file policemen, denied their regular payoffs, now found their meager paychecks inadequate.

Jueteng has its roots in poverty, as millions of poor Filipinos look upon it as a means of temporarily ameliorating or even, if they are almost impossibly lucky, escaping their dire circumstances. For the poor, jueteng plays a similar role as religion, and as such it is both understandable and forgivable. The same cannot be said of the corruption of the rich and powerful, particularly when public money is involved.

For someone who had participated in the toppling of a president on the grounds of his alleged corruption, and who had promised to tackle the issue with an "iron fist" during her own time in office, Gloria Macapagal Arroyo, along with her husband and members of her administration, attracted an astonishing number of allegations of graft, corruption and sheer crooked practice.

In October 2002, the German-based Transparency International deemed the Philippines to be the eleventh most corrupt nation of the 102 in its survey.[2] The following month, the World Economic Forum's Global Competitiveness Report ranked the Philippines bottom of 80 countries regarding "perception of bribes in connection with government policy-making" and next to bottom with regard to "illegal political donations."[3] And this was early in a period of office that would last for nine-and-a-half years.

*

The only major "reform" during Arroyo's first spell of government was the Electrical Power Industry Reform Act (EPIRA), and this was mired in scandal and controversy.

Passage of the EPIRA was urged upon the government by the World Bank and other international agencies and, indeed, the grant of a World Bank loan of $900 million was conditional upon passage of the bill. Although, when she assumed office, Arroyo said that she would shelve the legislation, she soon changed her tune. One section of the bill limited ownership of power distributors by generating companies to 15 percent, but the Manila Electric Company (Meralco) and the Aboitiz Group were eventually exempted from this restriction. Among major promoters of the bill were Senators John Osmeña, who was close to the Aboitiz family, and his cousin Sergio Osmeña III, who was married to a Lopez, the family controlling Meralco. According to *Newsbreak* magazine, the ban on cross-ownership was relaxed when the Osmeñas realized that the Lopez and Aboitiz interests were threatened. Congresswoman Etta Rosales complained: "The present situation is really no different from Estrada's time. The only new dynamic here is that Estrada's cronies have been replaced by the Lopezes and the

Aboitizes."[4]

Many of the civil society groups that had participated in EDSA Dos opposed the bill on the grounds that consumers would end up paying for the liabilities of the distributors. In the House, the bill was ratified by 131 to 14 at 4 a.m. on June 1, 2001, raising suspicions that it had been railroaded. In addition, it was claimed that members of Congress had each received a substantial sum in order to assure its smooth passage. In March 2003 Manuel Luis Sanchez, former head of the national electrification administration, alleged that expenditure of P470 million had been ordered by Mrs. Arroyo.[5]

In November 2002, the Lopez-controlled Meralco sustained a body blow when the Supreme Court ordered it to refund excess charges made between 1994 and 1998. As the company warned of bankruptcy and imminent collapse, the government suggested a rescue operation (owning 25.53 percent as opposed to the Lopezes' 17 percent,[6] the state was already Meralco's largest shareholder), but the Lopez family rejected the proposal. But government assistance would eventually be accepted by the Lopezes—although not for Meralco—and this would lead to a whole new controversy.

The company this time was Maynilad, which, jointly owned by the Lopez family's Benpres and the French company Ondeo, operated one of Metro Manila's two water concessions. In December 2002, having failed to obtain rate increases, Maynilad proposed it be released from the obligation to repay the foreign loans it had inherited from the Metropolitan Waterworks and Sewerage System (MWSS) in 1997. When this was turned down, Maynilad announced that it would hand back the concession to the MWSS. Then Ondeo threatened to pull out of Maynilad, asking the MWSS to take back its 30 percent participation in return for $20 million.

This deepened the crisis of the Lopez family, and the government now agreed to convert P8 billion of debt into equity, giving the government a 60 percent stake in Maynilad and the opposition further grounds to support its accusation that the Lopezes had done a deal with Mrs. Arroyo to persuade Lopez broadcaster (and, since June 2001, senator) Noli de Castro not to run for the presidency in 2004. When a Quezon City court placed a gag order on the precise details of what was called a "bailout," the justice department decided not to contest this, and was silent on a report in *BusinessWorld* in March 2004 that the deal released Benpres from guaranteeing payment of $47 million worth of debt in case of default.[7]

*

The "First Gentleman," Jose Miguel "Big Mike" Arroyo, attracted controversy early on. It was alleged, for example, that he had lobbied on behalf of those involved in a P41 million telecommunications franchise, and by July 2001, Joseph Estrada's Puwersa ng Masang Pilipino (Power of the Filipino Masses) party was challenging the Catholic Church and "other groups of moralizers" to denounce government corruption.[8] According to Senator Panfilo Lacson, the whole administration was "powerfully corrupt" and Mike Arroyo was "more than sharing power": he was said to head the "Department of the Underground," responsible for "assigning cronies to positions of power and making money out of them." He had, claimed Lacson, turned the Philippine Charity Sweepstakes Office (PCSO) into a "cash cow" for funding four of the administration's candidates in the May 2001 midterm elections.[9]

The Senate committee on the accountability of public officers and investigations (the "blue ribbon committee") said that it could find no hard evidence against Mike Arroyo. In November 2001, businessman Pacifico Marcelo wrote to the chairman of the committee to say that he was willing to testify. Mrs. Arroyo, he claimed, had in April vetoed two congressional franchises granted to his company and, giving evidence in December, he said that the lawyer representing Mrs. Arroyo's legal counsel had asked that 51 percent of the company be handed over in exchange for the reinstatement of his contracts.[10] Presidential spokesman Rigoberto Tiglao called him a liar and speculated that Marcelo might be part of a larger plot to destabilize the government.

In August 2003, Senator Lacson[11] used a privilege speech to unveil a series of claims regarding bank accounts said to be held by the "First Gentleman" that allegedly contained earnings from corruption, extortion and money laundering under the names of a number of "dummies," or fictitious names like "Jose Pidal." Mr. Arroyo filed a libel suit against his accuser, but in May 2005 this would be dismissed on the grounds that Lacson's remarks were covered by parliamentary immunity. The allegation bore, of course, a marked resemblance to

42

the "Jose Velarde" accusation made against Joseph Estrada. The inference was that Jose Pidal and Jose Miguel Arroyo were one and the same person, but police experts said their signatures differed.

On August 25, Eugenio Mahusay, Mike Arroyo's godson and former messenger, said at a press conference that he had seen the "First Gentleman" sign checks as "Jose Pidal." Then, in an extraordinary episode, Mahusay was "rescued" from the Lacson camp. Mahusay said he fled Lacson's "protective custody" because he feared he would be silenced, while the Arroyo camp said that Mahusay had an axe to grind, as he had been fired by Mike's secretary. The *Philippine Star* observed in an editorial that Mahusay "can't decide which camp is offering him the highest bid."[12] Some days later, the hapless "witness" recanted his allegations against Mike Arroyo and apologized to Lacson for using him in the vendetta.

The "First Gentleman" then claimed that "Jose Pidal" was in fact his brother Ignacio "Iggy" Arroyo, but Lacson argued that the latter (who had earlier claimed ownership of buildings in San Francisco, California suspected of being owned by the presidential couple) did not have the financial standing to justify this claim.

In a second privilege speech, Lacson declared that Big Mike and his secretary had two joint accounts containing P49 million and that, in addition, Mike had P79 million in other accounts.[13] When two of the named banks claimed to have no accounts in the name of Jose Pidal or Arroyo's secretary, the Lacson camp cried "cover-up" and displayed checks purporting to be from two of the accounts. At the Senate blue ribbon committee, Iggy Arroyo invoked the right to privacy 30 times, while Senator Sergio Osmeña III claimed that Mike Arroyo had investments managed by Morgan Stanley in the USA worth $5 million.[14] Pro-administration Senator Joker Arroyo then drafted a decision for the committee to the effect that Ignacio Arroyo would not have to reveal anything regarding the Pidal accounts as he had the right to privacy. Lacson, he said, had not demonstrated that the accounts contained public money or illegal proceeds, and so Mr. Arroyo could not be compelled to reveal their contents.

*

Members of Mrs. Arroyo's Cabinet and other leading officials would sometimes find themselves in the firing line. Justice Secretary Hernando Perez, who had acted as a prosecutor in Estrada's impeachment trial, was accused by Senator Lacson of having received a $2 million bribe connected with the approval of a power contract. Lacson said that the contract with the Argentine firm IMPSA had been turned down by Estrada, even though $14 million in bribes had been offered. Four days after Arroyo took office, following a legal opinion by Perez, the contract had been signed, the bribe money being, it was alleged, transferred to Coutts Bank in Hong Kong.[15] Having brokered the IMPSA deal, Mark Jimenez (shortly to be extradited to the USA where, having been convicted for making illegal political donations, he would spend over two years in prison), claimed in a privilege speech in the House of Representatives that Perez had extorted the $2 million from him early in 2001 and that he had wired the money to Coutts. Perez, he said, had regularly visited his home in January 2001 in an attempt to extort money from him.[16]

Perez claimed that his accuser was merely trying to delay his extradition but acknowledged that he had met Jimenez, although at the latter's insistence. He produced a letter from Coutts saying that he had never had an account with them; his brother, whom Lacson had accused of holding the account, had received a similar letter. Unfazed, Lacson now claimed that the account was in the name of Ernest Escaler, while Jimenez confirmed that Escaler had faxed him instructions.

As Perez went on a 30-day leave in early December 2002, vowing to return to his job, he filed libel suits against his accusers. On January 2, 2003, however, still denying the allegations but saying he wanted to spare himself and the president "undue stress," Perez resigned and Jimenez claimed victory.[17] With a Senate hearing underway, Lacson said that Jimenez had told him that $2 million had gone to Perez, $4 million had found its way to the presidential palace and that $1 million had gone to "the boys."[18]

In August 2003, a prosecuting magistrate in Switzerland requested the assistance of the Philippine judicial authorities in an investigation into Perez, his wife, his brother-in-law Ramon Arceo and banker Ernest Escaler, and three Swiss banks accounts in their names opened in 2001; three other accounts in the same names had been opened in Guernsey.[19]

But the wheels of Philippine justice, it seemed, turned very slowly where the prosecution of a former member of the government was concerned. Senator Sergio Osmeña III argued that Ombudsman Simeon Marcelo had in fact resigned over this issue, as Big Mike, the presidential spouse, had been urging him to go easy on Perez.[20] According to former Senator Jovito Salonga, Marcelo had also been investigating several people linked to the overpriced Diosdado Macapagal Boulevard who were close to Mike Arroyo[21] It was not until early January 2007 that the Ombudsman ordered the filing of charges against Perez, giving rise to speculation, on the one hand, that he would be cleared (Perez, said executive secretary Eduardo Ermita, "is one of our allies, and deep inside me I know what he is telling me is the truth."[22]), and, on the other, that the administration felt forced to at least look as if it was seriously combating corruption ahead of the May congressional elections. Jimenez now claimed that Arroyo did not profit from the transaction, insisting that he (Jimenez) had merely been the victim of extortion and that there had been no bribery. Some speculated that Jimenez's visits to the presidential palace might have played a part in the adoption of this line. He later dropped his own case against Perez, saying that he had "forgiven" him.

In 2008, the Sandiganbayan anti-graft court threw out several of the charges against Perez and his co-accused—on the basis that his rights had been violated by the fact that it had taken the Ombudsman six years to file the charges! Two charges were, and at the time of writing still are, outstanding—graft and the falsification of public documents.[23]

*

The count following the 2004 presidential election would take weeks, and while there may have been more than one reason for this, some of the delay could have been avoided if the polls had been automated. They almost were. The commission on elections (Comelec) purchased machines for P1.3 billion, but four months before the elections the Supreme Court voided the contract, ruling that it constituted a "clear violation of law and jurisprudence" and showed "reckless disregard" for the Comelec's bidding procedures. The Senate, after its blue ribbon committee found that the contract had been "egregiously fraudulent" and that the bidding had been rigged to favor the Mega Pacific Consortium, called upon all Comelec commissioners, with one exception, to resign.[24] But no one did.

Nor was that the end of the scandal. In June 2005, a panel assembled by then Ombudsman Simeon Marcelo recommended that the Comelec chairman, Benjamin Abalos, and its commissioners, with one exception, be impeached. A full year later, Marcelo having resigned (allegedly due, as we have seen, to pressure from Malacañang), his replacement, Merceditas Gutierrez, recommended the impeachment of several commissioners. In September 2006, a report submitted by one of the Ombudsman's field investigation officers recommended that graft charges be brought against Abalos, members of the Comelec's awards committee, and Mega Pacific executives. There was some consternation when, the following month, Ombudsman Gutierrez reversed her previous position and announced that no one at the Comelec could be held criminally or administratively liable for the contract.

*

The armed forces' Retirement and Separation Benefits Scheme was in such a bad way that it was announced it would be closed and replaced by a civilian-administered scheme. While the scheme had run into trouble due to bad investments, it was also a fact that 91 graft cases, not one of which had been resolved, had been filed against scheme officers.[25] Brig. Gen. (retired) Jose Ramiscal Jr., who was president of the fund during the Ramos administration, was charged concerning a real estate scam; in June 2011, he was sentenced to six years for graft and two years for estafa.[26] This, however, was merely the tip of the military iceberg.

Military corruption became a major issue when, in 2004, it was revealed that the previous December the wife of General Carlos Garcia, then the armed forces comptroller, had attempted to enter the USA with the undeclared sum of $100,000. The total wealth of the Garcia family, including two New York properties, would later be estimated at $2.3 million. The Garcias had some 40 bank accounts in the Philippines. Given his rank, Gen. Garcia would have earned around P40,000 a month. Interviewed by the US authorities, his wife helpfully explained that the general received travel money and expenses from European and Asian companies awarded contracts by the armed forces, and that there were also "gifts" and "gratitude" money.

Mrs. Garcia often accompanied her husband on his travels with, she said, "shopping money" of more than $10,000. Unbelievably, the general even had a "green card," a permanent US residence permit.

Garcia's name turned out to be just the first in a lengthening list. Lt. Col. George Rabusa, former chief of the budget division in Garcia's office, was said to have wealth of P50 million, including houses in the USA and the Philippines. Air Force Brig. Gen. Prospero Ocampo was also under investigation for unexplained wealth.[27] The House committee on national defense produced documents showing that the wife of retired Lt. Gen. Jacinto Ligot owned condominiums worth P20 million, but Ligot invoked the right of silence and failed to comment on the foreign trips his wife was said to have undertaken with the spouse of former armed forces chief Angelo Reyes.[28] Ligot was charged with amassing P135.28 million in ill-gotten wealth.

While the charges Garcia faced in a military court were thought to be relatively minor (he was, at the time, on the brink of retirement), left and nationalist opinion called for the government to charge him with plunder, which carried a potential death sentence (later abolished by Arroyo). Finally, in April 2005, such charges were brought. In December 2005, a court martial sentenced Garcia to two years' hard labor and gave him a dishonorable discharge. However, a military prosecutor said that no officer sentenced to hard labor had actually done any, as it was "inappropriate."[29] This turned out to be something of an understatement, as such a sentence is not implemented until endorsed by the president, and it was learned in September 2011 that either the documents had not been transmitted to Mrs. Arroyo or, if they had, she had not applied her pen to them. President Benigno Aquino III promptly did so, and Garcia was incarcerated in New Bilibid Prison without further ado (a source of further controversy, as some argued that one guilty of a military offense may only be imprisoned in a military facility). By the time Garcia was confronted with this unfortunate turn of events, he had been, as we will now see, at large for some months, having been granted bail by the civil court.

In the Sandiganbayan, the anti-graft court, Garcia was convicted of perjury regarding one of his statements of assets and liabilities and sentenced to two years' imprisonment, a sentence upheld on appeal in 2009. The plunder charge still hung over him, but in December 2010 a shocked nation learned that he had a plea-bargain deal under which, due to "weak evidence," the charge would be reduced and he would forfeit only P135 million of the P303 million specified on the original charge sheet. The court claimed that it had still not approved the deal, even though it granted him bail (plunder is non-bailable) on December 16. Demands were made by President Aquino and others for the deal to be quashed and Garcia to be taken back into custody. In May 2011, however, the Sandiganbayan approved the plea-bargain, although calls for its revocation continued. A criminal complaint was filed against the three judges by, among others, Danilo Lim, a former military rebel recently released by Aquino, and in June the presidential palace suspended a special prosecutor for 90 days, pending investigation into her role in approving the deal and allegedly ignoring or discarding evidence.

Ombudsman Merceditas Gutierrez had long attracted accusations of foot-dragging when it came to prosecuting those close to the Arroyos and there was speculation regarding her role in the Garcia plea-bargain deal. In March 2011, the House of Representatives voted to impeach her, but she resigned before the proceedings could commence. One of the first acts of her permanent replacement, former Supreme Court justice Conchita Carpio-Morales, was to order the appointment of a hundred lawyers to assist in the prosecution of outstanding cases.

So far, those on the list of senior officers alleged to have amassed unexplained wealth were all subordinate to Garcia, although it was argued that successive chiefs of staff must have known what was happening. This particular genie was released from its bottle after Arroyo had left office. In early 2011, former Lt. Gen. George Rabusa, Garcia's budget officer and one of the names that surfaced in 2004, was presented to a Senate investigation by Senator Jinggoy Estrada, son of the former president.

The first officer named by Rabusa was Angelo Reyes, who had been President Estrada's armed forces chief and, more than any other individual, had caused the latter's downfall in 2001 by announcing that the armed forces had withdrawn support from him. He had then been appointed as defense secretary by Mrs. Arroyo. After a mutiny of some 300 junior officers and soldiers in July 2003 (the "Oakwood Mutiny"), he resigned, as the mutineers had made allegations of high-level military corruption and claimed that Reyes had organized fatal bombings in Mindanao to lever more assistance from Washington. An inquiry dismissed the allegations, and within months Arroyo appointed him to another position.

Rabusa now claimed that upon his retirement Reyes had received $1 million in illicit funds as a sendoff, prior to which he had been in receipt of a P5-million "personal fund" each month. Reyes' name had often cropped up at congressional hearings into corruption during the Arroyo years. For example, it was established that his wife had undertaken 48 foreign trips between 1993 and 2004, and Rabusa now testified that she, like Mrs. Garcia, had regularly been supplied with up to $10,000 "shopping money."

Reyes' initial response was one of denial, and on January 31, 2011 he filed graft charges against Rabusa. On February 8, however, he visited his mother's grave and there committed suicide by shooting himself through the heart.

Rabusa admitted that he had himself received P500,000 a month and had accumulated a P200-million bank account.[30] Rabusa named two other former chiefs of staff: Diomedio Villanueva, for whom P160 million was withdrawn in tranches of P10 million—although he was unable to confirm that Villanueva had received it, as the money was handed to Garcia—and Roy Cimatu, for whom P60 million was withdrawn.[31] Cimatu promptly waived secrecy rights to his bank accounts. Defense secretary Voltaire Gazmin meanwhile announced, with some understatement, the formation of an investigating committee "to determine the weakness, if any, of the budgetary and financial system" of the armed forces.[32]

The Senate investigation heard that the wife of former Lt. Gen. Jacinto Ligot had eight US houses in her name. While Mrs. Reyes had made 48 foreign trips between 1993 and 2004, Mrs. Ligot had made 42 during the same period, visiting the USA, Singapore and Hong Kong. Her husband's monthly salary was P35,000.[33] Senator Franklin Drilon castigated Ombudsman Gutierrez for not filing graft charges against Ligot.[34] In June 2011, her successor would order that over P55 million of the Ligots' assets be forfeited.

Rabusa did not confine his accusations to military officers. On each of the several occasions that he met Commission on Audit commissioner Raul Flores, the whistleblower claimed, he had given him P200,000,[35] while Prospero Pichay Jr.,[36] former chair of the House committee on national defense, and a staunch ally of Mrs. Arroyo, had allegedly received P500,000 every time he visited the office of chief of staff Diomedio Villanueva.[37] Apart from kickbacks from contractors, a possible source of this mountain of cash was suggested by Neri Colmenares (a congressional representative for the Bayan Muna party-list group). According to Colmenares, the armed forces may have converted as much as P179.4 billion into slush funds during the Arroyo years, as he pointed out by way of example that in 2010 Congress had appropriated P41.3 billion for military salaries, while the defense department had requested only P19.4 billion.[38]

It should be noted that those accused in these investigations proclaimed their innocence. Some, like the five former chiefs of staff (Narciso Abaya, Hermogenes Esperon, Dionisio Santiago, Generoso Senga and Alexander Yano) who appeared before the House justice committee in February 2011, did so even though they had not been named, and on occasion a witness would offer alternative explanations, as when Brig. Gen. Benito T. de Leon, an alleged bagman named by Rabusa, denied the existence of a fund for bestowing gifts on retiring chiefs and, in admitting that he had receiving P10 million on Roy Cimatu's behalf, claimed that it was "intended to support the operational and administrative requirements of the Office of the Chief of Staff."[39]

*

After Mrs. Arroyo left the presidential palace, it was not long before it was discovered that matters in the prison service and the police were little better than in the military.

Ironically, had Carlos Garcia served his two years' hard labor earlier, he may have found the prison regime more congenial. In May 2011, four months before Garcia was transferred to New Bilibid Prison (NBP), there were calls for the resignation of Bureau of Corrections director Ernesto Diokno after Jose Antonio Leviste, former governor of Batangas province, was found in a public place. This would have been perfectly innocuous had it not been for the fact that Leviste should, as a convicted murderer serving out his sentence, have been securely held in NBP. During the ensuing investigation, it was discovered that prison superintendents sometimes granted "living-out" privileges. It also transpired that life might not be so grim for those "living in" either, subject to their possession of sufficient resources, as it was possible to have special quarters constructed and one source claimed that in NBP prostitutes were "peddled like fish to moneyed prisoners."[40]   According to justice secretary

Leila de Lima, it was not unknown for corrupt prison officials to receive as much as P5 million for ordering the transfer of rival drug dealers.[41]

Diokno resigned, and Aquino ordered "sweeping reform." There was, however, some dismay when, two months later, Aquino appointed retired Lt. Gen. Gaudencio Pangilinan Jr., facing a plunder charge filed by whistle-blower Rabusa, to replace Diokno.

In October 2008 Eliseo dela Paz, the recently-retired comptroller of the Philippine National Police (PNP) was prevented from leaving Moscow by customs officials, who had found that he and his wife were carrying around an undeclared 105,000 euros (P6.9 million). It was claimed that this was intended for the whole PNP delegation then on its way to an Interpol conference in St. Petersburg. Dela Paz said that the cash had been taken from the P10 million "cash advance bonded" that he had, as comptroller, authorized. However, the Directorate for Investigation and Detective Management reported that Dela Paz and others had "acted on their own" in releasing the money. The PNP director ordered that criminal and administrative charges be brought against them.

Although the PNP denied that the trip had breached any law or regulation, a Senate inquiry found that the it had violated several measures including, as far as Dela Paz was concerned, a regulation barring foreign trips within a year of retirement. It emerged that Russian authorities had relieved him of a further 45,000 euros, whereupon he claimed that a Chinese-Filipino friend had asked him to purchase watches in Vienna. He and his wife, he said, had planned to tour Europe after the conference, and apart from the 45,000 euros he had $20,000 in "personal funds." A PNP supplier confirmed to the Senate that he was the person concerned. Former PNP director general Avelino Razon Jr. later confirmed that he had forwarded the details of the trip (which entailed P2.314 million in fares and travel allowances) to the secretary of the interior and local government for approval, but that wives had not been included.

At a House inquiry in November, Dela Paz testified that he was prepared to reimburse the 105,000 Euros (which the Russians had still not returned) from his own pocket, and by this time the other seven officers had repaid all or part of their travel allowances, raising questions regarding the resources available to such officers. In March 2009, it was reported that Dela Paz had paid in the whole amount in cash and checks, and in August that year PNP director Jesus Versoza told the *Philippine Daily Inquirer* that, this being the case, he had been cleared, although his retirement benefits were withheld pending a clean bill of health from the Ombudsman.

However, in August 2010 the Ombudsman's field investigation office recommended that charges be filed against the officers and others, and in September Merceditas Gutierrez, who still occupied the position of Ombudsman, ordered the preventative suspension of six of the generals. It was not until July 2011 that the anti-graft court, having found probable cause to indict Dela Paz and his wife, ordered their arrest. At the time of writing, four years since the Moscow incident, a resolution is still awaited.[42]

As in other areas, some examples of police malfeasance only came to light after Mrs. Arroyo had left the presidential palace. Thus, in September 2011 interior secretary Jesse Robredo ordered an investigation of at least 36 PNP officers and personnel, along with six suppliers, regarding the alleged rigged bidding of "ghost" repair of 38 light armored vehicles in 2007.[43] At the same time, Robredo announced the discovery of a "ghost" PNP pensioner syndicate involving 2,000 pensions of at least P20,000 per month.[44] In September 2011, six PNP officers were charged with graft for the "irregular" purchase of 16 defective speedboats in 2009; that same year, rubber boats purchased were found to be incompatible with the outboard motors that came with them.[45]

In July 2011, Senator Lacson announced that he had proof that the former presidential couple had owned helicopters that had been "forcibly" sold to the PNP and priced as new at P105 million in 2009. Big Mike acknowledged that his company Lourdes T Arroyo Inc. (LTA) had at one stage owned a single helicopter, which it had sold to a private company. Flight records showed that Big Mike and son Congressman "Mikey" Arroyo had made extensive use of the two helicopters identified by Lacson between 2007 and 2009, and that they had also been used by lawmakers and entertainers. It was claimed that the aircraft had been owned by the Asian Spirit airline in 2004 and later leased to Lionair before being sold by the Manila Aerospace Products Trading Corp. to the PNP as new in July 2009. According to interior secretary Jesse Robredo, one of the pilots had later been a member of the PNP inspection team which certified the helicopter he had flown as new.

The two helicopters were among the five acquired by the presidential spouse for Mrs. Arroyo's controversial 2004 presidential campaign for which, according to documents, he paid a total of $475,000. Lionair owner Archibald Po told the Senate blue ribbon committee that he personally delivered $700,000 to Big Mike as payment for the two helicopters sold to the PNP. Arroyo's lawyer maintained that such statements were false and that there was no documentary proof that Mike had owned the helicopters. Brother Iggy then claimed that although LTA had leased the helicopters from Lionair, he had been president of the company from 2001 to 2010, as Mike had divested his shares in March 2001, reacquiring them in late 2010. Several opinion columns commented on the sense of déjà vu occasioned by this claim.[46]

Unimpressed, the Senate blue ribbon committee in October recommended that graft charges be filed against Mike and Iggy Arroyo and that charges also be brought against a number of police and former civilian officials, including former PNP director Gen. Jesus Verzosa.

*

Attempts to recover the allegedly ill-gotten wealth of former President Ferdinand Marcos and his family and associates had been ongoing ever since his overthrow in February 1986. Twenty years later, the presidencies of Corazon Aquino, Fidel Ramos and Joseph Estrada had yielded a mere fraction of the total.

Come 2006, the buzzword was "compromise." The Presidential Commission on Good Government's Ricardo Abcede, while agreeing to demands that full disclosure be a requirement, in late April 2006 announced that a compromise with Imelda Marcos was within reach, and that he was considering withdrawing some or all of the cases against her in return for a slice of a pie thought to be worth anywhere between $10 billion and $100 billion.[47] Days later, however, the judge hearing 32 criminal cases against Imelda said that the PCGG should not preempt the outcome of legal proceedings. The following month, Commissioner Abcede celebrated his 59th birthday at a party attended by Imelda. There continued to be some doubt as to whether a compromise was legally possible, with justice secretary Raul Gonzalez indicating that any grant of criminal or civil immunity would be outside the law. In August, at a board meeting of the Philippine Communications Satellite Corporation (Philcomsat), Imelda announced that she was unwilling to compromise, and that she had been misquoted earlier.

Over the years, there had been allegations that those appointed to recover Marcos's millions had themselves plundered sequestered assets. Now, Senator Juan Ponce Enrile in particular expressed concern that the assets of Philcomsat Holdings Corporation (PHC) appeared to have withered on the vine. At a Senate hearing in January 2007, PHC director Erlinda Bildner made a number of claims regarding how the assets of the company had allegedly been plundered by PCGG-appointed directors: P2 million to "buy" a temporary restraining order to stop her group from holding an election for new officers, to purchase T-shirts for Arroyo's 2004 campaign, and to wine and dine Supreme Court justices; P13.7 million spent on "entertainment representation"; P1.5 million booked as a tax payment when the tax bill was a mere P37,000; and P30 million for a call center costing P25 million. Being moribund, the company's only activity consisted of investing its money, and yet although it earned P111 million in one year, it claimed to have registered a loss of P21 million for that same year. Over a three-year period, senior officers and directors were paid P66.2 million in salaries, bonuses and benefits. "The PCGG people," said Bildner, "have been bleeding our company dry."[48]

The hearing at which Bildner testified was one of a series conducted by the Senate committee on government corporations and public enterprises between May 2006 and February 2007 into the various allegations concerning Philcomsat, the Philippine Overseas Telecommunications Corporation (POTC) and the Philcomsat Holdings Corporation (PHC). In its report, the committee summarized its findings as follows:

> Based on the evidence received throughout its investigation conducted pursuant to PSR No. 455, the Committee found overwhelming mismanagement by the PCGG and its nominees over POTC, Philcomsat and PHC resulting in deterioration of the financial condition of these corporations. Most notable of which are the soaring operating expenses of PHC, the generous compensation packages for government nominees, the PHC advances to its affiliates beyond the reach of PCGG comptrollers, and the existence of suspicious bank accounts.

> In numerous instances, the negligence of the PCGG in performing its mandate of preserving the interest of the national government interest is clearly so gross as to amount to bad faith.

> In the course of its investigation, the Committee came across a matter of

paramount public interest and concern: the lack of transparency and accountability of the PCGG. There is thus an urgent need to revisit the PCGG and put an end to its fraud, abuse and wastage.[49]

In 2011, the Bureau of Internal Revenue filed income tax evasion charges against three Philcomsat executives, one of whom was alleged to owe over P500 million.[50]

*

Was nothing sacred? Well, not much.

There were few places in Philippine society where corruption could not be found. It seemed to be assumed, moreover, that everyone was corruptible. Thus, in September 2005, around the time that the first impeachment complaint against Arroyo was thrown out by her congressional allies, according to documents of the Philippine Amusements and Gaming Corporation Cardinal Vidal and Archbishops Angel Lagdameo and Paciano Aniceto were offered "donations" of between P300,000 and P500,000.[51] They declined the offers, but such was not the case the following July, when, at a bishops' retreat shortly after the church had decided not to support calls for Arroyo's impeachment, envelopes containing between P20,000 and P30,000 were distributed by someone said to represent Malacañang.[52] Although presidential staff chief Mike Defensor ridiculed the allegation, Archbishop Lagdameo acknowledged that envelopes had been received. "It was only later that they realized the implication of the offer," he said in a statement. "Some, we know, returned their envelopes."[53] In 2008 Lagdameo, president of the Catholic Bishops Conference of the Philippines, lamented that the church had made a mistake with EDSA Dos, which had "installed a president who later on was judged by surveys as the most corrupt president."[54]

Several bishops, it would be revealed in 2011, had received rather more than envelopes from the former president. In June, the Philippine Charity Sweepstakes Office announced that it was investigating reports that Mrs. Arroyo had used its funds to buy the support of bishops. Archbishop Emeritus Oscar Cruz went a little further, urging those of his colleagues who might qualify for being known as the "Pajero Seven" to identify themselves. While the initial reports turned out to be inaccurate, this lay only in the fact that the four-by-fours were not Mitsubishi Pajeros. One of the magnificent seven, Bishop Juan de Dios Pueblos, who had recently suggested that Aquino resign, was revealed to have unashamedly written to Mrs. Arroyo in February 2009 to request such a vehicle for his birthday. Although claiming that they had been useful for work among their flocks in remote areas, the vehicles were returned.[55]

*

In 2006, a report by the commission on audit found that P494 million used to fund a hybrid rice program was unaccounted for, and that only 1,194 of the total 13,960 bags of seed had been received by agrarian reform beneficiaries.[56]

Two months after the ASEAN conference in Cebu in January 2007, it was disclosed that decorative lampposts installed for the event had been substantially overpriced. Although the Department of Public Works and Highways (DPWH) paid P50,000 for each lamppost, it turned out the true price should have been—at most—P11,750. Moreover, the cost of erecting them in Mandaue City was seven times that in Cebu City. Adding insult to injury, 30 posts had found their way into a private resort in Lapu-Lapu City (these three cities constitute Metro Cebu). Senior regional DPWH officials and the mayors of Mandaue and Lapu-Lapu were suspended.[57] The Ombudsman then began an investigation into 42 surveillance cameras purchased for the same event for P90 million—or P2.14 million per camera.[58]

Corruption is also to be found, of course, in Congress. Each year, congressmen and senators are allocated "pork barrel" allowances—allotments to be spent on approved projects at local level. It is widely believed that a large proportion of these funds end up in the pockets of the lawmakers, often by means of kickbacks from contractors. By way of example, in 2007 the *Philippine Daily Inquirer* published details of scams involving the use of "pork": 3,000 bottles of liquid fertilizer purchased for P1,500 each, when the actual price was P50 per unit; 15 irrigation pumps sold for P500,000 more than the actual cost[59]; and unbranded personal computers sold to state schools at P217,500 each, whereas the normal price would not be more than P50,000 each.[60]

56

In June 2006, the office of the Ombudsman estimated that in the previous five years the government had lost P1.2 trillion to graft; two years later, the Department of Budget and Management reckoned that P21 billion went the same way in the procurement of locally-funded projects.[61]

It would be wrong to assume that the Arroyo government took no action against corruption or similar wrongdoing. After senior staff at the DPWH confronted their boss, Florante Soriquez, with allegations that he had taken kickbacks (a claimed P210 million from district officers alone), Mrs. Arroyo demoted him to undersecretary and ordered the presidential anti-graft commission to investigate.[62] A number of public officials were suspended when lifestyle checks found that they were living beyond their known means.

In March 2006, Samuel Lee was arrested upon his arrival from Hong Kong, police having intercepted 62 container vans loaded with plastic resin that, instead of going to the bonded warehouse, were about to be driven to Valenzuela City, apparently on Lee's instructions. The police, who said that Lee offered them P300,000, also recommended that he be charged with bribery. They were angered when the Quezon City prosecutor's office recommended that Lee, who was said to be close to "Big Mike" Arroyo, be released. This was reversed, with the recommendation that he be charged with three counts of smuggling. The tax authorities then filed a complaint of tax evasion against Lee and his sister, claiming that they had under-reported some P1 billion worth of imports in 2001 and 2002.[63]

Lee was a big fish (although the cases against him do not appear to have been resolved at the time of writing), but the complaint was often heard that prosecution and punishment were either reserved for the small fry or, as in the case of Soriquez, only administered when it could no longer be avoided. Even the case of General Carlos Garcia was not straightforward: the civilian Ombudsman did not suspend him until October 2004, but the army had transferred him to other duties months earlier, maintaining a public silence in the interim. Many, recalling that Mrs. Arroyo would never have been installed as president if the armed forces had not withdrawn support from Joseph Estrada, suspected that debts were being repaid. Then again, for months the US authorities had maintained their own silence regarding Mrs. Garcia's attempt to smuggle in undeclared funds, leading Senate minority leader Aquilino Pimentel Jr. to claim that the revelations were eventually made to punish Mrs. Arroyo for her withdrawal of troops from Iraq.

The government's attempts to combat corruption were widely perceived to be either halfhearted or purely cosmetic and, thus, in a poll conducted by the Hong Kong-based Political and Economic Risk Consultancy, the results of which were released in March 2007, 1,476 expatriate businessmen regarded the Philippines as the most corrupt of the thirteen Asian countries included in the survey.[64]

But they hadn't seen anything yet.

*

On February 4, 2008, knowing that he could not defeat the motion of no confidence tabled against him, Speaker Jose de Venecia Jr. took the floor of the House of Representatives for an hour, reeling off a litany of sins committed by the administration he had served so loyally. "What is happening to our country?" he demanded. "Everything is for sale!"[65] According to the testimony of a Senate investigation witness just a few days later, the kickbacks on "anomalous transactions" — particularly one in which the presidential spouse was alleged to be involved — had climbed to unimaginable levels.

However, crusaders against corruption are not always what they seem. Jose de Venecia Jr. was ejected from the speakership because he had supported his son's allegations that negotiations for a contract with a Chinese company had involved corruption at the highest levels in the Philippine government; the fact that his son's own company had also bid for the contract did little to enhance the credibility of his anti-corruption speech.

In 2007 Comelec chairman Benjamin Abalos, already under attack for his alleged role in the 2004 election irregularities, found himself embroiled in a new controversy in which the Arroyo administration once again faced accusations of corruption. This involved an agreement with ZTE, a Chinese telecoms company, for the installation of a national broadband network (NBN) covering the whole country. It was alleged that Abalos was the intermediary with ZTE. While admitting that ZTE executives were his "golfing buddies," the 73-year-old Abalos at first denied the accusation.

In September, an anonymous businessman indicated that he was willing to testify that Abalos had offered the House Speaker's son, Jose "Joey" de Venecia III, $10 million to withdraw the bid by his Amsterdam Holdings Inc. (AHI) for the NBN contract, with the bribe coming from the overpricing of the deal.[66] According to Senator Lacson, this was small change, as the bribes were to have been divided as follows: $55 million for "a Comelec official," $75 million for two "highly-placed" individuals in government, and $68 million for use in the May elections. The contract, said Lacson, was overpriced by 300 percent.[67] As the controversy raged, Mrs. Arroyo discussed the matter with Chinese president Hu Jintao while at the APEC summit in Sydney, where both parties agreed to instruct their trade ministers to review the project. Even so, Arroyo barred trade secretary Peter Favila from attending a House "question hour" to discuss the deal.[68] Granting a petition by AHI and former congressman Rolex Suplico (now vice-governor of Iloilo), the Supreme Court issued a temporary restraining order against implementation of the contract, and in early October Arroyo cancelled the deal. (In February 2008, she would order the suspension of eleven projects funded by Official Development Assistance amid allegations that some of these had also been tainted with corruption.)

Meanwhile, the allegations made by the younger De Venecia took a sensational turn. In an affidavit, he swore that Abalos had admitted having bugged his phone, recording a conversation with ZTE in which De Venecia had claimed that Abalos had been demanding $130 million in kickbacks.[69] He then testified to the Senate that, at a meeting at Wack-Wack golf course, the presidential spouse had threateningly demanded that he "back off" from the NBN deal. Abalos denied both allegations, while "Big Mike" maintained that he had only a "chance encounter" with De Venecia.

Earlier in the year, Romulo Neri had been secretary of the National Economic Development Authority (NEDA) until, having approved the deal with ZTE, Mrs. Arroyo had relocated him to the Commission on Higher Education (where, he complained at the time, he had neither qualifications nor experience). Now, he testified that Abalos had told him that there was "two hundred in it" for him, which he interpreted as an offer of a P200 million bribe for approving the ZTE deal. After consulting his lawyers, he reported this to the president, who simply told him to ignore the offer and approve the deal. When pressed further on this discussion with Mrs. Arroyo, however, Neri invoked "executive privilege," a device popularized by Richard Nixon.

In late September, Rolex Suplico filed an impeachment complaint against Abalos, and while there were those who, like Bayan Muna congressmen Teddy Casiño, thought that the Comelec chairman "knows so many things about the administration to be dropped like a hot potato,"[70] the palace ordered a formal investigation into the alleged attempt to bribe Neri, and Speaker de Venecia (who was, admittedly, hardly perceived as impartial) called for a "conscience vote" on the impeachment complaint. Abalos resigned, thereby prompting opposition claims that he had taken the fall to protect Mrs. Arroyo.

Although some of the younger De Venecia's allegations (that, for example, transport secretary Leandro Mendoza was, along with others, plotting to kill him) strained credulity, his version of events was accepted by many. There were, however, alternative theories. According to Senator Miriam Defensor Santiago, the whole affair was little more than a dispute over kickbacks between the competing camps. Columnist Julius F. Fortuna detected the hand of Uncle Sam, suggesting that when, in April, Ambassador Kristie Kenney had written to NEDA to register the Washington's interest in the NBN deal, her subliminal message was, "Don't mess with us in this deal. You are in effect allowing China to dominate the cyberspace in Philippine territory which remains our sphere of influence. That is unacceptable."[71] In a sense, though, the important factor in this scandal was the fact that De Venecia's version was believed by so many, as this bore eloquent testimony to the popular perception of the depths to which the political and economic cultures had descended.

Enter Rodolfo "Jun" Lozada, the former president of the Philippine Forest Corporation who had acted as a consultant for NEDA, which Neri had headed. In late January 2008, the Senate issued a warrant for his arrest following his failure to appear at hearings, whereupon Lozada flew to Hong Kong. Upon his return to Manila on February 5, he texted his brother to say that he had been accosted at the airport, and there then commenced a series of allegations and denials in which Lozada claimed to have been abducted and forced to sign affidavits which departed from the truth. Lozada's allegations regarding the ZTE deal were sufficiently dramatic in themselves, however, that the reader may be spared the tortuous detail of the alleged abduction. (Suffice it to say that while a logbook at the Ninoy Aquino International Airport would indeed show that members of the Presidential Security Group were in the car that picked up Lozada, the official explanation was that he had requested security.[72]) He resurfaced at a press conference called at the La Salle School, Greenhills, where his family had previously taken refuge, and as he tearfully recounted his involvement in the NBN project it became clear that he had gone from fugitive to whistleblower. At the end of the day, he said, using a phrase that would enjoy a brief popularity in the opinion columns, his role in the NBN deal had become one of attempting to "moderate the greed" of some of the lead actors in the drama.[73]

Lozada said that he had known about the deal from its very inception, and that his participation had commenced in September 2006, when Neri had asked him to try to reconcile the ZTE project (which consisted of erecting the broadband network by means of a Chinese loan) with the build-operate-transfer project which he and Neri had put forward. When, however, he recommended Joey de Venecia's scheme, with Abalos as the supplier, he encountered problems, as Abalos was, said Lozada, insistent that the ZTE loan project, which he had brokered, should go ahead and that his $130-million commission should be protected. At one stage, Lozada claimed, Abalos had called Big Mike Arroyo to advise him of Neri's reluctance regarding the loan project. In December 2006, he had met Abalos and Mike for dinner, although Mike had contributed little to the conversation. The latter, however, denied that he had any involvement in the deal, or that he had dined with Lozada. The latter said that he had resigned as NEDA consultant after Abalos called him in January 2007 and, using rich language, warned him that he had plenty of police and military contacts.[74]

In the Senate, however, Lozada said that although he was aware of the content of the conversation with Mrs. Arroyo when Neri had reported Abalos's attempt to bribe him, he must refuse to divulge this as it was told to him in confidence.[75] This would become a major bone of contention, as we have seen that Neri himself claimed "executive privilege." The Supreme Court found that he was within his rights to do so; in a dissenting opinion, Justice Antonio Carpio said that executive privilege could not be invoked where a crime was being discussed. All nine justices subscribing to the majority decision had been appointed by Arroyo. Chief Justice Reynato Puno's was one of the six minority votes.

According to Joey de Venecia, ZTE had advanced at least $1 million to Abalos, and as at the time this had equated to more than P50 million, plunder charges might by appropriate.[76]

(Mrs. Arroyo, meanwhile, had ordered the justice department to decide who should be charged under the anti-graft and procurement laws regarding the ZTE deal, and some of the whistleblowers would in due course be presented with a nasty shock.) A few days later, the younger De Venecia would tell a rally in Makati that P10 billion of the P16 billion Chinese loan would have gone into "the pockets of First Gentleman Arroyo, President Gloria Arroyo, Abalos and their cabal in Malacañang."[77] The Chinese company refused to testify, saying that it could not "allow itself to be dragged into any political circus." However, it denied both bribery and overpricing, explaining that the price of the project increased to $329 million when it was expanded to cover the whole country, as opposed to the original 30 percent.[78]

According to Lozada, at a meeting at the Asian Institute of Management with Senators Panfilo Lacson and Jamby Madrigal, Neri had described Mrs. Arroyo as "evil," and had talked of an "ecosystem of corruption in government, and she was right in the middle of it." Neri, he recalled, wanted to resign as Arroyo had "lost all moral authority over him." Neri did not remember the "evil" remark, saying that he intended to remain in government as he had "hope" in Mrs. Arroyo and her administration.[79]

Mrs. Arroyo said that she had only been informed (by Neri) of the corruption allegations the night before the ZTE was signed on April 21, 2007, and did not stop the signing because it would have jeopardized Sino-Philippine diplomatic relations. She waited for five months before cancelling the deal in order, she said, to "properly advise" the Chinese government.[80]

In May 2008, Iloilo vice-governor Rolex Suplico claimed that on November 2, 2006, five months before she witnessed the signing of the agreement, Mrs. Arroyo had made a previously undisclosed trip to ZTE headquarters in Shenzen province for a meeting with company officials. There had, he said, been a pre-meeting game of golf, and he produced photographs to substantiate this.[81] That revelation was dramatic, but it was not proof of wrongdoing.

It was not until November 2009 that the Senate blue ribbon committee released its report on the ZTE affair, stating that Mrs. Arroyo had committed an impeachable offense (she had, said chairman Richard Gordon, allowed the signing of the deal to proceed even though Neri had told her that Abalos had attempted to bribe him), and recommending that eleven others, including Mike Arroyo, Neri, Joey de Venecia, Lozada and transport and communications secretary Leandro Mendoza, be prosecuted, although Senators Lacson and Escudero argued that the whistleblowers Lozada and De Venecia should be spared.[82] In fact, Joey de Venecia had filed an impeachment complaint against Mrs. Arroyo a year earlier, but that met the same fate as all impeachment complaints during Mrs. Arroyo's tenure, and one did not have to be too cynical to doubt whether criminal proceedings against Arroyo allies would, even if commenced, succeed.

Coincidentally (one must assume), the very same day as De Venecia filed his impeachment complaint in October 2008, the justice department's fact-finding panel had recommended that the Ombudsman investigate him and his father due to conflict of interest (the son was pursuing a government contract while the father was House speaker; according to communications secretary Leandro Mendoza, the elder De Venecia had "brazenly asked" him to approve his son's bid for the NBN contract).[83] In 2009, the Ombudsman (with the controversial Gutierrez inhibiting herself from the case) recommended the filing of charges against Abalos and Neri while rejecting complaints against the presidential couple. Neri was then suspended for six months from his position as head of the Social Security System, to which he had been recently appointed. The suspension was halted by an appeal court temporary restraining order but reinstated by the Ombudsman two weeks after the elections in May 2010. If Neri thought his problems were over following the election of Benigno Aquino III, he was mistaken, for in 2011 he was charged with income tax evasion.

The vagaries of the Philippine legal system were perhaps most clearly illustrated by the case of Jun Lozada who, having alleged that Mike Defensor had acted as an emissary of the presidential palace during his alleged abduction, offering him money and seeking to persuade him to drop the abduction story, was charged by Defensor with perjury. In May 2009, the case came before Manila metropolitan trial court judge Jorge Emmanuel Lorredo, who advised Defensor to arrive at a settlement as the case would be harmful to the latter's career and health. Some, he mused, said that Mike Arroyo was being punished by his heart problems.

I do not know if this is true, for I do not really know how our Lord works, for he does work in mysterious ways. But what I do know is that Lozada is being protected by the Church, by the priests and nuns. That must mean something. Defensor, take note: that must mean something...Now, why are all of these so important for Defensor to ponder on? Simple: if it is true that Mike Arroyo is being punished, Defensor may also be punished with some serious disease.

He went on to wonder whether Defensor was seeking political suicide, then suggested he consider the possibility that the defense would call the presidential couple, and if they refused to appear he (Lorredo) would have them arrested.[84] These remarks were not simply made in passing, or as humorous asides, but appear in the text of the order issued by Judge Lorredo. Doubtful that he would receive a fair judgment, Defensor dropped the case.[85] However, Lozada was still not out of the woods, as a malversation case filed against him in 2008 regarding his time at Philippine Forest Corporation was outstanding.

*

The truth of the ZTE-NBN case has still not been uncovered. Whoever was guilty, no one has yet been tried, found guilty and incarcerated. Nevertheless, it was blindingly obvious that *someone* (possibly everyone involved in the case, even) was guilty, and that graft and corruption was a problem at high levels of the Philippine political and business worlds; equally obviously, the justice system, even when it had not been corrupted, often proved to be, as in the Lorredo order, downright eccentric.

But people made their own judgments. Archbishop Angel Lagdameo, as we saw, somewhat belatedly concluded that the church had made a mistake with EDSA Dos. Michael Clancy, chief executive officer of the Philippine Business Leaders' Forum, consisting of around 40 transnational corporations, said that while elsewhere in the region investors usually budget for 10 percent in "facilitation" or bribes, in the Philippines it was more like 50 percent. According to Clancy, two years earlier government officials had rebuffed a European investment delegation with the words, "We don't need your money anymore, we have China now. We can get all the money we need from China."[86]

NOTES

1. As appalling as the levels of graft and corruption during the Arroyo regime may have been, it is necessary to inject a note of caution. A number of nationalist Filipinos have arrived at the realization that concern about corruption has been used as a smokescreen by some who do not necessarily have the best interests of the Philippines at heart. "The World Bank," says Herbert Docena, "insists that eliminating corruption requires economic reforms such as liberalization and deregulation 'to move toward a smaller, more efficient government'; privatization of corporations owned in part or in whole by the state; and opening domestic markets for products from abroad."

> Without the World Bank and the ADB [Asian Development Bank] singling out corruption as the reason behind the country's underdevelopment, they would not be able to argue for such "reforms"... Indeed..., "the case for trade liberalization, privatization, and deregulation often stands on the discourse of corruption. Without it, the case falters."

Thus, while corruption is a problem in the Philippines, it should be understood that it is not *the* major problem, that it is a symptom of a sickness rather than the sickness itself. It is, therefore, important to ward off attempts by the multilateral institutions to use the record of the Arroyo regime in this regard in order to peddle their questionable remedies. See Herbert Docena, "Corruption and Poverty: Barking Up the Wrong Tree?" in Walden Bello, Herbert Docena, Marissa de Guzman and Marylou Malig, *The Anti- Development State: The Political Economy of Permanent Crisis in the Philippines* (Quezon City: Department of Sociology, UP/Focus on the Global South, 2004), 298, 299.

2. *Philippine Star*, October 21, 2002.

3. *Daily Tribune*, November 16, 2002.

4. www.inq7.net, May 31, 2001.

5. *Philippine Daily Inquirer*, March 14, 2003.

6. www.inq7.net, November 23, 2002.

7. Cited in *Daily Tribune*, March 25, 2004.

8. www.inq7.net, July 30, 2001.

9. Ibid., October 4, 2001.

10. "Scandals," abs-cbnnews.com, July 18, 2009, accessed September 23, 2012.

11. Lacson had problems of his own. Several attempts were made to revive charges that, as a senior police officer, he had been involved in the Kuratong Baleleng "rub-out" case in 1995, in which eleven gang members had been killed. After Judge Theresa Yadao dismissed the charges in November 2003 (days later, she alleged that she had been pressured to deliver a decision against Lacson), the Supreme Court revived the case. Then it was alleged that Lacson and his wife had $278 million in US bank accounts. However, an Angelo Mawanag, who had previously testified against Lacson (he now claimed that intelligence chief Victor Corpus had threatened to implicate him in money laundering activity if he refused), alleged that, at Mike Arroyo's behest, he had manufactured all the documents detailing the alleged accounts, and that the presidential spouse had also instructed a lawyer to hack into Lacson's accounts. See *Philippine Daily Inquirer*, November 19, 2003, April 5, 2003 and *Malaya*, May 8, 2003 and May 9, 2003.

12. *Philippine Star*, August 28, 2003.

13. *Malaya*, September 2, 2003.

14. *Philippine Star*, September 9, 2003.

15. www.inq7net, November 14, 2002.

16. Ibid., November 26, 2002.

17. Ibid., January 3, 2003.

18. *Philippine Star*, January 15, 2003.

19. Ibid., August 19, 2003.

20. *Malaya*, October 20, 2005.

21. www.inq7.net, January 19, 2006. In October 2002, having the previous month

ordered the whole board of the public estates authority to take indefinite leave, Mrs. Arroyo suggested that directors alleged to have been involved in the overpricing of the new Diosdado Macapagal Boulevard (named after her father) resign while an investigation took place. The palace was also reported to have pressured Ombudsman Simeon Marcelo to slow down the prosecutions of Major General Carlos Garcia, Lt. General Jacinto Ligot (see later in this chapter) and presidential brother-in-law Iggy Arroyo. (Ernesto Maceda, "Mr. Expose," *Daily Tribune*, October 6, 2005.) Citing insiders at the Ombudsman's office, the *Daily Tribune* claimed that the last straw for Marcelo came with a shouting match with Defense Secretary Avelino Cruz (his former law partner) over Mrs. Arroyo's order effectively preventing officials from attending Senate investigations and instructions, allegedly from the president, to quash the cases involving Perez and the military officers charged with plunder. (*Daily Tribune,* October 7, 2005.).

22. www.inq7.net, 1/8/07.

23. inq7.net, November 25, 2008; *Manila Times*, November 25, 2008.

24. Editorial, "Hanging on," *Philippine Daily Inquirer*, December 15, 2005.

25. *Malaya*, October 7, 2006.

26. Ibid., June 15, 2011.

27. The foregoing originally appeared in Ken Fuller, "On the brink?", *Morning Star*, November 9, 2004.

28. www.inq7.net, February 10, 2005.

29. Ibid., December 6, 2005.

30. *Philippine Star*, January 28, 2011.

31. *Philippine Daily Inquirer*, February 4, 2011.

32. *Daily Tribune*, February 1, 2011.

33. *Philippine Star*, February 8, 2011.

34. *Philippine* Star, February 22, 2011.

35. Editorial, "Auditing the auditors," *Philippine Star*, February 8, 2011.

36. Having served the maximum three consecutive terms in the House, in 2007 Pichay made an unsuccessful bid for a Senate seat. He was then appointed as administrator of

the Local Water Utilities Administration (LWUA). In July 2011, the Acting Ombudsman ordered his dismissal from government service for unlawful use of government funds in acquiring a private bank in 2009. He and his deputy were permanently barred from government service and stripped of all benefits. (*Philippine Star*, July 5, 2011.) The Department of Finance filed charges of malversation of public funds and graft against him. Graft charges were also filed by LWUA employees. He was then charged with tax evasion as, although his net worth had increased by P58.5 million between 2008 and 2009, he had paid no tax. Pichay claimed political harassment. (*Philippine Daily Inquirer*, July 22, 2011.)

37. *Daily Tribune*, February 8, 2011.

38. *Philippine Star*, February 15, 2011.

39. *Philippine Daily Inquirer*, February 9, 2011.

40. *Philippine Star*, June 9, 2011.

41. *Philippine Daily Inquirer*, June 7, 2011.

42. www.inquirer.net, October 19, 21, 27, November 6, 11, 2008, March 2, 2009; *Philippine Daily Inquirer*, October 30, November 20, 2008, August 20, 2009; *Philippine Star*, September 10, 2010; *Manila Bulletin*, October 14, 2010.

43. *Philippine Star*, September 2, 2011.

44. *Manila* Times, September 2, 2011.

45. *Philippine Daily Inquirer*, September 28, 2011.

46. *Philippine Star*, July 6, 22, August 3, 2011; *Daily Tribune*, July 7, August 16, 2011; *Philippine Daily Inquirer*, July 20, August 1, 2011.

47. www.inq7.net, April 22, 2006.

48. *Malaya*, January 23, 2007.

49. Senate Committee on Government Corporations and Public Enterprises, "Committee Report on P.S. Res. No. 455," 2007.

50. Ibid., March 25, 2011.

51. www.inq7.net, July 13, 2006.

52. Ibid., July 12, 2006.

53. Ibid., July 15, 2006.

54. *Daily Tribune*, February 20, 2008

55. *Philippine Daily Inquirer.*, June 29, July 6, 14, 2011.

56. *Malaya*, October 25, 2006.

57. *Philippine Daily Inquirer*, March 23 and March 24, 2007.

58. Ibid., March 30, 2007.

59. Ibid., March 23, 2007.

60. *Philippine Daily Inquirer*, March 22, 2007.

61. *Philippine Daily Inquirer*, September 9, 2008.

62. www.inq7.net, February 10, 2005.

63. www.inq7.net, March 7, 8, 9 and 29.

64. *Philippine Daily Inquirer*, March 14, 2007.

65. www.inquirer.net, February 5, 2008.

66. www.inquirer.net, September 4, 2007.

67. *Daily Tribune*, September 5, 2007.

68. www.inquirer.net, September 11, 2007.

69. *Philippine Daily Inquirer*, September 14, 2007.

70. www.inquirer.net, September 27, 2007.

71. Julius F. Fortuna, "China bashing in the upswing," *Manila Times*, September 27, 2007.

72. www.inquirer.net, February 14, 2008.

73. www.inquirer.net, February 8, 2008.

74. www.inquirer.net, *Philippine Star, Malaya*, February 8, 2008, www.inquirer.net, February 9, 2008.

75. www.inquirer.net, February 8, 2008.

76. Ibid., February 11, 2008.

77. Ibid., February 15, 2008.

78. *Philippine Daily Inquirer*, February 15, 2008.

79. www.inquirer.net, February 18, 2008.

80. Ibid., February 23 and 24, 2008.

81. *Philippine Daily Inquirer*, May 14, 2008.

82. Ibid., November 11, 2009; *Philippine Star*, November 12, 2009.

83. www.inquirer.net, November 26, 2008.

84. Ibid., May 5, 2009.

85. *Philippine Daily Inquirer*, May 29, 2009.

86. *Malaya*, March 13, 2008.

4 "MORE OBEDIENCE TO GOD"

Ritual is a prominent –and largely negative—part of Philippine life, sometimes used to soften a harsh reality, often serving to simply hide the truth. Political leaders regularly use ritual to sing the praises of the poor and the workers, lament the divisions in society and even pledge to work towards overcoming them. At the time they say these things, they may even believe them. During ritualistic speeches, as much as the things that are said it is in a sense the speakers who are the fabrications. For it is as if they are in church, eyes tightly closed and hands clasped together, momentarily transforming themselves into citizens of a realm that does not exist. But after the speech is delivered, they leave the world-as-it-might-be and return to the world-as-it-is, where material interests, their own and those of their most powerful supporters, will ensure that whatever promises they have made will be unfulfilled.

On December 30, 2002, just three weeks after House Speaker Jose de Venecia Jr. had called upon her to form a government of national unity, Mrs. Arroyo delivered a speech at Rizal Park, Baguio, in which she said that Asia's first republic had, over the past 30 years, become its weakest, due to "the persistence of an outdated social system wherein vested interests and traditional politics have stunted development toward a strong and modern society." She talked of selfish interests exploiting poverty in order to maintain the status quo, and of a new generation of leaders who "will be our agents of change." The nation had become deeply divided, "symbolized by the polarity between Edsa II and the May 1 siege barely three months after." (Enraged by the manner of Estrada's arrest, in the early hours of May 1, 2001 huge numbers of his supporters, largely the urban poor, had marched to the presidential palace

71

where, virtually leaderless, they had been dispersed with gunfire, leaving an unrecorded number of dead and wounded. Mrs. Arroyo consistently refused to recognize the May event as "EDSA Tres.") As the 2004 elections promised to be bitterly contested, Mrs. Arroyo continued, and as "I am among the principal figures in the divisive national events of the last two or three years, my political efforts can only result in never-ending divisiveness."[1] This speech had only one place to go: she would not be running in 2004, and to demonstrate her sincerity she would soon announce her preferred successor. Speaker de Venecia said on January 2 that Arroyo had approved the formation, within 45 days, of a unity government that would include all opposition parties, along with the communist and Muslim groups.

It sounded wonderful, but the Arroyo speech had, of course, been an exercise in ritual on that most ritualistic of occasions, Rizal Day. (This honors the martyred Jose Rizal, author of the fiercely anti-clerical novel *Noli Me Tangere* executed by the Spanish authorities, confirming him as the number one national hero, an honor that, in the view of many progressive and nationalist Filipinos, should be conferred on Andres Bonifacio, leader of the revolution that Rizal had opposed.)

In the world-as-it-is, there was no government of national unity. As early as January 5, the presidential palace was cautioning supporters of the idea to be patient, as the proposal was being studied by the Cabinet oversight committee (whose members possibly suspected they were being asked to play the role of turkeys voting for Christmas). Communist Party of the Philippines (CPP) spokesman Gregorio "Ka Roger" Rosal rejected the proposal early on as it was "without any clear principled basis of unity."[2] Arroyo, meanwhile, had revived a presidential advisory body called the Council of State. Initially conceived as containing former presidents and senior serving officials, it was now suggested that some groups might be offered seats here, rather than in the Cabinet. However, presidential spokesman Ignacio Bunye specified that to gain access "militant groups" would need to adhere to the Constitution, the sovereignty and territorial integrity of the Philippines, and the rule of law. That seemed to rule out most of them. Indeed, the actions of the administration gave the clear impression that it had no intention whatsoever of forming a unity government. Why, if it intended to invite its opponents into the Cabinet, was it filling vacant positions?

And, of course, it would be another seven years before Arroyo would name her preferred successor, a distinction which would mark him for certain defeat in the 2010 election.

In any case, anyone with a reasonable attention-span would have recalled that, just a few weeks prior to her Rizal Day announcement, Mrs. Arroyo had appeared intent on postponing the 2004 elections, indicating that she would support the establishment of a parliamentary system (calls for constitutional change were raised throughout the Arroyo administration—see chapter 7) only if the terms of all elected officials, including of the president, were extended to 2007.[3] While there may, therefore, have been those who were surprised when, later in 2003, the ruling Lakas-Christian and Muslim Democrats (Lakas-CMD) began a petition campaign to "persuade" Arroyo to run, they were hard to find. Mrs. Arroyo now claimed that she had not yet decided whether she would be a candidate, saying in October that she would be guided by divine inspiration—following which, the outcome was never in doubt.

Augmenting the persuasive powers of the divinity, US ambassador Francis Ricciardone purred that, while the USA would be backing only one candidate—democracy—Mrs. Arroyo was a "first-class citizen of the United…" He then made light of his "slip," saying: "I think we admire her so much we might make her an honorary citizen."[4] It later emerged that Mrs. Arroyo had received further encouragement from the (then) almighty dollar, as during her recent trip to the USA, chairmen and CEOs of companies with Philippine interests had told her that greater investment would be available with political stability, which would itself be served by her candidacy.[5] On October 4, 2003, at a 40,000-strong rally on the former Clark airbase, she declared her candidacy, saying that for her this would mean "more sacrifice" and "more obedience to God."[6]

That the Arroyo camp did not see her victory as a foregone conclusion was demonstrated by its attempt to co-opt, pressure or sabotage potential rivals. Approached to run as Mrs. Arroyo's vice-presidential candidate, former education secretary Raul Roco responded: "As I have constantly said, the Philippines cannot afford six more years of President Gloria Macapagal Arroyo."[7] Following this rebuff, the Arroyo camp courted Senator Noli de Castro, then leading the pack of "presidentiables" in the polls. He agreed to "slide down" to the number two slot, leading to speculation that he was acting on behalf of the Lopez family, controllers of the ABS-CBN television station for which, regardless of his senatorial duties, De Castro still worked. In return for him settling for the vice-presidential position, ran the theory, troubled Lopez companies would receive government assistance.

If businessman Eduardo "Danding" Cojuangco decided to run, as he had in 1992, one thing was certain: his campaign would be well-funded. When in July 2003 the Sandiganbayan anti-corruption court ruled that 72.2 percent of the United Coconut Planters' Bank, claimed by Cojuangco and his nominees, was the property of the government, his supporters alleged the intention was to head off the possibility of his candidacy. The Presidential Commission on Good Government (PCGG) then began reviewing all cases involving the controversial coconut levy of the Marcos years to see if criminal charges could be filed against Cojuangco. If in July the stick was being wielded, it was the turn of the carrot in early October, when it was announced that the Sandiganbayan had lifted the freeze on the 20 percent of San Miguel Corporation shares claimed by Cojuangco. Many now began to ask whether Mrs. Arroyo had cut a deal with him. Whatever the truth, he did not run. Later, the PCGG would discuss the possibility of a compromise regarding some of Cojuangco's disputed wealth.

When movie idol Fernando Poe Jr. finally threw his hat into the ring in November, Arroyo's campaign managers were alleged to have met to discuss the possibility of bringing tax-evasion charges against him or of reviving questions regarding his citizenship.[8] Poe's father, also a movie star, had been of Spanish origins, while his mother had been American, and in January 2004 it was claimed that Poe was a US citizen and, as such, ineligible to run. However, a rather poor job had been made of forging the evidence, as an electric typewriter had been used on what purported to be a 1939 document. Then Senator Vicente Sotto III used a privilege speech to allege that Ricardo Manapat, whom Arroyo had appointed as director of the national archives, had masterminded the forgeries. The drama built as Manapat's staff confirmed this at a Commission on Elections (Comelec) hearing, while Manapat's driver testified in the Senate that, on two occasions in December 2003, he had driven Manapat to a building owned by Mike Arroyo, the presidential spouse.[9] Manapat, while filing perjury charges against his staff, went on indefinite leave. The Comelec, and later the Supreme Court, found that Poe was a Filipino citizen.

*

Mrs. Arroyo called her electoral vehicle the Koalisyon ng Katapatan at Karanasan sa Kinabukasan (Coalition of Honesty and Experience for the Future, or K4) and the theme of experience was emphasized throughout the campaign, but while Arroyo had the unusual bonus of being able to argue that she had already done the job for three years, the main purpose was to remind the voters that Poe, who would be her main opponent, had never before held elective office.

The sources of support for Arroyo were fairly predictable. Following George W. Bush's visit to Manila in October 2003, palace officials were keen to claim that he had "all but" endorsed her. They also cited a TV interview at the White House on October 14 in which Bush had said: "I know my friend is running again [a slip, as Bush had presumably forgotten the manner in which Arroyo gained the presidency in the first place] and she's got a strong agenda to run on. [She] has been very strong and I appreciate that and I appreciate my friendship with her." A few days before the election, she would receive a "Dear Gloria" letter of support from former Georgetown classmate Bill Clinton.

The business community seemed to be split. In late November, the president of the Philippine Chamber of Commerce and Industry (PCCI, which had been known to adopt nationalist positions) suggested that the next president should have emergency powers to implement reforms, in line with a plan for the first hundred days of the new administration that the PCCI was compiling. Entitled "Presidential Business Agenda," this described the Philippines as being "grossly mismanaged" and called for the tackling of poverty, the budget deficit and peace and order, the renegotiation of the foreign debt (Poe would be attacked for making the same suggestion) and the legalization of jueteng. The Makati Business Club (which is open to foreign business concerns) was more enthusiastic, a members' survey in January showing 47.6 percent support for her, and when she addressed a general membership meeting of the club in April, the event was described by one columnist as a "love feast."[10]

The Catholic Church played a role, even though Gaudencio Rosales had, upon taking over as Archbishop of Manila from the retiring Cardinal Jaime Sin, indicated that the Church would, while not withdrawing from politics, not endorse candidates. At a thinly attended celebration of the 1986 "people power" anniversary, the message of the now-retired Sin called for the people to vote for achievements and experience, while Bishop Socrates Villegas, the EDSA shrine prelate, also appealed for a vote for an experienced candidate. Decoded: vote Arroyo.

Essentially, there was only one issue in the 2004 presidential election: Gloria Macapagal Arroyo. Despite the depth of anti-Arroyo sentiment, however, she ran against a crowded field, and this undoubtedly contributed to her victory, legitimate or not. Even the main opposition grouping was unable to agree on a common candidate. After Senator Panfilo Lacson had been "tentatively" adopted by one section of the opposition, movie star Fernando Poe Jr., a close friend of Joseph Estrada, was persuaded to run. Soon to be universally known as "FPJ," Poe was subject to the same kind of mass adulation as Estrada, and therefore viewed as a winner. Before the campaign commenced, attempts to get Poe and Lacson to agree on a single candidate came to naught.

Raul Roco, a former senator and Arroyo's education secretary (until he was forced to leave the government after allegations he had used government resources to prepare for his presidential campaign), launched his bid at the Cultural Center in Pasay at the end of November 2003. Although at one stage he had topped the opinion polls (hence the early attempt by the Arroyo camp to co-opt him), he was now unable to announce a senatorial slate, and it was not until the end of December that he announced his running mate as former congressman Herminio Aquino, a relatively obscure member of that family. At a crucial point in the campaign, Roco would travel to the USA for medical treatment of a back problem, although it was later admitted that the ailment was connected with the prostate cancer that had been treated in the 1990s (and which the following year would claim his life). This further reduced his chances.

Eventually, there were no less than 84 candidates filing for the presidency, 22 for vice-president and 88 for Senator. The Comelec then whittled those down, eliminating "nuisance candidates" and those unable to demonstrate their ability to launch a nationwide campaign. At the end of the day, this process left a list of six "presidentiables": Arroyo, Poe, Roco, Lacson, Bro. Eddie Villanueva (leader of the Jesus Is Lord church) and obscure businessman Eddie Gil.

After the latter paid for accommodation for himself and his staff at a Cagayan de Oro hotel with a rubber check, he was debarred by the Comelec.

The Poe electoral vehicle was called the Koalisiyon ng Nagkakaisang Pilipino (KNP, Coalition of United Filipinos), but the "unity" appeared to be purely formal and not to everyone's taste. Senator Loren Legarda, another former broadcaster who had earlier defected from the administration team, was announced as Poe's vice-presidential running mate, and some within the KNP were upset at this decision, as she had played a key role in aborting Estrada's impeachment trial (and, therefore, opening the way for EDSA Dos). For the KNP Senate slate, three were taken from the administration ranks, and this was a further source of disquiet. Trade Union Congress of the Philippines general secretary Ernesto Herrera had, for example, been Visayas vice-president of Lakas-CMD until his non-inclusion in the administration ticket (in the race for 12 seats, he would come 21st). Veteran nationalist Alejandro Lichauco, initially an enthusiast, began to cool towards Poe, using his column to take him to task for the choice of Legarda and for being so heavily influenced by Senator Edgardo Angara. What chance, Lichauco asked, would Poe's anti-globalization thrust have (early on, Poe had talked of withdrawing from the World Trade Organization) if such influence went unchecked?[11]

The inexperienced Poe was given a crash course on the main electoral issues, and in the second half of February a 19-strong policy team was announced, whereupon spokesman Congressman Francis Escudero declared: "The blueprint for economic development will be guided by fundamental market principles and shall be founded on Mr. Poe's commitment to alleviate poverty, provide basic services efficiently and effectively, create more jobs and ensure equal opportunities to all Filipinos." There was little encouragement here for those looking for a break from the dysfunctional economic model currently in place, and even pro-opposition columnist Rod P. Kapunan was sufficiently dismayed to predict that the economic problems were here to stay, as Poe's advisers were the ones who had created them.[12] A disappointed Lichauco described the economic advisers as an "all-globalists' club," and cautioned Poe not to repeat the mistakes of Estrada, who had had a pro-poor platform but anti-poor policies.[13] Poe was given several very public invitations to debate the issues with Arroyo and the other candidates, but his camp refused every one of them.

Given the failure of the two main contenders to submit developed programs, the 90 days of the official campaign period allowed ample time for allegations of cheating, and they came thick and fast. Most were directed at the Arroyo camp and included claims that preparations had been made for the Arroyo vote to be "padded." When the Comelec released its lists of certified voters, the numerous anomalies caused an outcry. The number of registered voters in areas of Arroyo strength on the island of Cebu was, for example, found to have increased by 32 percent since 2001, while a locality in Laguna province with only 4,000 voters found that 38,186 were listed. On the other side of the coin, another Laguna village that found its 5,000 voters were reduced to 500 on the official lists.

Arroyo was, of course, in the unusual position of being a sitting president running for re-election as, due to the manner in which she had come by the office, the constitutional limitation of one six-year term did not apply to her. This gave her the opportunity to use government resources for campaigning purposes, and it was a widely- held perception that this opportunity was utilized (for example, Archbishop Oscar Cruz claimed that the publicly owned Philippine Gaming and Amusement Corporation had spent P68 million on Arroyo's campaign), but the Comelec dismissed complaint after complaint. It was further claimed that, by means of an "Oplan Checkmate," the major opinion polls would show Arroyo initially trailing Poe, then drawing level and overtaking him. In practice, they showed exactly this, but was the opposition merely concocting a conspiracy theory out of the unfortunate facts of life? For its part, the administration claimed that the opposition was planning, in the event that Arroyo won, a coup preceded by bombings, and an opposition lawyer became the subject of legal proceedings for, allegedly, falsifying government documents in an attempt to show that Arroyo had paid an actress P6.2 million for her support.

What of the opposition allegations?

Comelec chairman Benjamin Abalos, telling the security forces to be prepared for post-election violence, suggested that some of the allegations were being made by the opposition in order to condition the minds of supporters to believe that an Arroyo victory could only be achieved by cheating. This was a plausible thesis. But it was also the case that alternative polls and mock elections consistently showed Poe doing better than Arroyo. The opposition claimed to have inside information to the effect that even the polls privately commissioned by the administration camp showed Poe well ahead.

At the launch of a "Coalition of Hope," Archbishop of Manila Gaudencio Rosales warned that "at stake are the legal and ethical foundations of our democracy." The coalition's statement called on Filipinos to "move together to guard against those who would take advantage of positions and resources they hold in trust." That seemed clear enough. Then Rosales came forward with a further bombshell: junior police and military officers had confirmed to the church that there were plans to switch legitimate ballot boxes for those containing votes for a particular candidate. The church declined to name either its sources or the favored candidates for "security reasons," and in the absence of names, the Comelec refused to investigate the allegations, branding both coalition and bishops as "destabilizers."

While not all forms of fraud predicted by the opposition were used, as the reports came in after the May 10 polling day, it was alleged that many of them had been. A vast number of citizens found themselves disenfranchised, as their names did not appear on the voters' lists, while others found themselves assigned to the wrong precincts. At some precincts, there was no indelible ink (used to mark the voter's forefinger), and in other cases it was claimed to be all-too "delible." In several locations where the government claimed things went smoothly, the opposition alleged that no votes were cast, as gunmen has chased voters away as soon as the poll opened.

There were numerous claims that votes had been padded or shaved and it was found that in one Maguindanao town zero votes had been allocated to the other presidential candidates, while 17, 243 were said to have voted for Arroyo. According to the certificates of canvass, Poe had received zero votes in areas where he had both campaign managers and supporters. One method of achieving such incredible results was to simply buy up CoCs and then substitute phonies, and the opposition alleged that members of the Arroyo Cabinet and family were engaged in this activity in Mindanao.

According to former solicitor general Francisco Chavez (an unsuccessful senatorial candidate for Roco's party), there were eleven towns in Maguindanao where returns showed Arroyo receiving 98 percent, despite the fact that, due to intimidation, no voting had actually taken place there. (This piece of Maguindanao history would be repeated in the 2007 midterm elections—see chapter 8.) Chavez, who speculated that there could be a popular uprising if the election was shown to have been won by foul means, said that he had 31 sworn affidavits from all over the country alleging fraud.[14] In early June, after Chavez filed plunder charges against Arroyo, alleging that P728 million in fertilizer funds intended for farmers had been used in her campaign, "First Gentleman" Mike Arroyo brought a P10 million libel suit against Chavez and others. Chavez then filed a further plunder charge against the president and other officials regarding a second allocation of P1.1 billion, while Mike Arroyo filed libel suits, each claiming P10 million, against former Senator Francisco Tatad, the *Daily Tribune* and others for claiming that he had led the expedition to buy CoCs in Mindanao.

Another pattern had been established: when faced with allegations of wrong-doing, turn loose the presidential spouse. Libel is still a criminal offense in the Philippines, and by 2006 Mike Arroyo would have filed suits against more than 40 journalists, although he would withdraw these following a heart operation in 2007.

*

Polling day came and went, but it would be weeks before a result in the presidential race would be announced by either official means or the unofficial National Citizens' Movement for Free Elections (Namfrel).

Namfrel (established in its original incarnation by the CIA in 1951) was authorized to conduct an unofficial "quick count," and it had promised that it would have the result in seven days—a deadline that was passed several times over. It was alleged that one reason for the slow going was that it (like the Comelec) was "trending," i.e. counting first the votes from areas where Arroyo was genuinely strong to give the impression that her victory was inevitable; then, the theory went, the bogus CoCs would come into play, making her victory "real." By June, Senator Aquilino Pimentel Jr. was calling for the "quick count" to be halted on the grounds that

Jose Concepcion and Guillermo Luz, the two leading figures in the organization, had supported Arroyo during the campaign. Concepcion was a major industrialist, one of whose companies had produced bottled water bearing the name and image of Arroyo for distribution in the campaign, while Luz was a leader of the Makati Business Club, a prominent source of Arroyo support. (Long after it mattered, it would be discovered that Luz was a Canadian citizen.)

Well before the decision on the presidency, the results of the senatorial elections were declared: seven for the administration, five for the opposition. Arroyo supporters were quick to point out that this result mirrored Namfrel's partial count in the presidential race. One of the senators-elect was Jinggoy Estrada, son of the deposed president who, like his father, was facing plunder charges. The level of sincerity in the administration's professed desire for "national unity" was now demonstrated as government lawyers asked the Supreme Court to reverse the decision of the anti-corruption court to grant him bail.

The process leading to the proclamation of a president was long and convoluted. At each voting precinct, the votes were counted and an election return was sent to the board of canvassers at city or municipal level, which then collated all of these into a statement of votes. A certificate of canvass (CoC) was then issued by each city, province or overseas voting center, detailing the votes received by each candidate. These CoCs were used by the Comelec as the basis for its count. But it was not the Comelec that would declare the victor. Instead, the election materials were submitted to Congress, which would canvass the results before proclaiming the winner.

Congress began its work in late May, but the first week was consumed by a debate on the canvassing rules. One of the many demands made by the opposition was that the canvassers should have the right to compare the CoCs with the statements of vote and other materials, maintaining that ten percent of the CoCs were suspect. The administration forces adamantly refused to concede this.

The rules established, Congress then began opening the ballot boxes and scrutinizing the CoCs, a process that would take a further week. The purpose of this was to confirm the authenticity of the CoCs—something the opposition said was impossible because they were barred from consulting the statements of votes or election returns. There was plenty to complain about. Boxes from Arroyo strongholds had broken locks, Comelec seals were missing, envelopes had been opened, there were sometimes no statements of votes, and signatures on CoCs seemed to differ from those on the other documents. As an example of where this alleged tampering could have led, it was pointed out that the claim that Arroyo had won 92 percent of the vote in Cebu was "statistically improbable."[15] After all the boxes had been opened, an opposition motion to question the authenticity of some CoCs was voted down, and Senate president Franklin Drilon suspended proceedings, calling upon the joint canvass committee to commence its work.

The Namfrel "quick count" in fact took longer than the Comelec count, finishing on the evening of June 5. According to Namfrel's final "interim" report, Arroyo had won, with 9,674,597 votes against Poe's 9,158,999, a majority of 515,598. On this showing, Arroyo had taken 39 percent, Poe 37 percent; if nothing else, this demonstrated how wildly inaccurate the most widely-used opinion polls had been, lending credence to the opposition's claim that they had been rigged. But there were gasps of disbelief when it was realized that Namfel had only counted slightly less than 80 percent of the total votes, the remaining seven million being disregarded due to factors such as discrepancies with official numbers and illegible returns. In his *Malaya* column, Ducky Paredes posed the obvious question: "Did it stop its count because Namfrel did not want the true count to be revealed?"[16] This question was all the more pertinent in view of the fact that Namfrel was intended to be a "watchdog," and the Comelec, although it was not supposed to make its own count public until Congress had completed its canvass, had previously leaked the news that Arroyo had won by over a million votes.

The canvassing and the arguments dragged on. Opposition lawyers questioned CoCs found to have no watermark, and pointed to a major discrepancy when one CoC indicated that more overseas voters had voted for presidential candidates than had actually turned out (probably an "honest mathematical error," argued the administration lawyer[17]). The opposition made a number of suggestions and requests. If it was agreed that the election returns of two or three provinces could be opened, and if no irregularities were found, the opposition would accept all results at face value; if, however, discrepancies were found, it would then insist on examining the returns and statements of 25 boxes thought to be questionable. According to the administration lawyer, this would entail opening between 70,000 and 75,000 election returns and would take three years.[18] When the administration majority refused to set aside a CoC from absentee voters, despite discrepancies, Senate minority leader Pimentel went into a filibuster, speaking for several hours. Motions to deny the CoCs from the provinces of Bilaran and Quirino were voted down. In the case of the Hong Kong absentee voters, an election officer was caught on video, placing some ballot papers in a rubbish bin and others in the ballot box,[19] but a request by the Eddie Villanueva camp to show the recording was denied.

*

As the waiting period lengthened, there were suggestions that both sides were preparing to do battle. Security officials warned the opposition against plans to march to the presidential palace while, the second weekend after the ballot, text messages urged Arroyo to step down in order to avoid civil war. At the same time, Arroyo was said to have issued two classified directives — one to the armed forces, telling them to use force against opposition members who violated the law on demonstrations, and another asking local government leaders to exercise care in issuing rally permits and to delay those sought by opposition groups.[20] But Poe supporters were, in fact, proving much more patient than many had anticipated. There had been a "victory" parade in Metro Manila shortly after polling day, and now there was a round-the-clock vigil at which lawyer Oliver Lazano of the Freedom, Peace and Justice Movement (FPJM) predicted that Poe would be installed by peaceful "people power."

Even though crowds of "people power" proportions failed to materialize, there was, if not a circling of wagons, a visible closing of ranks by the administration and the establishment, and an attempt to portray the elections as history, the congressional canvass a mere formality. Senate president Drilon said as much, while Speaker de Venecia (even before the congressional canvass had got into its stride) went further, saying at a press conference that Arroyo had won, thus sparking calls by the KNP for his resignation. The Catholic Church hierarchy, said to be divided on the issue of the election, now rallied to the status quo: a full-page newspaper advertisement carried a statement signed by Archbishop Gaudencio Rosales, Bishop Socrates Villegas, former leader Cardinal Sin and Cardinal Vidal of Cebu, as well as the Makati Business

Club, the Jesuit-run Ateneo de Manila University and others, asserting "that in the absence of evidence of widespread fraud, in its [sic] totality the elections at the national level reflect the will of the people." The bishops' national secretariat for social action, once a source of support for "liberation theology," found the polls "generally clean, honest and peaceful."[21] Rosales would later lament the greed of those in government and complain that "our protected political system is such that families and interest groups hold on to government positions like it was theirs by right, by inheritance, as a domain or a dynasty."[22] But by then the damage had been done. Later, deputy presidential spokesman Ricardo Saludo would tell the press that "no amount of allegations could sway the Catholic hierarchy into withdrawing its support from President Arroyo."[23]

Not every church leader was on board: in his newspaper column, Bishop Teodoro Bacani agreed that the opposition had sufficient reason to treat the claimed results with suspicion and described Arroyo as "not a person worthy of trust."[24] He revealed that the Parish Pastoral Council for Responsible Voting had copies of diskettes containing inaccessible voters' lists. Moreover, he said the organization claimed that in Metro Manila alone a third of the five million voters had been disenfranchised.[25]

The Namfrel chairman in the province of Lanao del Sur, meanwhile, alleged at a press conference that the recent election had been the dirtiest in the province's history, and that votes had been shaved from Poe and added to Arroyo's total. According to Muslims for Law and Truth, cheating had been particularly rife in Muslim Mindanao, where it had cost Poe 800,000 votes,[26] while lawyers for Poe's coalition gave the press a Power Point demonstration of how 600,000 votes were shaved from Poe and added to Arroyo in just six provinces and one city in Mindanao, promising to provide additional proof showing that, elsewhere in the country, a further 1.3 million votes had gone the same way.[27]

Mrs. Arroyo, meanwhile, claimed that the "destabilization plot" had been "crushed" by lack of support and the plotters had "become a coffee shop cabal rather than a real challenge."[28] It began to look as if this assessment might be partly right, although a further factor was the atmosphere created by the government's regular announcements regarding the security situation. When the security forces said that, according to their intelligence sources, protest actions would culminate on Independence Day, June 12, and that sufficient police would be put on the streets to contain any trouble, the object may have been twofold: firstly to warn off "destabilizers," but secondly to create the impression that the whole episode was closed when, on June 12, protests turned out to be muted. The government put out the word that no protesters should be allowed to gather within the Quezon Memorial Circle near the Batasang Pambansa (national assembly) and when, on June 9, several thousand did, they were violently dispersed by riot police. That sent out a signal.

Things were not looking good for Independence Day, even if it was a Saturday. In an interview with the *Daily Tribune* two months earlier, the CPP's "Ka Roger" had doubted whether Arroyo could be defeated by electoral means, as she would cheat, so this would lead to "extra-constitutional action" by a broad united front.[29] But now the CPP and its mass and electoral organizations were quiet. While Eddie Villanueva had earlier complained of cheating, he had lately adopted a lower profile, and the administration had long ago congratulated Raul Roco for his "statesmanship" in conceding an Arroyo victory at a stage when it was far too early to tell who had won. The remaining candidate, Senator Lacson, said that the opposition was "just prolonging its agony" but also, possibly in an attempt to dampen speculation that his presidential bid had been part of a deal with Malacañang to split the opposition vote, added that the administration legislators were "trying their best to appear decent and democratic, but are actually committed to proclaim President Gloria Macapagal Arroyo on or before June 30."[30]

The pro-Poe FPJM had—ridiculously—vowed to turn out a million supporters for the Independence Day actions,[31] but the day came and there was hardly a sign of protest.

Fernando Poe Jr., having been fairly quiet since polling day, on June 15 spoke at a meeting in Malabon, Metro Manila, at which he accused the majority on the joint canvassing committee of "trying to protect their president, the president that has no mandate of the people and that mandate from the people will never be given her." However, although pledging that he and his supporters would fight to uphold the will of the people, he urged: "Let us not talk about an Edsa revolt for now."[32] A few days later, police clubbed a 1,500-strong demonstration at Mendiola into dispersal as Mrs. Arroyo dubbed the protesters "agents of anarchy and national ruin."[33] The Southern Police Division warned organizers against demonstrating in Makati and other parts of Metro Manila, saying that the "no permit, no rally" rule would be strictly enforced.

The joint congressional canvass committee worked through the weekend of June 19-20 and by the end of Sunday it had a result: Gloria Macapagal Arroyo, 12,905,808; Fernando Poe Jr., 11,782,232. For vice-president: Noli de Castro, 15,100,431; Loren Legarda, 14,218,709.

Would Poe concede? "We wait with baited breath," said an editorial in the *Today* newspaper, "the decision of this man portrayed by a bought and biased media as too dumb to be president; and dumber to think he would win if he only got more votes than his rivals without considering whether or not those votes might be counted; and if counted, tabulated; and when tabulated, reduced; and when reduced, left diminished by a canvassing committee whose majority saw their constitutional task as their last best chance of making up for what they lost or spent too much [of] in the last election: money and office."[34]

In the same newspaper, Bishop Teodoro Bacani addressed the question on the minds of many observers: where was the popular revolt? "Cheating in the recent elections," he wrote, "seems to have been perpetrated in a nonviolent, surgical way, with operations away from the voting crowd. This explains partly the lack of revulsion among the people."[35] Those who tried to protest, like the leaders of Anakpawis, the National Union of Students and the Student Christian Movement, who were preparing to march to Mendiola Bridge on June 21, were swiftly arrested. It was as if the elite politicians had suddenly woken to the fact that, not only did governments not *have* to fall because of mass rallies (two million people on the streets of Britain in February 2003 had, after all, not even achieved a change of policy on Iraq), but that the rallies could often be prevented in the first place.

But heavy police action and the point made by Bishop Bacani did not add up to a complete explanation. There was also the weakness of the opposition. Fernando Poe Jr. was, when push came to shove, no Joseph Estrada, a man who knew how, if only by rhetoric and ritual, to mobilize the masses. Estrada facing removal from office by impeachment had stalked the country, arousing the poor, telling them that the rich were not just doing this to him, they were doing it to *them* as well. Fernando Poe Jr., although claiming that he was being denied the fruits of victory by fraud, turned up now and again, would say that the joint canvass committee had no credibility, but would then advise the people not to take to the streets. One got the impression that, in fact, there were not many in the Poe camp with experience of mobilizing. They had, in addition, not much to offer: where was the radical programmatic alternative to another six years of Gloria Macapagal Arroyo?

A joint session of Congress was convened, and after a ten-hour debate Gloria Macapagal Arroyo was proclaimed president at 3.35 a.m. on June 24.

On June 29, the day before Arroyo's inauguration, there was one further attempt to fill the streets as yet another new organization, the May 10 Movement, dedicated itself to exposing fraud and called for a boycott of companies that had supported Arroyo. A few thousand (between two and ten, depending on which newspaper you read) approached the Mabuhay Rotonda in Quezon City, where they were met by police and the army's Scout Rangers wielding batons, water cannon and tear gas. In the wake of the dispersal, retired generals muttered their condemnation and Poe called on people "to resist this importunate effort to impose a tyrannical, cruel and illicit rule on our people."[36]

But it was, at least for now, over.

Just under six months later, Poe died after suffering a massive stroke. When Arroyo sent flowers to his wake, Poe supporters tossed them into the street and trampled them.[37]

*

Although proclaimed and inaugurated (no heads of state attended, the USA choosing to be represented by the Secretary of Veterans' Affairs and an admiral), Mrs. Arroyo's electoral problems were not yet behind her.

In early June 2005, presidential spokesman and concurrent press secretary Ignacio Bunye presented a press conference with two CDs, each containing a version of a wiretapped telephone conversation in which Mrs. Arroyo had participated in May 2004. Explaining that he was taking this step because a radio station had already aired one version, Bunye claimed that the genuine recording was of a conversation with one of Arroyo's political leaders called

"Gary," while the second, doctored version, which was soon universally referred to as the "Hello, Garci" recording, effected to be of a call to a Comelec commissioner, and the opposition would claim that this was Virgilio Garcillano. One interpretation of this "doctored" conversation was that Arroyo was asking Garcillano to ensure that she won with a majority of a million, even if it meant padding her votes. It was precisely this, of course, that the Poe camp had complained of, and the opposition now laughed at the notion that the recording had been doctored. Many in the capital joined in the laughter as, within days, the "Hello, Garci" greeting was available for purchase as a ring tone. Samuel Ong, former deputy director of the National Bureau of Investigation, then came forward to say that the tapes came from him, and that he received them from contacts in military intelligence.

For three weeks after the "Hello, Garci" recording came to light, Arroyo refused to comment on the matter, but then she blinked — twice. On June 27, as resignation calls grew, she made a televised address in which she confessed to having telephoned an electoral commissioner. Although admitting that this was a "lapse of judgment" and apologizing to the nation, she had, she said, not cheated, but had simply been concerned to ensure that the votes cast for her were protected. Having blinked once, she then did it again two days later when she announced to a business audience at the Manila Polo Club that husband Jose Miguel "Big Mike" Arroyo had volunteered to go into exile, removing "himself from any situation that cast[s] doubt on my presidency." (This latest development had been virtually predicted by the *Malaya* newspaper, which that very morning had carried a report that twelve Cabinet members, hinting at mass resignation, had persuaded her to confess her impropriety, banish her husband and sack his protégés.[38])

On July 8, 2005, Arroyo faced her greatest crisis as ten Cabinet members resigned and during the course of the day statements were issued by a wide range of organizations, including the Liberal Party and the Makati Business Club, calling upon her to do likewise. Late that afternoon, however, former president Fidel Ramos voiced a powerful declaration of support, following which all eyes were on the Catholic Bishops' Conference of the Philippines, which would be meeting at the weekend. When it delivered a statement straddling the fence, it seemed that Mrs. Arroyo had survived and, indeed, her grip on power strengthened in the days that followed as key players now had second thoughts (the Liberal Party, for example, would split, with Manila mayor Lito Atienza leading a pro-Arroyo faction).

Nevertheless, claims of electoral malpractice continued to be made. Later in the month, it was alleged that in January the previous year, four months before the election, Arroyo had used her private residence for a meeting with Comelec regional directors. Not only, the allegation ran, was Garcillano present, but Lilia Pineda, wife of alleged jueteng lord "Bong" Pineda, distributed jueteng money to the directors as bribes.[39] Then, in August, Michael Angelo Zuce, a former employee at the presidential palace, where he had worked in the political liaison office, claimed that he was also present at this meeting, that he had seen Lilia Pineda distribute the money, and that Mrs. Arroyo would also have witnessed this. The palace tended to dismiss Zuce as a minor functionary, and thus hardly likely to have been at such an event, but others recalled having seen him in various places in Mindanao during the election campaign.[40]

The Senate refused to let the controversy surrounding the 2004 election die. In late September 2005, Brig. Gen. Francisco Gudani testified that, as he had been suspected of favoring the opposition, he had been relieved as commander of the 1st Marine Brigade in Lanao del Sur province in Mindanao, and that presidential husband Mike Arroyo had brought in P500 million in two loads. Col. Alexander Bulutan told the Senate committee that Gudani's replacement had ordered him to support administration candidates and to relax the security arrangements at canvassing centers.[41] Both officers were relieved and told they would face courts martial. Arroyo made things difficult for the Senate by issuing Executive Order 464, forbidding government officials from appearing at congressional hearings without her prior approval. While some witnesses or resource persons would often fail to show for this reason, others were in hiding, like Virgilio Garcillano and former agriculture undersecretary Jocelyn "Joc-Joc" Bolante, who was accused of masterminding the transformation of money intended for the purchase of fertilizer into illicit campaign spending. Two days after former budget secretary Emilia Boncodin gave evidence to Senator Magasaysay's committee on the early release of the fertilizer fund in 2004, there was a fire in the computer records division of the budget department, leading Senate minority leader Pimentel to speculate that evidence had been destroyed; sure enough, when in December documents concerning the P728 million fertilizer fund could not be found, officials claimed they must have been destroyed in the fire.[42] In mid-December, the committee headed by Ramon Magsaysay Jr. issued a preliminary report, subject to further investigations, indicating the likelihood that the fertilizer fund allotments "were utilized to assure the victory of the administration in the electoral polls of 2004."[43]

As the congressional investigations grappled with the difficulties arising from EO 464, in November a "people's court" was established by the Citizen's Congress for Truth and Accountability, led by former vice-president Teofisto Guingona. Although, of course, the proceedings had no official standing, it soon became obvious that Malacañang had the jitters. Several pro-administration congressmen, all lawyers, sought to have the Supreme Court declare the proceedings unconstitutional (the distinction between unconstitutional and non-constitutional having apparently eluded them), and justice secretary Raul Gonzalez threatened possible sedition charges. As expected, the "people's court" heard that thousands of votes had been shaved from Arroyo's rivals and added to her own tally.

Apart from the hearings in the upper chamber, a further official investigation into the "Hello, Garci" recordings was being jointly conducted by five committees in the House. By mid-November, as Garcillano was still nowhere to be found, it looked as if these proceedings were coming to a close, and a draft report concluded that the palace had attempted a cover-up, as "no witness from the administration made a single contribution to arriving at the truth," and "no sincere cooperation was ever extended by the administration..."[44] Given the fact that the opposition members involved in the investigations were outnumbered, this was somewhat surprising, but the report had been drafted by the chairmen of the five committees, and it *was* only a draft. A day after the news broke that Garcillano had resurfaced, the chairmen of all five committees (three of whom had voted for Arroyo's impeachment in September) were replaced.

Anybody who expected a chastened Virgilio Garcillano to emerge from the shadows was due for a surprise. Through his lawyer, he made it clear that, while he was prepared to attend the House hearings, he would not countenance an appearance before Senator Rodolfo Biazon's committee. He vowed to sue anyone in possession of the "Hello Garci" tapes and to refuse to answer questions about them or their content as, being illegally obtained, they were inadmissible. Jocelyn Bolante returned to the country in mid-November. When he failed to appear before the Senate the following month, having flown to Hong Kong, he was cited for contempt and a warrant was issued for his arrest. His name next hit the headlines in July 2006, when he was detained by US immigration officials after the US embassy in Manila, following an approach by Senator Magsaysay, revoked his visa.

In November 2005, *Newsbreak* magazine came forward with a bold account of the whole poll-fraud operation. This gave details of alleged military involvement and the influencing of opinion polls, and claimed that pre-determined votes were distributed among 30,000 voting precincts in 11 provinces. The account claimed that wiretaps were placed on Garcillano (as he was, surprisingly, suspected of also working for the opposition) and Ronaldo Puno (he was thought to be channeling funds into his own congressional campaign). A "Mr. Antidote," who had previous worked clandestinely for former presidents Ramos and Aquino, was alleged to have sneaked "corrected election returns and statements of votes into the ballot boxes" held in the national assembly complex. *Newsbreak* said that the interviews it conducted indicated that the actual wiretapping of Garcillano had been conducted by officers of the armed forces' intelligence service.[45] Senate president Drilon, who had withdrawn his support from Arroyo, lamented that even now there appeared to be no military investigation, and that the job had been left to the police. Days later, the armed forces surprised everyone by saying that an investigation had been ongoing for six months. The fact that this had been previously unannounced did not inspire confidence.[46]

In February 2006, Demaree J.B. Raval, one of the lawyers for recent vice-presidential candidate Loren Legarda, announced in his *Daily Tribune* column that he had received photographs showing the creation of the fake election returns. The forgers had, he said, used official Comelec paper and borrowed machines for printing and numbering the documents, and once the job was finished the fakes were smuggled into the national assembly complex during four visits in January and February, 2005.[47] Later, *Newsbreak* magazine would run a similar story, reporting that security officers had recorded the alleged break-in by six House employees, who took election returns from 38 provinces and replaced them with fakes. However, rather than immediately blowing the whistle, the security officers had attempted to sell the evidence, now compiled on a CD.[48] Five years later, Senior Supt. Rafael Santiago came forward to claim that he had led the operation, in which a Comelec supervisor had participated and which had been aimed at demonstrating that Arroyo had won if, as a result of the election protest filed by Poe's widow Susan Roces, a recount was ordered.[49] (It was later ruled, however, that Poe's election protest had died with him.)

As each wave of revelation broke, one would wonder if this was the one which would drag Mrs. Arroyo under. But it never was.

NOTES

1. *Manila Bulletin*, December 31, 2002.

2. *Philippine Star*, January 6, 2003.

3. *Daily Tribune*, December 1, 2002.

4. *Philippine Daily Inquirer*, October 2, 2003.

5. This was claimed by former defense secretary Orlando Mercado in a studio
    discussion on the day of George W. Bush's visit to Manila, NBN, October 18, 2003.

6. *Philippine Daily Inquirer*, October 5, 2003.

7. Ibid., October 3, 2003.

8. *Daily Tribune*, November 27, 2003..

9. *Daily Tribune*, February 3, 2004. Three years later, Manapat was reportedly living in
    Australia (*Malaya,* June 16, 2007). He returned to the Philippines in 2008, dying in
    December that year.

10. Beth D. Romulo, *Manila Bulletin*, April 20, 2004.

11. Alejandro Lichauco, "Analysis," *Daily Tribune*, January 8, 2004.

12. Rod P. Kapunan, "Backbencher," *Daily Tribune*, February 26, 2004.

13. Alejandro Lichauco, "Analysis,' *Daily Tribune*, March 11, 2004

14. *Daily Tribune*, May 21, 2004.

15. *Daily Tribune*, June 3, 2004.

16. Ducky Paredes, "Goodbye Namfrel," *Malaya*, June 7, 2004.

17. www.inq7.net, June 7, 2004.

18. Ibid.

19. *Daily Tribune*, June 12, 2004.

20. Ibid., May 24, 2004.

21. Ibid., June 2, 2004.

22. Ibid., June 12, 2004.

23. Ibid., June 18, 2004.

24. *Today*, June 1, 2004.

25. ABS-CBN News, June 19, 2004.

26. www.inq7.net, June 2, 2004.

27. *Daily Tribune*, June 10, 2004.

28. www.inq7.net, June 7, 2004.

29. *Daily Tribune*, June 12, 2004.

30. www.inq7.net, June 9, 2004.

31. *Daily Tribune*, June 12, 2004.

32. Ibid., June 13, 2004.

33. *Daily Tribune* and inq7.net, June 19, 2004.

34. *Today*, June 21, 2004.

35. Teodoro Bacani, "Bishop's Move," in ibid.

36. *Today*, June 30, 2004.

37. *Philippine Daily Inquirer*, December 16, 2004.

38. *Malaya*, July 29, 2005.

39. www.inq7.net, July 30, 2005.

40. Ibid., August 8, 2005.

41. www.inq7.net, September 28, 2005.

42. *Daily Tribune*, December 7, 2005.

43. www.inq7.net, December 16, 2005.

44. Ibid., November 16, 2005.

45. Miriam Grace A. Go, "Madam Operator?" part 1, and "In the Shadows," *Newsbreak* online edition, November 24, 2005.

46. An investigation led by Vice-Admiral Mateo Mayuga had commenced in July 2005, after a number of dissident officers had threatened a mass leave. Although this was completed in October, the report was not submitted until January 20, 2006 (Mayuga, meanwhile, had been promoted to Navy chief in December), following which it remained with armed forces chief Generoso Senga and defense secretary Avelino Cruz for several months. Mayuga read a two-page summary on late-night television in April 2006, clearing senior officers of electoral irregularities. He recommended that several lower-ranking officers be investigated and that the practice of assigning military personnel to election duties be reviewed. Despite calls by the media, junior officers, the opposition and the church, the full report was not released until Mrs. Arroyo had left office.

47. Demaree J.R. Raval, "Enquiry," *Daily Tribune*, February 19, 2006.

48. www.inq7.net, March 13 and 14, 2006.

49. *Philippine Daily Inquirer*, July 28, 2011.

5 "INSUFFICIENT IN SUBSTANCE"

Gloria Macapagal Arroyo faced a number of attempts to unseat her during her nine-and-a-half years in presidential office, and she survived them all. Confronted with hostile investigations in the Senate, she issued Executive Order 464, which forbade government officials from testifying without her express permission. In fact, this measure, like the proclamation of a state of emergency in February 2006 (see chapter 6), had the effect of reducing her popularity still further, and yet she still survived, largely because popular revolt and impeachment had both been rendered impractical.

Neither the mainstream opposition nor the left was able to assemble the kind of numbers necessary for a "people power" exercise, and there were a number of possible reasons for this. Many with memories of the march on the presidential palace on May 1, 2001 to protest the arrest of Estrada would have recalled that the huge number participating had, as they reached their destination, been virtually leaderless and, as they met gunfire at the gates of the palace, left to their own devices. Since then, local mayors had been persuaded to issue permits to rally sparingly, and when rallies did take place, they were often dispersed violently by the authorities. And, finally, the one component which had done so much to ensure the success of EDSAs Uno and Dos—the Catholic Church—now, divided on the question of the Arroyo presidency, tucked up its frocks and sat astride the fence.

So as Arroyo, with the assistance of former president Fidel Ramos and the Catholic

Church hierarchy, recovered from her Black Friday in July 2005, the opposition, having failed to assemble the kind of crowds that might keep alive the possibility of toppling her by "people power," switched its focus to the impeachment avenue.

The first impeachment complaint had been filed by lawyer Oliver Lozano in June 2005. Corazon "Dinky" Soliman, one of the resigned Cabinet members, claimed that on June 27 she had witnessed Mrs. Arroyo order political adviser Gabriel Claudio to ensure that this complaint was immediately endorsed in the House. It was. The opposition took the view that the Lozano complaint was deliberately weak and filed as a spoiler, the Supreme Court having previously ruled that only one complaint could be filed against a particular official in any one year. To dispel this fear, Lozano indicated that he was willing to withdraw his complaint if the opposition, which he criticized for its disunity, wished to file a more substantial one. This path was closed when, in early July, a second complaint was filed, this time by lawyer Jose Rizaldo Lopez, receiving immediate endorsement by a congressman from Arroyo's own party. Faced with this situation, the opposition decided that the wisest course was to amend the Lozano complaint and then argue that it still qualified as the first one filed in the year.

It soon became clear that it would not be plain sailing. By mid-July the Liberal Party, having vowed a week earlier that it would support impeachment, now, faced with dissension in its ranks, said that it would allow its congressmen to follow their consciences. And, of course, there were claims of bribery. According to the opposition *Daily Tribune*, Malacañang gave P200,000 to each of its supporters in the House.[1] Congressman Eulogio Magsaysay of the party-list organization Alliance of Volunteer Educators (AVE) claimed that he had been offered this amount, plus a further P300,000 during the impeachment process itself, and funding for a number of projects that brought the total to P5 million, plus a secure slot for the AVE in the 2007 elections.[2] There were reports that Arroyo had visited Imelda Marcos to promise that her late husband would receive a burial at the National Heroes' Cemetery (he had lain embalmed since his death years earlier, in anticipation of just such an event) if daughter and congresswoman Imee would withdraw her support for impeachment.[3] House minority leader Francis Escudero claimed that Arroyo had been telephoning congressmen, their families and friends in a desperate attempt to have the impeachment process aborted.

The opposition filed an amended version of the Lozano complaint in late August, signed by 42 congressmen. In order to have the complaint automatically transmitted to the Senate, 79 signatures (one third of the House) were required. Against this, by early August House Speaker De Venecia was claiming that no less than 189 members were committed to preventing transmission to the Senate "whatever the evidence" (a tacit admission that the outcome would be determined by simple arithmetic rather than adherence to the principles of justice). The following weeks saw a "battle for signatures," with the opposition campaigning for additions and the administration urging those who had already signed to withdraw.

With insufficient signatures, the complaints were referred to the House committee on justice, which spent long days in technical arguments. As thousands rallied in late August to denounce the plan to kill the impeachment process, the committee decided that the amended complaint was separate and distinct from that filed by Lozano., and that sealed the fate of the whole process. When the chair ruled out further debate on this matter and disallowed the request by the hitherto pro-administration Robert "Ace" Barbers to deliver a privilege speech on "Dinky" Soliman's accusation that Arroyo was behind the endorsement of the Lozano complaint, the opposition walked out of the proceedings. The committee next agreed that the Lozano complaint was sufficient in form, which may have brought about a temporary lifting of the spirits of those still sufficiently optimistic to have faith in the proceedings, but went on to rule that it was insufficient in substance. The amended complaint and that filed by Jose Rizaldo Lopez were then ruled out on the "one per year" principle.

The opposition was still not counted out, however, as the report of the justice committee now had to be considered in plenary session, and 79 votes could still send the amended complaint to the Senate. The opposition complained that administration officials were visiting the homes of key congressmen with large amounts of cash and the odd threat in an attempt to persuade them to absent themselves from the plenary. At this stage, the battle lines were far from clearly delineated: Congressman Benjamin Agarao announced that he might eventually resign from the *opposition* Laban ng Demokratikong Pilipino (LDP) if party colleagues continued to pressure him to withdraw his support for impeachment. LDP luminary Senator Edgaro Angara was forced to deny that another congressman had switched to the anti-impeachment camp due to pressure from him.[4] Administration congressman Jose Salceda would later acknowledge the role of the Iglesia ni Kristo (Church of Christ) which, having previously played a role in slowing the signature process, now called upon congressmen it had helped get elected to ensure there were sufficient votes against impeachment.[5] The voting process was completed at around 3.30 a.m. on September 6, by which time 158 had voted to accept the committee report, and just 51 had voted against.

Gloria Macapagal Arroyo therefore survived once more. Had she paused for reflection, she would have seen that her deliverance from the impeachment process had been due to many of the ills afflicting the body politic in the Philippines: bribery, opportunism, disunity, religious interference and self-interest. Needless to say, this was not the way she saw it. Instead, she claimed in an interview with ANC television that "the Lord" had not abandoned her at the height of the crisis, and that it was the will of the deity that the impeachment complaint should not be transmitted to the Senate.[6]

Filipinos were now confronted with the prospect of almost five more years of the Arroyo presidency, and the disturbing possibility that she really believed this kind of thing—unless, of course, the fortunes of the impeachment camp improved in 2006.

*

Even though the 2006 impeachment bid came just months after a brief and unpopular state of emergency, Mrs. Arroyo's control of the House of Representatives was as firm as ever. This time, the complaint considered by the House justice committee contained no less than 22 charges (that she had violated the Constitution, betrayed public trust, and was guilty of graft and corruption and other crimes), but the committee found by a vote of 56-24 that it was "insufficient in substance." Ten days later, a plenary session of the House voted by 173-32, with one abstention, to accept the report. In fact, no less than eight complaints were filed that year, but the justice committee ruled that seven of these breached the one-year rule. Opposition members who had wished to present the evidence contained in seven boxes were not allowed to do so. The House, it must be said, did not reflect public opinion, as a Social Weather Stations survey found that only 30 percent agreed with the burial of the 2006 complaint, as against 45 percent who disagreed.[7]

*

By the time impeachment season came around in 2007, the controversy surrounding the ZTE-NBN deal (see chapter 3) had been hogging the headlines for months, virtually guaranteeing that the impeachment process would become entangled with the issue of Jose de Venecia Jr.'s continued occupancy of the House speakership.

Although the role of his son in the ZTE affair had hardly endeared him to Mrs. Arroyo, and rumors were circulated that an attempt would be made to unseat him, in September, a complaint was filed against him at the House ethics committee for, allegedly, having hosted a meeting at his home to discuss the ZTE deal, but at this stage some sources maintained that Mrs. Arroyo was dissuading her allies from moving against him.[8] The following month, however, De Venecia rejected her suggestion that, after an impeachment complaint was filed against her, he should take a leave of absence, and now it was said that she had told congressional allies to topple him.[9] The *Daily Tribune* reported a weekend meeting called by Mrs. Arroyo at which eight congressmen discussed the ouster move, Prospero Nograles being the favored replacement.[10] Nograles, however, maintained that he was no threat to De Venecia. The Speaker, meanwhile, called on Arroyo to establish a new administration to purge government of corruption and, in a letter of October 20, gave her 100 days to "complete initial reforms" aimed at reducing corruption and poverty.[11] A few days later, Mrs. Arroyo and De Venecia held a closed-door meeting with Fidel Ramos and Vice-President Noli de Castro, following which it was claimed that the "cold war" was over, both having agreed to work on a "joint vision" of reforms.

It was possible, of course, that the threat of deposal had been held over De Venecia's head in order to ensure that he played his usual role during impeachment season. Certainly Oliver Lozano seemed intent on reprising his 2005 role, filing a complaint in July that was so widely regarded as a spoiler that no congressman endorsed it. He tried again in September, with a similar result. The following month, lawyer Roel Pulido, who had previously represented the defendants in the Oakwood Mutiny proceedings (see chapter 6), filed a complaint on the grounds that Mrs. Arroyo had failed to act against the attempted bribing of officials in the ZTE case. However, the fact that it was endorsed by one of her congressional allies immediately set alarm bells ringing, and Senator Lacson warned that the complaint was, like Lozano's in 2005, "nothing but an immunization shot to at least keep her safe in office for one year."[12] Anak Pawis's congressman Crispin Beltran claimed that a Kampi officer had offered him P2 million if he would support the complaint, and three other congressmen also said they had been offered bribes.[13] The theory here was that an attempt was being made to give the complaint an air of legitimacy.

De Venecia said that, as the complaint was now tainted with bribery, he might delay sending it to the appropriate committee. When, in the presence of Arroyo, his five deputies pressured him to transmit it immediately, he refused, whereupon Deputy Speaker Raul del Mar referred it to committee, setting the one-year clock ticking.

At precisely this time, a further (and, some claimed, related) scandal erupted when, on October 11, Arroyo called congressional supporters to a breakfast meeting at the presidential palace. It was alleged that at the close of the meeting congressmen were handed packages containing between P200,000 and P500,000. A few hours later, those attending a meeting of provincial governors and mayors were, it was claimed, recipients of similar generosity, and the recently-elected Governor Ed Panlilio of Pampanga displayed the cash before the media.[14] Mrs. Arroyo denied any knowledge of the cash distribution and, following a rising tide of criticism, ordered an investigation. Arroyo apologists variously explained that the gifts were "tokens of remembrance," gifts for Christmas (the season starts early in the Philippines), or assistance for village elections due on October 29—which would still be illegal, as the law required these polls to be nonpartisan.

There were, of course, those who believed that this distribution of largesse was connected to the latest impeachment complaint. In denying this, one congressman was disarmingly frank (possibly unintentionally so) in saying that the amounts were too "measly" to influence the impeachment vote[15] and, of course, governors and mayors were not involved in the impeachment process.

Meanwhile, the opposition had to decide what to do about the Pulido complaint. In the end, the United Opposition decided to file an amendment, although it was widely anticipated that this would be rejected. The stance adopted by the House speaker might well be crucial. Here, the news was not good for the opposition, for although it was claimed that a group closely identified with De Venecia was ready to defect and oust him at any stage (in which case, presumably, the latter would have rallied his supporters to the impeachment cause), Arroyo, De Venecia, Ramos and around a dozen other Lakas luminaries met on the evening of November 3 to patch up their differences. Mrs. Arroyo then issued a statement indicating that leadership controversies in the House "shall be put to an end."[16]

And so they were—for three months. Once the Pulido complaint had been found to be "insufficient in substance" in mid-November, De Venecia had served his purpose.[17] A few weeks later, by a vote of 174 to 35, with 16 abstentions, he was finally ousted. Just before 1 a.m. on February 5, 2008 Nograles was, as predicted four months earlier, elected to replace him. In his *Daily Tribune* column, Ernesto Maceda cited rumors that those voting against De Venecia had received between P500,000 and P1 million each, funded by backers of the ZTE deal,[18] while Joey de Venecia claimed the amounts were far higher—P4 million a head, starting off "as P1 million plus pork barrel projects."[19]

*

If the 2008 impeachment complaint demonstrated anything, it was that after the once-powerful Jose de Venecia Jr. had been ousted from the speakership, his influence had almost completely evaporated.

On October 13, an impeachment complaint was filed by Jose "Joey" de Venecia III, UP lawyer Harry Roque and others, citing Mrs. Arroyo's role in the ZTE affair, the allegedly overpriced Northrail project, and a joint marine seismic undertaking with China in the Spratly islands (these are claimed by both countries, along with four others, although in the event it was said that the undertaking was conducted in areas where the Philippines had undisputed ownership). Oliver Lozano mailed his complaint but was beaten to the punch by the De Venecia group. The new speaker of the House, Prospero Nograles, intimated that the process would be dealt with as in the past and that the merit of the arguments would count for little, as impeachment "is a political exercise and we will deal with it head on. At the end of the day it will be a numbers game."[20] Later that month, Nograles's predecessor called a press conference at his home to announce that he would endorse the complaint, although he would not be campaigning to secure other endorsements, as congressmen should be guided by their consciences.[21] This was the realist speaking for, bereft of the speakership and the patronage that came with it, De Venecia obviously knew that he would be able to shift few if any of his congressional peers. Nograles now threatened that De Venecia might be sanctioned by Lakas-CMD, as the "stand of the party is not to support any impeachment filed against our chairman,"[22] providing further proof that as a means of arriving at the truth the impeachment process was practically useless.

The De Venecia complaint at least made it over the first hurdle, as the justice committee threw out two others (one of them Lozano's) and a motion of intervention by Manuel L. Quezon III which sought to expand the complaint, as breaching the one-year rule. The committee was due to vote on the substance of the remaining complaint on November 26. According to the elder De Venecia, on November 25 "gifts" of P500,000 were distributed by a palace ally at the Linden Suites in Pasig City.[23] Shortly before the committee voted the following day, Gabriela Representative Liza Maza referred to the report of De Venecia's allegation in the *Daily Tribune* and put forward a motion calling for the incident to be investigated. This was rejected and the committee went on to decide, by a vote of 42-8, that the impeachment complaint was lacking in substance.[24] A few days later, a plenary session of the House adopted the justice committee report with a vote of 183-21, with three abstentions.

By now, it was obvious that it would be impossible to remove Mrs. Arroyo by means of impeachment by the current Congress. In the meantime, there had been an attempt to use a military rebellion or mutiny to arrive at the same end, and that had fared no better.

NOTES

1. *Daily Tribune*, July 22, 2005.

2. www.inq7.net, July 22, 2005.

3. *Daily Tribune*, July 29, 2005.

4. www.inq7.net., September 2, 2005.

5. Ibid., September 7, 2005.

6. *Daily Tribune*, September 20, 2005.

7. inq7.net, October 17, 2006.

8. Ibid., September 20, 2007.

9. Ibid., October 12, 2007.

10. *Daily Tribune*, October 16, 2007.

11. www.inquirer.net, October 23, 2007.

12. Ibid., October 8, 2007.

13. "VP Noli urged to take a stand on corruption controversies," www.gmanetwork.com, October 19, 2007.

14. *New York Times*, October 18, 2007.

15. www.inquirer.net, October 12, 2007.

16. *Philippine Daily Inquirer*, November 5, 2007.

17. In November the following year, the elder De Venecia confirmed that he and others had received P500,000 in return for their support of the Pulido complaint and that when, on the same day, he had resisted her pressure on the issue, he knew that he would lose the speakership. (*Philippine Daily Inquirer*, November 24, 2008.) That same month, he told the House justice committee that Arroyo's bribes in 2007 could have totaled P100 million. (Ibid., November 25, 2008.) The fact that the complaint was spurious was amply demonstrated by the voting figures: 43-1 in committee and 184-1 in the plenary session.

18. *Daily Tribune*, February 5, 2008.

19. *Philippine Daily Inquirer*, February 6, 2008.

20. www.inquirer.net, October 13, 2008.

21. *Daily Tribune*, October 27, 2008.

22. www.inquirer.net, October 27, 2008.

23. *Daily Tribune*, November 26, 2008.

24. www.inquirer.net, December 2, 2008

6 "A STATE OF PANIC?"

The political crisis that had gradually intensified since Gloria Macapagal Arroyo's questionable seizure of power in January 2001 seemed interminable for the simple reason that none of the contending parties were able to resolve it in their own interest. Regardless (or perhaps because) of the repressive measures taken by Arroyo, resistance to her rule persisted, but the efforts of her opponents to unseat her, whether by "people power" or impeachment, came to naught. In early 2006, therefore, there was an attempt (or strictly speaking two attempts) to rally rebel military elements to this cause. On this occasion there were indications that, in proclaiming a state of emergency, Mrs. Arroyo was seeking not merely to survive, for the military threats had been dispensed with by the time of her proclamation, but to slice through the Gordian knot by assuming powers which would enable her to finally end the crisis. But this, like her opponents' attempts to remove her, would fall flat and the crisis would continue.

*

Despite the fact that the often sensational claims made in congressional investigations were so obviously failing to provoke critical levels of outrage and mobilization, the government adopted an increasingly authoritarian stance.

Thus, the hard line against dissent, evident since the 2004 election, continued, and opponents claimed that Arroyo was preparing to impose some form of emergency rule. Executive secretary Eduardo Ermita first called for a moratorium on demonstrations, fearful that Arroyo would face embarrassment when she addressed the UN General Assembly, then announced that the policy of "maximum tolerance" would be scrapped, with rallies being dispersed if they had no permits. And even if permits were granted, said justice secretary Raul Gonzalez, the palace could use its "police powers" to revoke them if the "general welfare" was endangered. Arroyo complained that the rallies in the financial district of Makati (where the mayor, Jejomar Binay, was also leader of the United Opposition and, thus, only too willing to issue permits) had cost millions and could not be allowed to continue; so, "maximum tolerance" would be replaced by "calibrated preemptive response" (CPR). Thereafter, even very small "rallies" saw arrests and/or the wielding of police batons. And unlike Binay, pro-administration mayors toed the line, doing all they could to limit public expression of discontent.

The hard line on rallies, while an example of an increasing authoritarianism that may have kept people off the streets, also served to stoke the bitterness of Arroyo's opponents, as did the crudity of government warnings. Advising the public not to attend rallies called for September 12, 2005, Raul Gonzalez had alluded, as a possible consequence, to the tragic occurrences at Hacienda Luisita in Tarlac province the previous November, a reference to the dispute at the huge plantation owned by the family of former president Corazon Cojuangco Aquino, during which several pickets and supporters were shot dead. (The workers had been demanding the revocation of the stock distribution scheme by means of which the Tarlac branch of the Cojuangco family had evaded land reform, and this was later conceded. Needless to say, there were suspicions that herein lay the explanation for Mrs. Aquino's transformation into a determined anti-Arroyo campaigner.)

That same month, it was claimed that the justice department had drafted a proclamation stopping just short of martial law. Officials obligingly explained that all that was under consideration was the possibility of a government takeover of key industries in the event of an economic crisis. It therefore seemed possible that talk of martial law was, as claimed by presidential spokesman Ignacio Bunye, "hogwash."[1] Five months later, things would look rather different. In October, a palace source told the *Daily Tribune* that Arroyo had already signed an executive order declaring a national emergency and empowering the police and military to crack down on political dissent; release of the order would, it was claimed, be preceded by bombings in Metro Manila.[2]

To some, it began to appear as if the Arroyo administration was gradually assembling measures that would constitute a regime of undeclared martial law. A week after Arroyo ordered the crackdown on rallies came Executive Order 464, effectively neutering the system of checks and balances by denying Congress the opportunity to hold government officials accountable. According to Manuel L. Quezon III, Mrs. Arroyo wanted to declare martial law late in the year, retreating when she met opposition from her defense secretary, the armed forces, and Washington.[3]

The role of the latter has now been confirmed by US Embassy cables made public by Wikileaks. These reveal that a government aide memoir claimed that, as those seeking to destabilize the government had concluded an alliance with communists, and terrorists were linked to al-Qaeda (probably a reference to a dissident military faction's talks with the CPP in the first case and the Abu Sayyaf group in the second), the situation merited emergency rule or martial law. On November 7, 2005 the US charge d'affaires Paul Jones told Mrs. Arroyo that the US "did not share in the analysis in the aide memoir or believe the circumstances would justify extreme measures." In a meeting four days later Eric John, US deputy assistant secretary of state for Southeast Asia, warned that "the invocation of emergency measures could trigger a review of US defense-related and other forms of assistance to the Philippines." Nevertheless, House speaker De Venecia would advise Jones of impending emergency rule, arguing that the government required extra powers to arrest media practitioners and others who were paid or controlled by the NPA.[4]

Then, in January 2006, speculation was rife that Arroyo was poised to strike at the Lopez business empire, as had Ferdinand Marcos during his martial law regime.

Times had changed since, just a few years earlier, Arroyo had been accused of pledging to support Lopez interests if Noli de Castro could be dissuaded from entering the presidential race. The issue leading to a parting of the ways concerned an agreement made by the Lopez-controlled electricity giant, Meralco, to purchase specified amounts of power from the National Power Corporation (Napocor). Instead, Meralco seemed to prefer to buy from Lopez-owned power producers, leading the government to demand payment of billions of pesos in penalties. In his "Mr. Expose" column, Ernesto Maceda reported a source as saying that pressure was also being exerted on the Lopezes to relinquish control of their ABS-CBN television station. In the same issue of the *Daily Tribune*, editor-publisher Ninez Cacho-Olivares claimed that Arroyo was preparing to take over Meralco, a two-page Malacañang paper having indicated that "friendly businessmen" had given the thumbs-up to temporary state control. Arroyo was expected, having taken over, to reduce power rates for poorer consumers, thus contributing to her political survival.[5] Although energy secretary Raphael Lotilla denied any takeover plans, the alleged scheme struck a chord with those who recalled the declaration of a state of emergency drafted by the justice department just three months earlier—as, indeed, it might with those who read the *actual* declaration made just a month later, on February 24.

*

There had been rumblings from military and police sources for some time, and in mid-October 2005 the clandestine Young Officers Union of the New Generation (YOUNG) issued a "final warning" to Arroyo, telling her to go if she wished to avoid bloodshed. YOUNG was, in fact, in touch with Laban ng Masa (Mass Struggle), a coalition of left-wing groups, most of which had broken from the CPP in the 1990s, formed earlier that year. At a 1,500-strong "people summit" called by the coalition in September, the president of Alab Katipunan (the mass organization of one of the coalition members) declared: "We are calling on patriotic officers and members of the [armed forces] and [police] to unite with the masses in the struggle to oust the GMA regime, end elite rule and bring about fundamental changes in the system…" A labor leader explained that this call to military dissidents was aimed at ensuring that the elite opposition and the church hierarchy would not be able to, as they had in the past, use the masses and then sideline them, along with their agenda.[6] According to an anonymous source who spoke to the *Inquirer*, the junior officers wished to ensure that the people would be with them, and thus some argued that they should not act until a critical mass of civilians was visible on the streets.[7] But this was a problem that would evade resolution, for as we have seen, the assembly of such a "critical mass" was beyond the capability of the left and the mainstream opposition.

Capt. Nicanor Faeldon, detained for his alleged involvement in the Oakwood Mutiny of 2003, escaped in December 2005 and thereafter set up a website on which he claimed that, visiting military bases with little danger of arrest, he had found that he was supported by all but the most senior officers. The following month, another captain and three lieutenants also escaped, issuing a call for their comrades to take action against the "corruption, illegitimacy, and neglect...and repression of a bogus regime."[8] During a court appearance, leading Oakwood mutineer Lt. Antonio Trillanes IV was given time to speak to the media, telling the public that the time would soon come when every Filipino would have to choose sides and "whichever side the public takes, the [armed forces] will be there."[9] The fact that this media appearance was allowed by Trillanes' superiors suggested — or so it was thought at the time — at least passive support at senior levels.

When CPP spokesman Gregorio "Ka Roger" Rosal publicly offered the escaped military rebels sanctuary in NPA-controlled areas, the government pounced on this, chief of presidential staff Mike Defensor citing "intelligence reports" that indicated a possible alliance between military and communist rebels.[10] National security adviser Norberto Gonzales (who, according to the Wikileaks material was a firm martial law advocate[11]) made the more extreme claim of a plot to assassinate Arroyo by the Oakwood escapees, the NPA and some opposition members.[12]

YOUNG claimed that its central committee had met to plan Arroyo's ouster and that its list of 200 "hard targets" included 40 congressmen, 47 smugglers, 32 drug lords, 30 illegal gambling lords and 22 tax evaders.[13] While that might have sounded like empty boasting to some, Senator Rodolfo Biazon said that his sources advised that talks were taking place between YOUNG and the original Young Officers Union (YOU); if true, this would mean that rebellious junior officers now enjoyed support from their more senior comrades, as veterans of YOU, formed in the late 1980s, now occupied the rank of colonel and above.

The rebel cause suffered a setback when Faeldon was recaptured driving to his safe-house. In mid-February, the four remaining escapees issued a statement in which they called upon people to take to the streets and wear red armbands — a call that, like Faeldon's suggestion that flags be flown at half-mast, was both tame and widely ignored. The remaining Oakwood prisoners, escorted by 300 heavily-armed troops, appeared in court on February 14. During a break, members of left-wing groups handed the soldiers red roses. Leaving the court, one of the junior officers told the media: "The regime change is near. It's near."[14]

Then Reuters reported that two anonymous generals had unveiled a plot involving a mass escape and the holding of military commanders hostage at the military academy in Baguio. Confirming this, the armed forces' spokesman said that "Oplan Hackle" would have also involved the seizure of military camps and the deposing of Arroyo; two politicians (one with a military background) and several retired generals were said to have been the masterminds. Later, it would be claimed that the plan had been discovered as early as December 2005. Some 200 active officers and men had, it was stated, been recruited, but they had been "confronted" by their commanders.[15]

The Oakwood escapees hit the headlines again when, on February 21, Lt. Lawrence San Juan was recaptured. According to the authorities, he had been attending a meeting with the CPP, and the military component of this unlikely alliance was said to be an organization called the Makabansang Kawal ng Pilipinas (MKP, or Patriotic Army of the Philippines), allegedly led by Gregorio Honasan. The security forces claimed that Honasan and other former rebels of his vintage had been recruiting within the armed forces since December 2004, the plan of the CPP-MKP alliance being to launch a program of activity which, commencing on February 24, would peak in May. The plot was discovered, it was said, when some MKP members baulked at the alliance and advised their superiors. San Juan claimed that evidence, including a disk containing the CPP-MKP agreement and minutes of the meeting held the previous day, was planted by the military.[16] Later, he would go over to the government side.

Large rallies were expected on February 24, as the nation commemorated the twentieth anniversary of EDSA I. Later, it would be alleged that, on the evening on February 23, Jose "Peping" Cojuangco, brother of Corazon Aquino, hosted a meeting of businessmen and officials at which Pastor Saycon (formerly a member of the coalition that assisted Arroyo in ousting Estrada, but now an opponent) called a US official regarding the post-Arroyo group's plans; it was claimed that he put through another call to someone called "Delta," thought to be Brig. Gen. Danilo Lim, who advised him that it was "all systems go." Significantly, Saycon was alleged to have assured the Washington official, "You will still be our friend, not China."[17] Cojuangco would claim that what had taken place at his home was a reunion of certain EDSA I personalities, and that there had been no plotting. The following morning, news broke that Lim, a founder of YOU in the 1980s and now commander of the First Scout Ranger Regiment, had been relieved after armed forces chief of staff Gen. Senga had persuaded him not to go through with a plan to attend the civilian rally. In the early hours, unusual levels of activity were reported at Malacañang and Camp Aguinaldo, the armed forces headquarters.

Later that morning, Arroyo went on television to declare a state of national emergency.

*

In Presidential Proclamation 1017, Arroyo complained that elements of the opposition had "conspired with authoritarians of the extreme Left...and the extreme Right, represented by military adventurists..." and that they were "now in tactical alliance and engaged in a concerted and systematic conspiracy...to bring down the duly constituted Government..." The claims of these groups had, moreover, "been recklessly magnified by certain elements of the national media." Therefore, Arroyo, in her capacity as commander-in-chief, ordered "the Armed Forces of the Philippines, to maintain law and order throughout the Philippines, prevent and suppress all forms of lawless violence as well as any act of insurrection or rebellion and to enforce obedience to all the laws and to all decrees, orders and regulations promulgated by me personally or upon my direction; and as provided in Section 17, Article 12 of the Constitution do hereby declare a State of National Emergency."

There were several questionable aspects to this brief proclamation. First, the charge that opposition members had "conspired" with elements of the extreme right and left, hurled on a number of occasions by members of the administration, was here stated as fact—although no proof was offered, and no member of the congressional opposition, apart from left-wing party-listers and Gregorio Honasan (who was out of office), were ever charged. However, *Newsbreak* magazine later took the view that the claimed meetings with the CPP (in November 2005 and on February 20, 2006) appeared to be genuine, and that at the latter gathering it was agreed that action on February 24 would be a dry run, with the real push coming at the end of March or even as late as May 1, Labor Day.[18]

Why did the administration choose to concentrate its fire on the CPP when other left groups openly supported the idea of an intervention by military rebels? The left-wing alliance Laban ng Masa had on January 24 called on rebel soldiers to unite with the people to overthrow Arroyo and change the system, a call reissued by the alliance's chairman, former University of the Philippines president Francisco "Dodong" Nemenzo, on February 10. It would be late April before the justice department filed formal rebellion charges, and no one from Laban ng Masa would, at that stage, feature in the list; indeed, the only members of even the CPP-influenced organizations who were immediately charged were those sitting in Congress—Satur Ocampo (Bayan Muna), Teddy Casiño (Bayan Muna), Joel Virador (Bayan Muna), Crispin Beltran (Anakpawis), Rafael Mariano (Anakpawis) and Liza Maza (Gabriela)—and this raises the possibility, with midterm elections due the following year, that they were the real targets; it would be several months before National Democratic Front leaders Jose Maria Sison and Luis Jalandoni would be charged, along with Honasan (already charged, shortly after the declaration of the emergency, with involvement in the Oakwood Mutiny of 2003, since when he had been in hiding), a number of retired officers, Lt. San Juan, Nemenzo and others.

While the opposition to Arroyo was very widespread, was it sufficient to justify the imposition of a state of emergency? The trend in mass mobilizations had been dispiriting, with usually only a few hundred demonstrators at a time taking to the streets. This would have been a key factor in the planned enterprise, as YOUNG wanted "people power" to precede military action, while the Magdalo group (the organization formed with the Oakwood prisoners at its core) saw this coming after it had taken action. Either way, the signs were hardly promising. In addition, one needs to ask what form of military action was planned. Although the word "coup" was bandied about, all the rebels planned was a declaration that military support had been withdrawn from Arroyo. This had been found to be acceptable in January 2001 and so how, the rebels argued, could it be deemed unconstitutional now?

Thus, on the evening of February 23, Lim and Col. Ariel Querubin had gone to see their chief of staff, Gen. Generoso Senga, to advise him that their men were planning to join civilian demonstrations the following day and that they did not think they would be able to stop them. Their hope was that Senga would bow to what they claimed to be the prevailing wind and agree to join them, announcing on EDSA that Arroyo no longer had the support of the military.

Instead, he talked them out of it and suspended Lim. So where, now, was the threat? Why the need for a state of emergency? Manuel L. Quezon III might have had a point when he characterized PP 1017 as "the concrete manifestation, in legal language, of a state of panic."[19]

Unless there was a hidden agenda. The reference to Section 17, Article 12 of the Constitution was distinctly puzzling, for this does not, as claimed by PP 1017, provide for the declaration of a state of emergency. Instead, it states: "In times of national emergency, when the public interest so requires, the State may, during the emergency and under reasonable terms prescribed by it, temporarily take over or direct the operation of any privately owned public utility or business affected with public interest." What was happening here? The justice department had, as we have seen, drafted a declaration just a few months earlier that would have had the government taking over utilities in the event of an *economic* crisis, but that was not the rationale here. Was this merely a case of sloppy drafting, with some of the earlier draft incorporated without a check of the actual wording of the Constitution? Or was there a sinister intent?

Later, Congresswoman Imee Marcos would comment that Arroyo's emergency proclamation was a "copycat" exercise based on her father's declaration of martial law in 1972. This was not particularly far-fetched. Marcos had exaggerated the threat posed by the NPA, and certain events (such as an "assassination" attempt on Juan Ponce Enrile, his defense secretary) had been staged. Now, it seemed that the ability of the NPA to make a significant contribution to a takeover of state power was again being given rather more credence than it deserved, but that plot had been blown with the arrest of San Juan, and the suspension of Lim (who had been liaising with the Laban ng Masa coalition) had removed the most potent immediate threat. With martial law in place, Marcos had attacked the Lopez family, taking over much of its economic empire; and here was Arroyo, the Lopezes having turned against her, citing Section 17, Article 12 of the Constitution…

In addition, Arroyo, just like Marcos, was obviously aiming to silence, or at least mute, the voices raised against her—that much was made clear in her proclamation. Thus, not only were arrest warrants issued, but at around 12.30 a.m. on February 25 police officers entered the offices of the *Daily Tribune* and took away a mock-up of the current edition. Although the paper continued to come out, police would stay there for the duration of the "emergency," and the premises of the opposition *Malaya*, its sister paper *Abante*, and the Lopezes' ABS-CBN station, would be surrounded. National telecommunications commissioner Ronald Solis asked for "balanced reporting," saying that broadcasters should not air statements from parties that "incite[d] to sedition" or were "rebellious." His commission, he warned, would not balk at recommending closure of any company violating the "rules."[20]

The adoption of imitative tactics was not confined to the administration. The plan to oust Arroyo rested upon the ability to repeat the key element in the success of EDSA Dos: the withdrawal of military support. But in 2001, the church had been filling the tanks of its more unquestioning followers with anti-Estrada venom for three or four years, so all it had to do at the crucial point was open the faucets. And defense establishment collaboration in the plot had taken place at the highest levels—chief of staff and defense secretary. Presumably, that was why Lim felt that he had to attempt to bring Senga on board, but the latter, casting his eye over the political terrain, could have seen nothing to join. The "rebellion" failed at that point.

This was not, though, the end of the drama. On Sunday, February 26, Maj. Gen. Renato Miranda was relieved of his command of the Marines, to be replaced by Brig. Gen. Nelson Allaga. Col. Ariel Querubin called for "people power" at Fort Bonifacio in order to protest the relief of Miranda and "protect us from aggression." Here was the copycat syndrome once more, although this time it was obviously the early stages of EDSA I (when a modest number of military rebels, along with defense secretary Enrile and deputy chief of staff Fidel Ramos, had mutinied and called for civilian support) that Querubin was attempting to replay. It seemed a strange way to go about it, however, as the relief of a commanding officer was hardly a cause around which many civilians would rally. Nevertheless, over the course of a few hours, into Sunday night, some civilians turned up. Cory Aquino, doubtless replaying the events of February 1986 in her mind, was on her way with family and supporters, but was stopped, and by the time they arrived the gates of Fort Bonifacio had been closed. Along with Bishop Teodoro Bacani, she stationed herself at Gate 3 and prayed the rosary. Meanwhile, around 1,000 students and members of left-wing groups gathered at the Diliman campus of the University of the Philippines, preparing to march to Fort Bonifacio.

As time passed, it was presumably an increasingly forlorn Querubin who said, "I hope the bishops will not forsake us."[21] But there was never a chance of significant support from the church, and, in fact, even the Marines were not, despite Querubin's pleading, united, as a proposal to withdraw support from the chain of command had been defeated by nine votes to six.[22] Just before 11 p.m., after Querubin had agreed to stand down, the protesters at Fort Bonifacio began to disperse. It was over.

*

If the Arroyo emergency was intended as an imitation of Marcos's martial law, it was a fairly pale one (which was all that political circumstances, both domestically and internationally, would allow), and it would achieve little apart from making it clear that the occupant of Malacañang was willing to adopt drastic measures in order to safeguard her hold on power. For one, few voices were muted, let alone silenced. Despite a last-minute ban on rallies marking the 20th anniversary of EDSA I, they went ahead in Manila (30,000 according to organizers, 5,000 according to the police), while a thousand were out in Davao City, and 3,000 were dispersed in Cagayan de Oro.[23]

It soon became clear that the authorities were going about their business in a way hardly likely to inspire confidence either domestically of internationally. Crispin Beltran, the first party-list congressman to be arrested, was shown a warrant issued in the 1980s. Members of the administration appeared to have different scripts, for while defense secretary Avelino Cruz said that warrantless arrests were not among Arroyo's powers, justice secretary Raul Gonzalez did not rule them out. (Manuel L. Quezon III says that what actually occurred here was, in effect, a rebellion by certain Cabinet members, forcing Arroyo to relinquish plans to "round up opponents and muzzle the media."[24]) It was not long before protests from home and abroad, particularly from media organizations, began to roll in.

The government, desperate to justify its actions, on February 27 issued a chronology of events leading to the proclamation. Far from reassuring the public that the actions taken were justified, this gave rise to increased alarm, as most of the actions or planned actions (rallies and vigils) enumerated were perfectly legal. During and after the short-lived emergency, this would become a trend, with government spokespersons' definitions of "sedition" being broadened to include actions that, while against government, were not aimed at its unconstitutional overthrow.

It is true that the emergency had some effect on dampening democratic life. The Senate cancelled a hearing on the fertilizer fund scandal for fear that witnesses such as Danilo Ramos, leader of the CPP-inspired KMP peasant organization, might be arrested, and *Daily Tribune* columnist Herman Tiu Laurel complained that his radio program was "momentarily in flux because management has been threatened with closure if they allow me free rein."[25] But, by and large, those whom the government aimed to intimidate refused to play along, and there was, if anything, an increased cohesion among the hitherto disparate opposing forces, as when, just before the emergency was lifted, representatives of the Gloria Stepdown Movement, Bayan (both influenced by the CPP), Akbayan (led by one of the groups that had broken away from the Maoists) and the College Editors Guild visited the offices of the pro-Estrada *Daily Tribune* to pledge support.

As the authorities attempted to hold an inquest, Anakpawis's Crispin Beltran (the only party-lister actually in custody, where he would remain until June 2007, when the Supreme Court threw out the charges against the party-listers) refused to recognize the proceedings or take a seat. When their time came, his five party-list comrades similarly refused to participate in attempted inquests. At the University of the Philippines, teachers and students walked out of classes, and the University Council declared the Diliman campus "a refuge for those who are subjected to political arrests and other forms of harassment."[26]

It looked, then, as if the match was drifting toward a goalless draw. Although Jose de Venecia reminded all who would listen that the state of emergency had staved off a "military-communist dictatorship," and hardliner Raul Gonzalez warned that, as captured documents indicated that the situation would remain dangerous until May, it was not yet time to lift the emergency, they were outnumbered. The Makati Business Club, supported by the economic cluster within the government, favored an immediate lifting, as did Vice-President Noli de Castro, and in the House even Arroyo's allies aligned themselves with this group. Arroyo asked Gonzalez, defense secretary Avelino Cruz and police chief Arturo Lomibao to assess the situation and let her have their recommendations by midday on March 4. On March 1, US assistant secretary of state Christopher Hill flew in to meet Arroyo, security officials, Ramos and

Aquino, saying the next day that he had been given "a very clear understanding of the situation" and was confident that the crisis would soon be over.[27] One day later, March 3, Arroyo lifted the state of emergency.

As the "rebellion" had already failed by the time of Arroyo's proclamation of a state of emergency, it is difficult to see how the latter could have been justified. There remain two possibilities: Arroyo either panicked, as suggested by Manuel L. Quezon III and Fidel Ramos, or she had a "copycat" model of her own, and was seeking to use emergency powers (which, the Supreme Court would later point out, she did not constitutionally possess) to resolve the five-year political crisis by silencing her opponents and cowing the business community into submission by a takeover of parts of the Lopez empire. If this was the case, she failed to accurately read the balance of forces at home and internationally.

NOTES

1. www.inq7.net., September 25, 2005.

2. *Daily Tribune*, October 9, 2005.

3. Manuel L. Quezon III, "The destruction of the presidency," *Philippine Daily Inquirer*, April 3, 2008.

4. "US rebuffed Gloria Arroyo on martial law plan," *Philippine Daily Inquirer*, September 7, 2011."

5. *Daily Tribune*, January 18, 2006.

6. Ibid., August 18, 2005.

7. www.inq7.net, September 11, 2005.

8. *Daily Tribune*, October 1, 2005.

9. www.inq7.net, January 17, 2006.

10. *Daily Tribune*, January 21, 2006.

11. "US rebuffed Gloria Arroyo on martial law plan," *Philippine Daily Inquirer*, September 7, 2011."

12. *Daily Tribune*, January 25, 2006.

13. www.inq7.net, January 22, 2006.

14. *Daily Tribune*, February 15, 2006.

15. www.inq7.net, February 17 and 18, 2006.

16. Ibid., February 21 and 28, 2006.

17. Bryan Walsh, "Dinner with Coup Plotters," *Time*, February 26, 2006.

18. Glenda M. Gloria, "More to Come," *Newsbreak* online edition, viewed on March 15, 2006.

19. Manuel L. Quezon III, "A state of panic," *Philippine Daily Inquirer*, February 26, 2006.

20. www.inq7.net, February 24, 2006.

21. Ibid, February 26, 2006.

22. Ernesto Maceda, "Mr. Expose", *Daily Tribune*, March 1, 2006. A later report had it that Allaga, on being asked to take command, had asked five key officers where they stood, whereupon the commanders of three brigades voted to follow the chain of command, isolating Querubin. (Marites Danguilan Vitug, "Sunday Standoff," *Newsbreak* online edition, April 15, 2006.)

23. www.inq7.net, February 24, 2006.

24. Manuel L. Quezon III, "The destruction of the presidency."

25. *Daily Tribune*, March 1, 2006.

26. www.inq7.net, March 1, 2006.

27. Ibid., March 2, 2006.

7 "THE CRY OF THE PEOPLE"

Since the adoption of the current Constitution of the Philippines in 1987, most of the exhortations for its amendment or revision (called "charter change," swiftly evolving into "cha-cha") had been utilitarian and lacking in principle. When President Corazon Aquino found, to her dismay, that giving the Senate the final say on foreign treaties meant waving goodbye to the US military bases, she was like the child who, having lost the game, suddenly discovers imperfections in the rules. President Ramos found it inconvenient that the basic law limited him to one six-year term and, adding insult to injury, allowed the Senate to impede the swift passage of bills devoted to his declared aim of pro-market reform. It was during the abbreviated Estrada regime that the proposal to remove the constitutional restrictions on foreign ownership and investment came to the fore. And now Gloria Macapagal Arroyo favored both a parliamentary system *and a* savaging of the nationalist safeguards.

Talk of cha-cha had recommenced shortly after Arroyo took over the presidency in 2001. Although the Senate expressed little enthusiasm for its own abolition, there seemed to be fairly broad support for a shift to a parliamentary system. There were several motives here, the most healthy of which was to speed up the passage of legislation, but there were also those who had never forgiven the Senate for voting against renewal of the US military bases agreement in 1991: the upper chamber was perhaps the one arm of the state (or half of one) which took the separation of powers seriously, maintaining a sometimes awkward independence, and occasionally adopting a nationalist stance. But as the clamor for constitutional surgery continued after the 2004 election, many suspected that Arroyo saw the possibility, by having herself elected prime minister, of occupying the number one spot indefinitely and, at the same time, staving off civil prosecution.

It was in her state of the nation address in July 2005 that Arroyo signaled that cha-cha would henceforth be high on her agenda. Having recently survived the crisis occasioned by the mass resignations of the Hyatt 10, and with an impeachment complaint yet to be decided by Congress, Arroyo, distrusted in the capital, had assembled an audience into which local power-brokers had been drafted to stiffen the ranks of her congressional allies. And it was to them she spoke—of federalism, which would enhance their powers.

Federalism would accommodate the strong regional loyalties within the Philippines, but would have very real drawbacks. Dr. Eric Langenbacker of Georgetown University identified dangers in the possibility of the emergence of competing tax rates and incentives to entice investors, leading to a "race to the bottom."[1] One did not need a crystal ball to envisage the result of such inter-regional competition: nationalist consciousness would be diminished and regional consciousness augmented as the federal components degenerated into little more than expanded "ecozones." The national economy would be further dislocated, and the pressures would be such that the nation might well, in any real sense, cease to exist.

The proposal to dismantle the nationalist economic safeguards received little attention at this stage, although that little was highly significant. Augusto B. Sanchez, the new head of the National Economic Development Authority, thought that the constitutional limits on foreign investment should go, a position with which trade secretary Peter Favila agreed. Finance secretary Margarito Teves remarked that, while at the end of the day it would be up to Congress, he was in favor of reviewing the Constitution's economic provisions. Senator Ralph Recto argued that such a review would serve to "dignify" cha-cha, transforming it into "a civic enterprise [rather] than just a trivial pursuit of politicos..."[2]

While, perhaps deliberately so, this issue was given a low profile in the cha-cha campaign, periodically during the next year voices would be raised, as if to ensure that it did not drop off the agenda. Some, like journalist Jarius Bondoc, a member of the charter change advocacy commission that Arroyo would create, put forward propositions that were extremely debatable, e.g., that Filipinos did not have the capital to come up with the 60 percent for ownership of a utilities franchise.[3] (See the contrary argument in the final chapter of this book.) From time to time, foreign capital would make a direct intervention, as in July 2006, when the joint foreign chambers of commerce and industry wrote to socioeconomic and planning secretary Romulo Neri to seek the removal of the restrictive provisions.

Thus it seemed clear that, for those who fought on the economic front, armed with ideological weapons manufactured in Washington and Brussels, the real objective was the last redoubt of Filipino nationalism.

At this stage, voices from the business community raised against these proposals were few and far between and, as was often the case, the most sensible stance was adopted by a Filipino-Chinese, on this occasion John Gokongwei, who argued that the Philippines should choose an Asia model of government—and industrialize.[4]

*

There were three methods by which the Constitution could be amended or revised: a constitutional convention (dubbed Con-Con), the delegates to which would ideally be elected (although in 1986 Corazon Aquino had appointed them) and which, therefore, was ruled out as too costly; a people's initiative, which was essentially a signature campaign; and the convening of both chambers of Congress into a constituent assembly (known inelegantly as Con-Ass).

In pursuit of the latter, the House in August 2005 approved a joint session with the Senate, but this was unlikely to happen, as a significant number of senators objected to the notion of constitutional change while Arroyo remained in office. Thus, Constantino Jaraula, chair of the House committee on constitutional amendments, warned that the lower chamber would come forward with amendments on its own if the Senate refused to play as, he argued, this would be constitutional as long as each amendment attracted sufficient votes. This would form the basis of a long-running dispute, as the Constitution provided that its amendment or revision could be proposed by the "Congress, upon a vote of three-fourths of all its Members," which cha-cha zealots interpreted as implying the possibility that the House could on its own adopt proposed amendments (which would then go to a plebiscite) if the positive votes equaled or exceeded 75 percent of the members of both chambers, while opponents were adamant that what was required was 75 percent of each chamber, voting separately.

Having foreseen continuing intransigence in the Senate, the administration had already begun to hedge its bets, with justice secretary Raul Gonzalez saying that the government was considering a "people's initiative," which provided for constitutional amendments to be proposed upon the signatures of 12 percent of all registered voters, and of at least three percent of all such voters in each electoral district. The justice secretary did not appear to notice the paradox of the *government* proposing a *"people's* initiative." For the time being, cha-cha opponents scoffed at the very idea anyway, as the Supreme Court had already ruled it out. In 1996, a People's Initiative for Reforms, Modernization and Action had attempted to use this route to secure an extension to term limits, allowing Fidel Ramos to remain in Malacañang, but the following year the court had pointed to the fact that the Constitution stated that "Congress shall provide for the implementation of this right," i.e. pass an enabling law, and that the current law was inadequate. The chances of such an enabling law being passed were now non-existent, as Senate approval would be required.

But while the law had not changed since then, circumstances had: the Supreme Court decision had not been unanimous and, with the retirement of Chief Justice Davide, both the front-runners for the vacant chair were dissenters. Towards the end of the year, there were rumors that Congressman Ronaldo Puno, the Kampi leader, would be plucked from Congress and appointed as local government secretary, a post he had held under Estrada and in which he could now utilize his network of contacts to carry forward a "people's initiative" campaign.

It would have been a mistake to believe that Mrs. Arroyo was inclined to relinquish any of her powers, let alone leave the political stage. Having only weeks earlier suggested that the adoption of a parliamentary system could provide her with a "graceful exit," by late July 2005 Ramos was saying that, as she had been convicted of nothing, she would be free to run for the post of prime minister under a parliamentary system. Jose Abueva stated that she could serve as both transitional prime minister and head of state. Moreover, he said this in a book entitled *Charter Change for Good Governance*—a further indication (he also chaired the Citizens' Movement for a Federal Philippines) that the man whom Arroyo had chosen to head the constitutional consultative commission (predictably referred to as the "Con-Com") may not have had an open mind on the issue. The members of the Con-Com, the task of which would be to undertake public consultations and make recommendations to Congress, were named in

September, 2005 and given until mid-December to complete their brief.

At this stage, nationalists were scandalized to learn that the administration had been seeking funding from a foreign power (the USA) for the proposed constitutional reform exercise, and that an agreement had been signed with lobbyists Venable LLP by, unaccountably, national security adviser Norberto Gonzales, for a retainer said to be $75,000 per month.[5] Executive secretary Eduardo Ermita and budget secretary Romulo Neri denied knowledge of the agreement, while in his own defense Gonzales claimed that no public monies would be used, as the contract was being funded by private donations; moreover, he said, Venable had been hired mainly to chase defense aid, and cha-cha had been an afterthought. While it was just believable that private individuals with an interest in cha-cha might have come up with the money, it was rather more difficult to envision them doing this for defense aid. Arroyo ordered the agreement scrapped on September 18, whereupon her spokesman Ignacio Bunye declared that the matter was closed. It was not, of course, for the Senate decided to conduct an investigation. Here, Gonzales refused to identify the donors or to say whether he had signed the contract with Arroyo's authority, whereupon he was detained for contempt. When he complained of high blood pressure, he was removed to the Philippine Heart Center, from where it was reported that he had suffered a mild stroke during the Senate hearing.

*

The recommendations of the Con-Com, delivered in December, were as follows.

- All elected officials would be exempt from election in 2007, serving until 2010. (This became known as the "no-el" scenario.)
- The interim parliament would consist of all members of the Senate and House, a third of the cabinet (appointed by the president), and thirty experts.
- The interim prime minister would be elected by MPs.
- The president would serve as both head of state and government leader, with powers to appoint the cabinet from MPs, and with supervisory powers over

the prime minister and cabinet.

- The 40 percent limit on foreign ownership in certain sectors would be deleted.

- Foreigners would still not be able to own agricultural and reclaimed lands, but would be able to obtain leases, with Congress determining the maximum permitted area. They would also be allowed to own franchises and public utilities, although Congress should legislate that only large public utilities should be franchised to corporations with majority foreign ownership.

- Congress would be empowered to allow foreign ownership in the mass media and advertising.

- From 2010, executive and legislative powers would be exercised by a unicameral parliament, elected from constituencies based on population. MPs would serve a term of five years, with no restriction on the number of terms that, subject to re-election, could be served. Candidate MPs would need to be at least college graduates.

There is some doubt as to whether these recommendations faithfully reflected the public consultation, as the *Inquirer*, in reporting a Makati meeting held on November 23, said that, although Con-Com members claimed an overwhelming majority of business and labor organizations had supported the opening up of various sectors to foreign interests, the workshop on economic reforms had seen 19 out of 30 voting for retaining the ban on foreign ownership of mass media. In the workshop on the form of government, only eleven had voted for a parliamentary system, with twelve undecided, given their inadequate knowledge of the system.[6] Moreover, a Con-Com source told the *Daily Tribune* that the original draft of the report had proposed a cut in Arroyo's term and claimed that there had been no discussion of the "no-el" proposal.[7] Abueva acknowledged that the commission had first of all voted 18-16 against the latter proposition, but then, following a motion for reconsideration, had adopted it by 22 votes to 19.

As was made clear by a series of articles by Raissa Espinosa-Robles in the *Manila Times*, there were distinct similarities between the proceedings of the Con-Com and the way business had been conducted in Ferdinand Marcos's constitutional convention (Con-Con), which had led to the adoption of the 1973 Constitution.

Like its predecessor, the Con-Com had split up into subcommittees and "special committees," inserting new presidential powers into the draft report submitted to a plenary session at the last moment (i.e., the day before the commission was dissolved); the rules were suspended, members were told to hasten approval, and amendments were refused, although unauthorized insertions were made at the last moment. The deliberations of the Con-Con had dragged on for 17 months, and thus in October 1972 the rules were suspended and a special committee was established to draft the Constitution. Secretary to this committee was none other than Jose Abueva, and the draft was completed in a week. Apart from former president Diosdado Macapagal (father of Gloria, he had been defeated by Marcos in the election of 1965), another person "silently fashioning the intricate details of suspending the rules" was Gilberto Duavit, whom Arroyo had appointed to her Con-Com.[8] Just as Marcos, having promised to cancel elections, had created citizen's assemblies to approve his Constitution, so the Con-Com inserted a provision canceling the 2007 elections, and now cha-cha supporters would attend barangay assemblies to commence the "people's initiative" campaign (see below).[9] The commission had, it seemed, fallen victim to the copycat syndrome.

If the administration entertained high hopes regarding the manner in which the Con-Com recommendations would be received, these were dashed. There were certainly some inflated claims from the palace: back in November, the presidential spokesman had predicted that, with the immediate adoption of cha-cha, the Philippines would enter the ranks of the First World countries in 20 years. But the Senate did not budge, senators of all persuasions raising their voices against the report. The pro-administration (if awkwardly so) Senator Joker Arroyo charged that the recommendations plagiarized the Marcos constitution. In the *Inquirer*, Amando Doronila used his column to observe sourly that the proposals were "an ill-disguised subterfuge to keep [Arroyo] in power until 2010," as the "transitional proposals lock us in the stalemate of the crisis over Mrs. Arroyo's legitimacy. They have brought the country to a dead end."[10] In the House, Rep. Roilo Golez called the proposed cancellation of the 2007 elections a bribe and a "shameful political, self-preservation ploy..."[11] Even Fidel Ramos commented that such a cancellation would be a "monumental blunder."[12]

When people like Golez criticized the "no-el" proposal as a bribe, they did so in the knowledge that it would amount to rather more than granting incumbents an extra three years in office without the inconvenience of an election. Significant funds are expended on election campaigns, and thus cancellation would have entailed big savings; moreover, anti-corruption campaigners argued that such expenses were often looked upon as investments, to be recouped with interest once in office, so "no-el" offered the prospect of continued income from corruption for zero investment. Even so, under pressure from some big guns (most notably former president Fidel Ramos), Arroyo appeared to back off, claiming that it had never been her intention and pointing out that it was, anyway, up to Congress.

This was not the only demand put forward by Ramos, for he also wanted Arroyo to step down in 2007. The ruling Lakas-CMD (originally founded as Ramos's electoral vehicle in 1992) talked, however, of a developing consensus for her to remain as president under a new parliamentary system, serving out her term until 2010 with key powers, although the prime minister would be the political leader. This matter would, the party said, be resolved at a national caucus on January 14, 2006.

It turned out that the "no-el" proposal had not been dropped, for at the caucus this was one of the proposals adopted, along with a parliamentary, unicameral system, five-year terms, a ban on party-hopping, the creation of autonomous regions in preparation for a federal system, and the lifting of restrictions on foreign investment. Arroyo told the gathering that she had no intention of stepping down in 2007, and those present dutifully passed a motion to this effect.

The group of CPP-influenced party-list congressmen introduced a House motion that sought to reject "no-el," dubbing the proposal "immoral, unethical" and something that could be seen as an "opportunistic, self-serving ploy to perpetuate incumbent officials...in power."[13] But everyone knew that the party-listers and the mainstream opposition lacked the numbers to do much damage on their own, and thus Arroyo loyalists carried on regardless. The House committee on constitutional amendments adopted a working draft on the proposed changes and then began to debate and adopt each proposal.

The real problem for Arroyo lay in the Senate, and Richard Gordon, chairman of that chamber's committee on constitutional amendments, let it be known that there would be no plenary debate on the issue until after the 2007 elections. At a Council of State meeting (where, even Arroyo's official spokesman admitted, eighty percent were opposed to "no-el"), Fidel

126

Ramos warned that cancellation was "a disaster waiting to happen."[14] It was not until the Catholic bishops exerted pressure on Malacañang that Arroyo's spokesman confirmed that the 2007 elections would go ahead, although Arroyo would remain in office until 2010. The House committee fell into line, rejecting (for the time being, at least) any constitutional amendment that sought to cancel the elections or extend terms.

At least within administration circles, the cha-cha issue now began to gather momentum, with the creation of a charter change advocacy commission (eleven members of the Con-Com, with Jose Abueva serving as adviser and chair emeritus), which was given eight months to complete its work. Ronaldo Puno was, as predicted, appointed as secretary of the interior and local government, and announced that Kampi would collect 195 signatures from both Houses to endorse the formation of a constituent assembly. The opposition immediately warned that, based on its own interpretation of the Constitution, this would give rise to a constitutional crisis.

The administration then opened the second front, with Speaker de Venecia announcing the formation of a "people's initiative" campaign by some 100 members of NGOs and people's organizations. Thus, in mid-February 2006, before an audience of 10,000 at the Ninoy Aquino Stadium, Manila mayor Lito Atienza publicly launched the campaign, called Sigaw ng Bayan: Pagbabago sa Saligang Batas Ngayon Na! (The Cry of the People: Charter Change Now!). Even though he had still not resigned from Congress, Puno called all regional, provincial and city directors to a two-day conference on this campaign, leading the opposition to point out that the use of public funds for such a purpose was illegal.

*

With the lifting of the state of emergency in early March 2006, cha-cha opponents re-emerged, their determination unshaken, with no less than 22 Senators (out of 23, Ramon Magsaysay Jr. being out of the country) signing a resolution advising the House that it could not convene as a constituent assembly on its own.

But then the cha-cha proponents unleashed their forces in an attempt to bypass both houses of Congress. The Sigaw ng Bayan movement took out half-page ads in the national press, and the "people's initiative" was off and running, cunningly timed to coincide with the day when, all over the country, barangay assemblies would be held. It soon emerged that these were being used to pass resolutions in favor of cha-cha and to collect signatures.

The *Daily Tribune* claimed that barangay chiefs had each received between P20,000 and P50,000 in return for signatures. The palace denied any involvement, saying that any money spent must have come from the local governments (which would still, of course, have been illegal).[15] According to the *Inquirer*, cash and rice was being offered for signatures, and a barangay leader in Valenzuela claimed that an instruction to give P200 to every signatory came from an undersecretary at the department of the interior and local government (DILG), while it was said that in Olongapo City barangay officials had been promised P1,000 for every five pages of signatures.[16] The following month, Senate minority leader Aquilino Pimentel Jr. claimed that a DILG source had told him that an average of P500,000 per voting district had been released for the signature campaign.[17] Naturally, Sigaw ng Bayan leader Raul Lambino denied that money had changed hands and claimed that the majority of the assemblies had voted for cha-cha. Senate leader Franklin Drilon dubbed the use of the assemblies as "Marcosian," a reference to the time when, by a variety of dubious means, people had been induced to raise their hands at citizens' assemblies in support of Marcos's proposals. Incredibly, the campaign claimed to have already collected four million signatures.

A Pulse Asia survey at this time found that 43 percent were in favor of cha-cha, up from 36 percent the previous October and 29 percent in March. Those opposed amounted to 48 percent, down from 55 percent in October.[18] Thus, although it seemed that the cha-cha proponents would still not win a plebiscite at this time, the trend was moving in their direction. More significantly, however, the survey also found that 66 percent had "little, almost none or no knowledge at all about the 1987 Constitution,"[19] and a little over a week later a Social Weather Stations survey would find that between 64 and 76 percent of respondents belonged to these categories.[20]

This last finding was of no little importance, for the claims of the campaign organizers implied that the purported millions knew what they were signing and fully understood the issues. It was unlikely that this was so, as an appraisal of the contents of the petition would demonstrate. The petition form began with an abstract, which by law was required to be reprinted on every page of signatures. This read:

> Do you approve of the amendment of Articles VI and VII of the 1987 Constitution, changing the form of government from the present bicameral-presidential to a unicameral-parliamentary system of government, in order to achieve greater efficiency, simplicity and economy in government, and providing an Article XVIII as Transitory Provisions for the orderly shift from one system to another?

If between two-thirds and three-quarters of those attending the assemblies had "little, almost none or no knowledge at all" of the Constitution, it was unlikely that they would have been familiar with the provisions of Articles VI and VII, let alone have understood such terms as "bicameral-presidential" or "unicameral-parliamentary." And what of the "transitory provisions?" A full understanding of all these terms would have necessitated a careful consideration of the full contents of the petition—some 2,140 words. It must be doubted whether there was time available for such consideration, let alone questions, explanation and discussion of the proposals.

By and large, the petition followed the Con-Com proposals and those of the House committee on constitutional amendments, although there was no requirement for MPs to have a college education. Quite cleverly, there was provision for the continuation of the party-list system, whose MPs would comprise one-sixth of the parliament. The post of president would be retained, but only as head of state, with executive power being vested in a prime minister, who would be elected from and by all MPs. Under the transitory provisions, the current president and vice-president would serve until 2010 unless impeached by a vote of two-thirds of MPs. The interim parliament would consist of all congressmen and senators, those cabinet members who headed executive departments, and the vice-president; the implication, therefore, was that the 2007 elections would be cancelled, although the petition failed to state the date of the first parliamentary election.

These transitional provisions were not spelled out in the question posed to signatories, and the time available would hardly have allowed a full airing of them. Moreover, the full petition proposed a further provision whereby, within 45 days of the amendments being ratified, the interim parliament would convene to propose further "amendments to, or revisions of, this Constitution consistent with the principles of local autonomy, decentralization and a strong bureaucracy." This could only be interpreted as a reference to federalism, of which there was no mention in the question posed to potential signatories. Undoubtedly, this was in part due to the fact that a "people's initiative" was constitutionally limited to one issue, and was thus unable to undertake wholesale revision of the Constitution.

Possibly for the same reason, the petition also failed to mention the economic provisions of the Constitution. On the one hand, this omission strengthened the argument of those who took the view that cha-cha was, first and foremost, all about preserving Arroyo's immunity from prosecution: under the transitional provisions, she would probably be safe from impeachment until 2010, at which point she could stand for election as an MP and, possibly, be elected as prime minister by her peers. On the other hand, it was quite possible that the leaders of the "people's initiative" had concluded that it was simply unnecessary to include the proposals to dismantle the economic provisions, for whereas three-quarters of the votes of each chamber voting separately was currently an impossibility, and a vote in the House which mobilized the equivalent of the sum of these was practically difficult and constitutionally questionable, there would be less of a problem in an interim parliament made up of the current crop of congressmen and senators, beefed up by the heads of executive departments and the vice-president.

As might be expected from the above, complaints of sharp practice were not long in appearing. It was reported that in the island province of Bohol, many residents attending the assemblies had refused to sign as they were given insufficient time to comprehend the issues, and, thus, barangay officials in the provincial capital of Tagbilaran City and some towns were conducting house-to-house forays for signatures. If there had been insufficient time at the assemblies to explain the issues, it is difficult to see that the local officials would have the time to give detailed explanations to individuals, particularly as, according to one councilor, a senior officer had confirmed that they had been given the astronomical target of collecting the signatures of 55 percent of registered voters by a "letter of instruction from higher authorities…" At the same time, a senior municipal official claimed that barangay officials had each received P1,000 in "expenses" for the assemblies.[21] Officials in La Trinidad, Benguet, demanded that all signatures collected in the thirteen towns and 140 barangays of the province be declared null and void, as people had been asked to sign without being informed of the issues.[22] An anonymous Comelec official revealed that "ghost" and dead signatories had been identified in two provinces, in one of which twelve percent of those signing were not registered voters. And why, he asked, if this was a "people's initiative," were DILG officials visiting Comelec regional offices to request that the signatures be verified?[23] In Makati, Mayor Jejomar Binay declared he had evidence of signatures of people long dead.[24] Later, four Makati residents would complain to the prosecutor's office that their signatures had, with others, been forged. Among the alleged forgeries was the signature of a former barangay captain who died in 2005 and that of his successor, one of the complainants. In Caloocan, residents also complained about the methods used in obtaining their signatures, one official having reportedly asked a couple to sign in order to verify their names on the voters' lists.[25]

The cha-cha proponents hardly missed a trick. When in May the charter change advocacy commission laid out its stall before an association of senior military officers, executive secretary Eduardo Ermita assured a skeptical media that this did not mean that members of the armed forces were being politicized, as it was merely an information campaign, and no harm would be done if the commissioners sought the support of the military so that the campaign for constitutional reform would be successful. Sigaw ng Bayan's Lambino then announced that the commission would tour military camps. Sigaw foot-soldiers met with rather less success the following month when, alerted by concerned faculty members, students at the Polytechnic University of the Philippines denied them access to the campus.

In Makati, the "people's initiative" campaigners faced special problems, as Mayor Binay was also leader of the United Opposition. In April, Lambino complained that his campaigners had been prevented from gathering signatures in both Makati and San Juan (where J.V. Ejercito, Joseph Estrada's son, was mayor). For his part, Binay warned that petitioners would be arrested if they offered money, as he had heard that anywhere between P20 and P200 was being offered for each signature, and that some residents had been told that the aim of the petition was to remove Arroyo from office, others that they would be denied benefits by the local government if they refused to sign.[26] By June, Lambino conceded that Binay and Ejercito appeared to be winning, as the two electoral districts in Makati and one in San Juan were the only ones in the country where the campaign had failed to attract signatures from the requisite three percent of registered voters.[27]

The following month, Binay claimed that a group led by former vice-mayor Roberto Brilliante was aiming for 20,000 "real signatures" in Makati, with a network of cadres in each of the 33 barangays, and payments to leaders, foot-soldiers and signatories that would amount to P10 million. The Makati Comelec office, meanwhile, certified that in one barangay only 53 of 3,909 signatures appeared to be authentic[28] (hence the need, presumably, for "real signatures").

Like so many of the administration's dubious political successes, it was hoped that the people's initiative campaign would triumph through sheer force of numbers, and thus great claims were made for this "democratic" exercise. Addressing foreign donors at a meeting of the Philippine Development Forum, Arroyo claimed that the signature campaign reflected the "true power of the people," while Speaker De Venecia asked the Supreme Court to reconsider its 1997 decision, arguing somewhat irrelevantly that there had at that time been no signatures. "How," he asked, "can the Supreme Court or Malacañang or Congress be higher than the sovereign will of the Filipino people?"[29] The director of the Supreme Court's press office, while saying that an enabling law was required, pointed out that two of the six justices who gave a dissenting opinion in 1997 still sat on the court and that one of them, Artemio Panganiban, was now the Chief Justice.

Justice secretary Raul Gonzalez, sometimes known to be less than discrete, admitted that the 1997 ruling was inimical to the "people's initiative," but added that if the Comelec verified the signatures, "I am sure someone will go to the Supreme Court about it," and he expressed confidence that the court would reverse its decision.[30] This, it would become clear, was a key component of the administration's strategy. Yes, the Supreme Court had ruled almost a decade earlier that there was no sufficient enabling law to give effect to the people's initiative, but it could change its mind, just as it had when, following pleas from the government to provide an incentive for foreign mining interests to return to the country, it had reversed its own ruling that the mining law was unconstitutional.

*

There was a plethora of anti-signature organizations. Claiming that residents had been told the petition was a census, an assurance to avoid eviction, or even proof that they were not members of the NPA, the KMP (the CPP-influenced peasant organization) opened Oplan Bawi Pirma (Operation Cancel Signature), by means of which people who had been asked to sign by dubious means could now rescind their signatures. Bayan, the KMP's sister-organization and a member of Peoples Movement Against Arroyo's Charter Change (PEOPLE'S MARCH), began collecting signatures against cha-cha and asked the Catholic church to open all parishes to assist groups in such activity, while the Tanggulan ng Obrerong Pilipino (TOP, or Defense of Filipino Workers) kicked off a drive to collect 11 million signatures (equaling the number of votes received by Estrada in the 1998 presidential election) in support of snap elections. The Young Enlisted Active and Retired Military and Police for Solidarity (Yes Arms) urged support for a signature campaign to cut short Arroyo's term and establish a transitional government. A more elite initiative saw Corazon Aquino, congressmen, senators, religious, civil society and business groups involved in Sa Tamang Oras at Paraan (STOP, Right Time and Reason), which planned a roadshow in its education and information campaign. In June, yet another group, purporting to be multisectoral and non-partisan, appeared—One Voice, led by Christian Monsod, a former Comelec commissioner.

The existence of this wide array of organizations, often with differing aims, was open to two interpretations: that it was provoked by such a widespread feeling of outrage that the administration and its proxies in the "people's initiative" campaign would soon be engulfed by protests; or that this was a further illustration of the lack of unity and coordination among the ranks of the government's opponents. The latter would seem to be the more accurate of the two. Not only were the actions largely uncoordinated and, thus, wasteful of effort, but some of the proposals were patently unrealistic. Seeking to have signatures withdrawn would, for example, be just as (if not more) time-consuming as the original signature-collection campaign, and, in addition, the cha-cha opponents did not possess anything approaching the national network that, courtesy of local government officials, was enjoyed by Sigaw ng Bayan. As a further example, how could TOP ever hope to collect 11 million signatures with, again, no national network? And, of course, the fact that there were so many proposed campaigns with different aims simply reduced the chance that any one of them would succeed.

Hardly surprisingly, then, these initiatives achieved very little except, possibly, to raise the level of public awareness on the issue, and the more realistic protests took the legal route. A number of local courts were asked, as there was no enabling law to permit it, to stop the Comelec verifying signatures, and a number of temporary restraining orders were issued. At the end of the day, however, as appeared to be the administration's intention, the matter would end up with the Supreme Court.

With the reputation of the Comelec already tarnished by its alleged involvement in the 2004 election irregularities, its chairman Benjamin Abalos appeared to be courting further controversy when from the outset he maintained that the organization would verify the signatures, and that a plebiscite was possible for July.[31] The *Inquirer* editorialized that the electoral body was "making itself a party to the most ruthless and, in a sense, reckless assault on the concept of checks and balances. It is helping to make irrelevant the Supreme Court and its decisions. It is actively assisting a partisan political exercise. There is no clearer, and more glaring, example of the tyranny of numbers, than the so-called people's initiative that has received President Gloria Macapagal's blessing."[32] Nevertheless, head of presidential staff Mike Defensor urged mayors to follow the example of their Manila colleague Lito Atienza in getting the poll body to verify the signatures, arguing: "The sooner our local officials have the signatures for charter change verified by the Comelec, the sooner we can move to the next step which is a plebiscite."[33] Incoming solicitor general Eduardo Nachura vowed that he would defend the Comelec officials if called upon to do so, while executive secretary Eduardo Ermita also defended the Comelec's role as, he said, the controversy would be resolved by the Supreme Court. Such interventions did little to persuade a skeptical populace that the "people's initiative" was really anything of the kind.

*

If the Sigaw campaigners were looking to the religious sector for consolation, they were disappointed, for a little more than a week into the campaign, the Catholic Bishops Conference of the Philippines (CBCP) declared that the campaign was "dangerously unclear and open to manipulation by groups with self-serving interests." A pastoral letter from CBCP president Archbishop Angel Lagdameo said that the bishops viewed the petition activity with alarm, as "[s]ignatures were apparently collected without adequate information, discussion and education."[34] House majority floor leader Prospero Nograles retorted that cha-cha was a political initiative, and thus none of the church's business. He was apparently unaware that, days earlier, presidential spokesman Ignacio Bunye had expressed the hope that the church would support the "people's initiative." Having declined to take the lead in the campaign against cha-cha due to the church's non-political status (a fiction as breathtaking as the claim by administration officials that the signature campaign was a grassroots initiative), the CBCP nevertheless expressed alarm again in May, saying that reports received from its social action centers indicated that the campaign was "deceptive, lacking in adequate information and discussion, and not initiated by the people."[35] When Bohol governor Erico Aumentado, president of the union of local authorities, claimed that he had secured CBCP support for cha-cha at a meeting in Iloilo, Lagdameo set him straight by retorting that the bishops favored an elected constitutional convention — but not until 2010.

Bro. Mike Velarde, meanwhile, vowed to mobilize his El Shaddai (a numerous evangelical Catholic sect) against cha-cha, as the "people's initiative" was obviously directed by the government. The protestant National Council of Churches also took the view that the aim of the exercise was to perpetuate Arroyo and others in office, and thus it, too, opposed cha-cha. It was only the Philippine Council of Evangelical Churches (which had been represented on the Con-Com) that came out in support of the campaign. Given the fact that one of the big claims advanced by cha-cha proponents was that growth and development of the economy would accelerate at such a rate that First World status would be achieved in 20 years, further disappointment must have been registered when the Makati Business Club warned that the hasty adoption of a parliamentary system would in fact have negative effects, and that, anyway, a constitutional convention or a constituent assembly would be required.

Apart from a blip in July, when Pulse Asia found that 40 percent, with 38 percent opposing, favored immediate revision of the Constitution (an "historic turn in public opinion," claimed Speaker De Venecia[36]) the polls indicated that the "people's initiative" was in trouble. But, rather than placing all their eggs in one basket, cha-cha proponents were simultaneously pursuing a constituent assembly. At the very time the signature campaign was launched in late March, De Venecia had pointed to the desirability of the Con-Ass, as the "people's initiative" would restrict the exercise to the single issue of a switch to a parliamentary system. A month later, Constantino Jaraula filed House Resolution 1230, containing a package of constitutional amendments and a call for a Con-Ass. By mid-May, its supporters were saying that they had 180 signatures, 15 short of the amount required (according to their interpretation of the Constitution) to convene the assembly.

*

In late August, Sigaw ng Bayan and the union of local authorities submitted their "people's initiative" petition, with 8.9 million signatures, 6.3 million of which had been verified, to the Comelec. Within days, the poll body unanimously rejected it, citing the 1997 ruling. Everyone had expected this, and so there were no long faces in the administration camp. Eyes now turned to the Supreme Court.

By now, ten of the fifteen Supreme Court justices had been appointed by Arroyo, and a cynical public had long been of the view that the court would do her bidding. With the appointment of Artemio Panganiban as Chief Justice, this suspicion was strengthened, but then the court came out with a series of disarming rulings in April and May, indicating that the skeptics may have got it all wrong. First, the court ruled that parts of Executive Order 464 were unconstitutional, although the president could request a closed-door session if it was felt that national security required it. Then, by a vote of 13-0, it declared the administration's policy of "calibrated preemptive response" with regard to rallies unconstitutional, although the legality of the Marcos-era Batasan Pambansa 880, under which rallyists were required to obtain permits, was upheld. Finally, by a vote of 11-3, it was held that Presidential Proclamation 1017, Arroyo's declaration of a state of emergency, was "constitutional insofar as it constitutes a call by the President for the [military] to prevent or suppress lawless violence," but that the way the proclamation was implemented, with a crackdown on street protest, warrantless arrests and the raid on the *Daily Tribune,* was "unconstitutional and illegal." It was further found that the proclamation's "extraneous provisions" exceeded constitutional limits, as in the granting of express or implied power to issue decrees, direct the armed forces to enforce all and sundry laws and impose standards on the media. The president could not, said the court, take over companies or utilities without prior legislation. Arroyo could declare a national emergency, which was merely a description of a situation, but emergency powers could only be obtained with congressional support, unless she declared martial law.

It therefore appeared that the system of "checks and balances" was back in play, with the Supreme Court acting as a brake on the anti-democratic impulses of the executive branch. Such was the corrosive nature of the cynicism bred by the post-war political culture, however, that there were still doubters. With these three decisions (which, after all, concerned administration devices that had, to a certain degree, already served their purposes), had the court merely been seeking to establish a public perception of itself as a fearless, independent body, so that a future ruling on cha-cha favoring the government would be more likely to be accepted as fair and impartial?

When, in late September, the Supreme Court heard oral submissions concerning the "people's initiative," yet another hole was blown in the fiction that this was truly a popular initiative when solicitor general Eduardo Nachura, who had earlier vowed to defend Comelec officials prosecuted for verifying signatures, now appeared for the petitioners (i.e., *against* the Comelec). Chief Justice Panganiban expressed the view that the signature drive was more in the nature of a survey than a people-initiated campaign, for to comply with the Constitution, the people (and not, for example, the governor of Bohol) should propose. Associate Justice Angelina Sandoval-Gutierrez asked how the 6.3 million verified signatures had been collected, as some of her relatives had been asked to sign without being given an explanation of the exercise. Associate Justice Reynato Puno (who, along with Panganiban, had dissented from the 1997 ruling), asked how, as the petition was in English, people in remote areas had been able to understand the "people's initiative." It seemed to be going the opponents' way; but then, before he gave both sides 15 days to submit memoranda on whether the three percent target had been met in all electoral districts, Panganiban conceded that there might be a need to revisit the 1997 ruling.

Prior to the Supreme Court decision, Panganiban admitted that justices had been subject to pressure. Indeed, at a reception for delegates to the Global Forum on Liberty and Prosperity, at which Panganiban was present, Arroyo chose to make a plea for "cha-cha," while Speaker De Venecia urged the justices to consider with their hearts as well as their minds—almost as if the law were not the major consideration. But if there was pressure, most justices resisted it, and on October 25 the court delivered a decision that, by 8 to 7, threw out the petition. There was, said the majority decision penned by Justice Antonio Carpio, no reason to revisit the 1997 decision because the petition "dismally fails to comply with the requirement...that the initiative must be 'directly proposed by the people...'" The signature forms had failed to display the draft of the proposed changes, and the signatures were "deceptively gathered."

It was not quite the end of the line for Arroyo's cha-cha aspirations, for the petitioners indicated that they would file a motion for reconsideration. Should that fail, attempts would be made to convene a constituent assembly without the participation of the Senate. There was, in addition, a potential problem for cha-cha opponents: Chief Justice Panganiban, who had done so much to re-establish the integrity and independence of the Supreme Court, was due to retire on December 7. Thus, when Sigaw's motion for reconsideration was mailed from Bohol, critics claimed that the aim was to play for time. Maybe it was, but Panganiban and his colleagues doused administration hopes by coming up with a decision on November 21, denying the motion with finality by the same 8-7 vote. Close though it may have been, this particular "people's initiative" was stone dead.

Speaker De Venecia was not a particularly good loser, suggesting that Panganiban and Antonio Carpio, the justice who had worded the original decision with barely concealed contempt, should be impeached, as "the dream of millions of Filipinos to pursue constitutional change was finished." This was presumably a reference to that large body of citizens who, having signed attendance sheets at the barangay assemblies back in March, had later learned that their signatures were being passed off as endorsements for Sigaw's petition, so although De Venecia protested that he was unable to prevent "the people" from filing impeachment cases,[37] they were hardly likely to do any such thing.

Nevertheless, some Filipinos—in the administration camp, anyway—did continue to

138

dream of constitutional change, and so the pro-administration majority in the House went ahead, amending the rules on constitutional amendments by deleting the requirement to treat these in the same manner as bills (Senate concurrence would not, therefore, be required). At 5.37 a.m. on December 7, 2006 the House approved a resolution to convene as a constituent assembly, set for December 12.

At last, the feeling in the country seemed to move beyond indignation and outrage to preparedness for activity. The Catholic bishops, confronted with something to which they could object on "moral" grounds, called on people to express their opposition. Mike Velarde of El Shaddai urged attendance at protests. United Opposition leader Jejomar Binay promised rallies. "Our nation," said Joseph Estrada, protesting that democracy was being murdered by the House majority, "has become known as a nation of liars, a nation of cheaters, and a nation of thieves. If we do not move now and do something about this, we will also be known as a nation of cowards."[38] Most forces were now organizing for a rally on December 12 — the mainstream opposition, the left, and, at last, the church.

There had, of course, been promises of action before, but this time it felt different, and the administration knew it. Governor Singson of Ilocos Sur (significantly, he was chairman of the league of governors), without whom Gloria Macapagal Arroyo would never have entered Malacañang in January 2001, now urged caution. Fourteen congressmen who had hitherto supported cha-cha signed a resolution opposing postponement of the May 2007 elections. Even the union of local authorities, one of the moving forces behind the defeated "people's initiative," asked Arroyo to withdraw support for the proposal for a constituent assembly, as it feared this could give rise to "people power." To great embarrassment, the government now postponed an ASEAN summit due to take place in the island province of Cebu, ostensibly due to Typhoon "Seniang" (which would not touch the conference site); although there were, apparently, warnings from several intelligence agencies of a terrorist plot to disrupt the summit, the *Manila Times* reported sources as saying that the promised protest actions played a part in the decision.[39]

Then, on December 9, the administration bloc virtually surrendered as, at a press conference, Speaker De Venecia affirmed support for the May elections and called for an elected constitutional convention; Malacañang signaled its agreement. The following week, the House scrapped its resolution calling for a constituent assembly. According to Senator Joker Arroyo, cha-cha was now dead and the administration supporters had been bluffing all along, having never possessed sufficient numbers.[40]

The church went ahead with the planned rally anyway—with some amendments. First, the venue in Rizal Park had been already booked by the Philippine Amusement and Gaming Corporation, so the date was shifted to December 17. Second, it was now made clear that this would be a "prayer rally." There would be no placards, no slogans, no speeches from politicians, and only celebrants of the mass would be allowed onstage. The upshot of this was that, of the 500,000 promised by their graces, only 30-40,000 (a police estimate) or 100,000 (the estimate of left groups) turned up.

This obviously led some in the administration camp to wonder whether they could, after all, have gotten away with it, and whether it might be safe to risk another attempt. The day after the rally, therefore, executive secretary Eduardo Ermita indicated that Arroyo had not dropped cha-cha. In Arroyo's speech at the 40th anniversary of the Asian Development Bank, cha-cha was no longer a hot potato but "a platform commitment of [the] administration that will be pursued with urgency and fervor," although there was "a need for a unified national consensus on the means and the timetable…"[41] Then it looked as if the union of local authorities was going to come forward with another "people's initiative," this time for a unicameral *presidential* system, while the Sigaw group was said to be still wedded to a parliamentary system.

By this stage, opponents of cha-cha, faced with the possibility of another round of negative campaigning, must have been clutching their heads in their hands. But they need not have worried: having been floored in the eleventh round, the cha-cha campaign could not summon sufficient strength to beat the count.

NOTES

1. www.inq7.net, August 7, 2005.
2. *BusinessWorld*, July 29, 2005.
3. *Daily Tribune*, April 30, 2006.

4. www.inq7.net, August 11, 2006.

5. www.inq7.net, September 14, 2005.

6. Ibid., November 25, 2005.

7. *Daily Tribune*, December 20, 2005.

8. Raissa Espinosa-Robles, "President's Charter campaign copies FM's," *Manila Times*, May 1, 2006.

9. Raissa Espinosa-Robles, "How they copied from Marcos's book," *Manila Times*, May 2, 2006.

10. *Philippine Daily Inquirer*, December 19, 2005.

11. Ibid., December 19, 2005.

12. Ibid., December 22, 2005.

13. Ibid., January 16, 2006.

14. *Daily Tribune*, January 25, 2006.

15. Ibid., March 25, 2006.

16. *Philippine Daily Inquirer*, March 25, 2006.

17. *Daily Tribune*, April 2, 2006.

18. www.inq7.net, March 28, 2006.

19. *Daily Tribune*, March 28, 2006.

20. www.inq7.net, April 6, 2006.

21. *Bohol Chronicle*, March 29, 2006.

22. www.inq7.net, April 5, 2006.

23. Ibid., April 7, 2006.

24. *Malaya*, April 20, 2006.

25. *Daily Tribune*, March 31, 2006.

26. www.inq7.net, April 6, 2006.

27. Ibid., June 27, 2006.

28. *Daily Tribune*, July 20, 2006.

29. www.inq7.net, March 30, 2006.

30. Ibid., March 31, 2006.

31. www.inq7.net, March 30, 2006.

32. Editorial, "Force of numbers," *Philippine Daily Inquirer*, March 31, 2006.

33. www.inq7.net, April1, 2006.

34. Ibid., April 7, 2006.

35. Ibid., May 12, 2006.

36. Ibid., July 26 and July 28, 2006.

37. *Malaya*, November 24, 2006.

38. *Daily Tribune*, December 8, 2006.

39. *Manila Times*, December 9, 2006.

40. www.inq7.net, December 9, 2006.

41. www.inq7.net, December 19, 2006.

8 "A VERY WELL DEVELOPED DEMOCRACY"

When, in August 2006, the House threw out the second complaint against Mrs. Arroyo, it was perfectly clear that impeachment could never succeed in the chamber as it was currently composed. Thus, the only hope for the pro-impeachment camp lay in ensuring that, as a result of the midterm elections in May 2007, this composition was radically changed.

It was possibly in preparation for this challenge that in the latter part of 2006 the Arroyo administration began an attempt to drive a number of local officials from office. When the mayor, vice-mayor and councilors of Pasay City were suspended on graft charges, Makati mayor Jejomar Binay warned that this heralded a crackdown on local officials opposed to the administration. In September, Binay, his wife and others were charged with irregularities, and the following month, as rumors of an impending suspension circulated, officials and employees shuttered the ground floor offices of the city hall, and when the suspension was ordered supporters blockaded the building. The tension was relieved when the Court of Appeals granted Binay a temporary restraining order (this was extended indefinitely in December).

January 2007 saw a second wave of suspensions based on allegations of corruption. When, taking a leaf out of Binay's book, Governor Niel Tupas of Iloilo barricaded himself in the provincial capitol, police stormed the building but were unable to find him. He then obtained a temporary restraining order, as did Governor Armando C. Sanchez of Batangas. Unable to obtain such an order, the mayor of Jaen, Nueva Ecija, stood down. The administration camp was divided on this issue, for while the hardliners warned that officials refusing to vacate their offices would be charged with sedition, and that the suspensions would continue into the electoral period, there being 200 cases outstanding[1] (of which little was thereafter heard), others, such as Manila mayor Lito Atienza and Ilocos Sur governor Luis "Chavit" Singson, urged caution. Their counsel seems to have prevailed, although it is possible that the initial suspensions, and the threat of more to come, had had the intended effect, for at the end of February Senator Panfilo Lacson observed that opposition support had suffered as a result, as some had joined administration parties in order to "survive the onslaught," whereupon the pressures had ceased.[2]

There was, however, one more attempted suspension. Less than two weeks before polling day, the Bureau of Internal Revenue (BIR) asked 34 banks to freeze the assets of the city of Makati, along with Mayor Binay's own assets, due to an unpaid tax bill of P1.1 billion. According to Binay, who was facing an electoral challenge from actor-Senator Lito Lapid, he had been dealing with the BIR and thus Malacañang must have pressured its officials into taking this action. A former councilor then filed plunder charges against Binay, his wife, the city treasurer and an accountant, following which the Ombudsman issued a six-month suspension order against mayor and treasurer. Once again, Makati city hall was besieged by Binay supporters, and two days later, as the administration's senatorial team complained that it would suffer from the backlash, the presidential palace postponed the suspension and all but one of the bank accounts were unfrozen.

Although the administration had been forced into another climb-down, the episode did not augur well for the conduct of the elections.

*

By and large, Philippine politics is the preserve of the principalia, the ruling class formed during the Spanish period by the intermarriage of traditional leading families with Chinese traders and the Spanish. Even now, the principalia is largely a mestizo class. Economic strength accumulated during the centuries of Spanish rule was translated into political influence when the Americans introduced representative government (in an extremely limited form) in the early 20th century, as elections were initially subject to literacy and property qualifications. While, historically, membership of the principalia was closed, more recently it had admitted more members as newly-successful business people (along with a sprinkling of entertainers and sports personalities) had built political dynasties, and skillful politicians had used their offices to amass wealth for investment. Electoral politics being to a large extent the preserve of the rich, many votes were simply bought—indeed, they had to be, as money was very often all that the candidates had to offer. As Simbulan says:

> As representatives of both the landed and business interests, elite politicians cannot attract voters' support on the basis of issues arising out of differences in political principles—there are none. Consequently, one of the major areas of competition lies in the field of spending, that is, in the use of the economic resources that they possess and control to buy voters' support. Patronage distribution, favor, and dole-giving, even blatant vote buying, figure prominently in this contest.[3]

Nor are such politicians willing to spend large sums simply to satisfy their egos.

> Public office is looked upon by the elite as an avenue to more power, prestige and wealth. This is the reason why elite politicians spend hundreds of millions of pesos just to win positions that pay them a small fraction of what they spent. They regard expenditures in politics as an investment which will not only be easily recovered once public office is won, but will also pay handsome dividends, perhaps tens, or hundreds of times the "investment" they made. For the elite politician is really a capitalist in public office. He is what we may call a bureaucrat-capitalist, looking at government not as a place where he/she will render service to the people but as a place where he can earn millions, perhaps even billions, while in office.[4]

In 2007, many of the candidates for the Senate and the House of Representatives would be members of the principalia. Some would come from political dynasties (forbidden by the Constitution but not yet outlawed by legislation—indeed, how could they be, when the

145

legislators came from the principalia?), families with landed or business wealth that had been politically dominant for generations. (According to the Center for People Empowerment in Governance, there were 250 political families, members of which occupied 160 congressional seats in the outgoing Congress.[5]) This would also be true of a number of candidates for the positions of provincial governor and city mayor, while the lowlier positions would be pursued by many who were aspirants to eventual membership of that elite class. While, therefore, these elections might determine whether or not Arroyo was impeached, or whether or not there would be constitutional change, they would signify little else—apart from chalking up another victory for the principalia.

*

Attention was first focused on the Senate, half of which was now up for election on a national basis. Given the major role played by opportunism and personal ambition in Philippine elections, the drafting of a slate was not a straightforward exercise for either camp. The opposition had long claimed that the administration would have trouble filling its own twelve slots, due to the unpopularity of Mrs. Arroyo. There was the possibility that there would be three coalitions fighting it out, as the "Wednesday Club," named for the day on which a handful of like-minded senators (Manuel Villar, Joker Arroyo, Francis Pangilinan and Ralph Recto, along with Vice-President Noli de Castro) usually met, was considering running as a "middle force." Eventually, Arroyo (no relation to Gloria) and Recto went with the administration. They were joined by re-electionist Edgardo Angara (obviously realizing he was going to be dumped by the opposition), congressmen Prospero Pichay and Miguel Zubiri, palace functionary Mike Defensor, Sultan Jamalul Kiram III (a Muslim royalist, one of the claimants to the sultanate of Sulu), and governors Luis "Chavit" Singson (Ilocos Sur), Vicente Magsaysay (Zambales) and Carlos Jericho Petilla (Leyte). The remaining two administration candidates had both defected from the opposition camp: former senators Tessie Aquino-Oreta (sister of the late Benigno "Ninoy" Aquino Jr., she made no secret of the fact that her decision was occasioned by little more than the fact that her nephew "Noynoy" had eased her out of the

146

opposition slate[6]) and Vicente Sotto III. Realizing that his was not a household name, Petilla swiftly withdrew, and his slot was taken by movie actor and director Cesar Montano. The slate adopted the name "Team Unity" (TU), the first word standing for "Together Everyone Achieves More."

The initial "Genuine Opposition" (GO) team consisted of re-electionists Francis Pangilinan, Manuel Villar and Panfilo Lacson, incumbent congressmen Francis Escudero, Alan Peter Cayetano, Benigno "Noynoy" Aquino III and Aquilino Pimentel III, Sonia Roco, military rebel Antonio Trillanes IV, and former senators Nikki Coseteng, John Osmeña and Loren Legarda. Gregorio Honasan, who had been arrested some weeks earlier for alleged involvement in the 2004 Oakwood Mutiny, decided to run as an independent from his jail cell; well into the campaign, Ernesto Maceda would divulge that the Aquino group had objected to Honasan's inclusion in the GO team as the former military rebel had led several coup attempts against Corazon Aquino in the 1980s.[7]

The adoption of this slate gave rise to the criticism that the opposition was perpetuating the role of dynasties: Cayetano's sister was already in the Senate, where their late father had also served, and his wife would slip into his congressional seat; Escudero came from a leading political family in Sorsogon, and his father would return to the House by picking up Francis's seat; Aquino was, of course, a member of the famous Tarlac clan; if elected, Pimentel would be sitting alongside his father; Roco was the widow of the late presidential contender Raul; the Osmeñas had long dominated Cebu politics (although challenged more recently by rival dynasties); and Villar's wife was an incumbent in the House.

The GO team soon found that it was one man short, as Francis Pangilinan made it clear from the very outset that, while he was grateful for the opposition endorsement, he considered himself an independent and had been surprised by the decision to adopt him. This was an early indication that the GO campaign was not going to be problem-free. In the first weeks, shortage of cash led to the cancellation of a number of provincial rallies. Some problems were not of the opposition's own making, as when lawyer Oliver Lozano, who had played a pivotal role in killing the first impeachment complaint against Arroyo, assisted a "Joselito Peter Cayetano," a clerk for a Davao City stevedoring company, in filing his candidacy for the Senate. The Comelec eventually disbarred the latter as a "nuisance candidate." Then it was alleged that the GO's

Alan Peter Cayetano was a US citizen (the same ploy used against Poe prior to the 2004 presidential election) and thus Cayetano produced his Filipino passport, complete with a US visa, which he would hardly have required had he been a citizen of that country; the case was dismissed. "Noynoy" Aquino was also faced with a same-name rival when second cousin Theodore Aquino filed his candidacy.

Neither camp had a developed program that would persuade any voter that this election was about anything other than gaining or retaining office. The untitled program of action featured on the Team Unity website simply promised more of everything: more food, books, classrooms and teachers for schoolchildren, more cops and patrol cars, health insurance for more people, more irrigation, more prosecutors to fight corruption, etc. There were few items in this wish-list (railway subsidies and the development of alternatives to fossil fuels might just qualify) to convey the impression that serious thought had been given to the exercise, and the inclusion of a promise already broken (the provision of safety nets against the effects of globalization) tended to give the game away. A statement by Team Unity spokesman Joseph "Ace" Durano purporting to spell out the slate's "legislative program to create more jobs, sustain growth" promised that unspecified measures would "form a new financial architecture that would enable the country to entice more capital from abroad and maintain business confidence, plug all tax leaks to help the government sustain its revenue base, keep the peso stable, provide credit access even to small farmers and wage-earners, keep the price of basic goods stable, and provide more financial opportunities to overseas Filipino workers wanting to invest their hard-earned dollars." The statement concluded by repeating Mrs. Arroyo's spending plans for infrastructure, but in the whole 750 words not a single concrete legislative measure was mentioned.[8] Team Unity issued a call for the creation of a Commission on Labor, which would study emerging labor trends, and for changes in the Labor Code to take account of developments such as business process outsourcing, but it was difficult to tell from this vague statement whether this would be good news or bad for the labor movement.[9]

The opposition's general program was distinctly disappointing, its ten points promising:

* more labor-intensive infrastructure projects
* more cash for education

* lower-priced medicines

* lower transport and power costs by developing renewable energy

* prosecutorial powers for the Commission on Human Rights, and de-
   emphasis of the military approach to counter-insurgency

* no new taxes, but improved tax administration

* a contribution to the arrest of global warming

* more support programs for overseas Filipino workers

* strengthening of the media's watchdog role against graft and corruption by
   decriminalizing libel and increasing penalties for harm done to media
   practitioners

* "other meaningful economic reforms."[10]

Apart from the promise of no new taxes, the approach to human rights and media freedom (important enough in themselves, admittedly), there was little here to distinguish the program from that of the administration. One had to assume from this that the opposition had no intention of breaking with the "export-oriented" economic model and blazing a nationalist trail—unless such a departure was concealed within "other meaningful economic reforms."

One only had to turn to a statement issued by John Osmeña on April 30 to see the extent of the opposition's bankruptcy in this regard. According to Osmeña, "there is no employment in this country and there will not be any employment for a long time." He therefore called on each overseas Filipino worker to recruit one more person to work abroad—a possible total, in his reckoning, of 10 million. Successful recruiters would be rewarded with three months' salary. Leaving aside the absence of nationalist vision, it is unlikely that the former senator from Cebu had paused to consider the consequences of, in the event of total success, a Philippines with 10 million less tax-payers forking out the equivalent of 2.5 million person-years' salary to the recruiters. As part of this scheme, the Philippines would offer the host economies further subsidies by retraining overseas Filipinos vacationing at home, enabling them to gain wage increases and/or promotion upon their return overseas. At the same time, students would be encouraged to study subjects which, like nursing, would be more likely to gain them foreign employment.[11] Only someone who had abandoned all hope of national development could have

149

come up with such a scheme.

In view of the above, it was perhaps not surprising that there were no public debates during the campaign. The administration issued such a challenge after the opposition published a statement questioning Mrs. Arroyo's economic "achievements," but once it was accepted Arroyo insisted that there should be no personal attacks, no "political grandstanding," and no access to the public other than via television — in other words, no politics.

*

A vote of only one-third of the House was required to transmit an impeachment complaint to the Senate, and so it was not surprising that the administration seemed keen not merely to fill as many party-list seats as possible, but also to reduce the number occupied by pro-impeachment representatives.

The party-list system had made its first appearance in 1998, its aim being to cater for the representation of the marginalized. Party-list seats (each group being limited to a maximum of three), which the Constitution said should constitute 20 percent of the whole House, were initially allocated one the basis of one for each 2 percent of the total party-list vote gained, until it was realized that the full complement of seats would never be filled on this basis, following which amendments were made. Party-list groups inspired by the Communist Party of the Philippines and some of the groups which had broken away from it in the 1990s had won several seats from 2001 onwards, although still constituting a small minority.

After complaints in March 2007 that the Army was harassing supporters of left party-list groups in the capital, it soon was revealed that soldiers had been deployed on such "duties" as early as the previous December and were now in 26 Metro Manila barangays.[12] According to the military, this was a component of its "holistic approach" to the CPP-NPA insurgency and, in any case, slum residents had themselves requested the deployments.[13] Alarmingly, the head of the Commission on Human Rights (CHR) in the national capital region appeared to go along with this, saying that, as the residents appeared to support the soldiers' presence, there would be no call for a withdrawal — although this was "suggested" by the CHR at national level.[14]

Officialdom seemed to be blithely ignorant of the impropriety of such military activity, particularly during an election period. Arroyo's spokesman said that he would leave it to the military to offer an explanation, while his boss paid the troops a visit in working class Tondo in order to congratulate them.

According to Satur Ocampo, national security adviser Norberto Gonzales led a group with the aim of thwarting the election of left-wingers, and as part of this project he and fellow party-listers Rafael Mariano, Teodoro Casiño and Liza Maza were accused of involvement in three murders perpetrated between 2001 and 2004,[15] and thus disqualification cases were filed against their parties (Bayan Muna, Anak Pawis and Gabriela). The obviously flawed allegations were not dismissed until June, the month after the elections, and so it is possible that the three parties lost votes as a result. An attempt was also made to link Bayan Muna's Satur Ocampo to killings conducted during the CPP's campaign against infiltrators twenty years earlier, and as a result he spent some time in custody.

The administration's opponents claimed that it was also funding party-list groups of its own. Apart from enabling the administration to count on successful candidates as anti-impeachment votes, the tactic of creating bogus parties would (given the reasonable assumption that the administration allies would mobilize supporters to cast their votes for such parties) also increase the total party-list vote, thus making it more difficult for the left-wing groups to clear the thresholds required to win seats.

As early as February, the Partido ng Manggagawa (Workers' Party) was calling for the Comelec to delist groups allegedly sponsored by Malacañang, such as Bigkis Pinoy (said to be supported by Efraim Genuino, boss of the Philippine Gaming and Amusement Corporation, and Mike Arroyo), the Alliance of Nationalism and Democracy (an anti-communist group backed by national security adviser Norberto Gonzales), Biyaheng Pinoy (purportedly an organization for tricycle drivers, this had Dr. Arsenio Abalos, brother of the Comelec chairman, as a director and nominee[16]) and Kasangga sa Kaunlaran (identified with Mrs. Arroyo's sister-in-law[17]). Various sources alleged that accreditations and "victories" were being sold by Comelec-connected operators, for which the palace-created parties were using funds supplied by Malacañang's Office of External Affairs.[18]

Given the principle that party-list seats should be filled by representatives of the marginalized and underrepresented, critics asked how the son of *Manila Times* publisher Dante Ang could be a nominee for Ahon Pinoy (Emerge Filipino, said to represent overseas Filipinos), and why Bantay had as its lead nominee recently-retired Gen. Jovito Palparan, long notorious for the human rights abuses committed in areas under his command.[19] (Palparan explained that the "marginalized" constituency he would be representing included communities "terrorized by leftists."[20])

In April, two NGOs asked the Supreme Court to disqualify no less than 34 party-list groups on the grounds that they did not represent the sectors they claimed as their constituencies. The court, however, ruled that the Comelec was the appropriate body to hear such challenges. The opinion polls, meanwhile, indicated that the administration tactics were meeting with some success, as support for left groups had dropped and those parties alleged to be palace fronts were picking up support.

*

In the race for the 219 House seats elected by district, it became apparent that the opposition had never had a chance of gaining sufficient numbers for a third impeachment attempt, let alone forming a majority. In April, executive secretary Eduardo Ermita claimed that 199 of the candidates likely to win were administration allies, as were 77 of the 81 incumbent governors and 115 of the 120 incumbent city mayors.[21] Even allowing for some exaggeration, this added up to not only a significant potential majority, but also a formidable campaign machine. Less than two weeks later, GO admitted that only half of its 144 House candidates had a good chance of winning, and that only a third were "sure."[22] The fact that the opposition lacked the organizational network to mount challenges in more than a third (or, perhaps more realistically, a half) of the congressional districts exposed its basic weakness. At the core of the opposition was a coalition of disparate interests united (if that is not too strong a word) only by the desire to see Gloria Macapagal Arroyo impeached. While this may have been an important aim, it was hardly the same as having a common vision of national development around which an organizational network could have been constructed and large sections of the public mobilized.

The administration and its supporters were, outside of the impeachment issue, different in one respect only: due to their incumbency, the whole infrastructure of patronage and electoral influence lay at their disposal. In the House, they could not lose.

At the congressional and more local levels, especially in areas where the opposition had failed to put forward candidates, the campaign saw an unseemly free-for-all between the two major members of the ruling coalition. Lakas-CMD and Kampi each announced that they would be fielding 10,000 candidates; even leaving aside candidates of the other coalition partners like the Nationalist People's Coalition and Liberal Party (Atienza wing), the combined total exceeded the 17,813 positions available.[23] In several areas, Arroyo's Kampi raided Lakas-CMD, poaching their candidates. In the province of Isabela, the reverse process could be observed, with 20 Kampi members, most of them in the running for mayor and vice-mayoral posts, joining Lakas. Often, you had to be a clever candidate to work out where the ball would be when the wheel stopped spinning. In Batangas province, gubernatorial candidate Armand Sanchez miscalculated, and after he, along with 15 mayors, defected from the Liberal Party (Atienza wing) to Kampi, Lakas decided to run Vilma Santos (actress, mayor and wife of senatorial re-electionist Ralph Recto) against him. Then Kampi decided that it, too, would back Santos, leaving Sanchez in need of a new sponsor.

In late March, Arroyo ordered Kampi to stop the raids on Lakas, but much blood had been spilt by this time. According to Kampi president Luis Villafuerte, the party had grown "five-fold."[24] A number of things were happening here. On one level, we might say that these intra-coalition clashes disclosed the real content of the electoral exercise: a naked battle for power and influence in which the principalia families, in fighting it out between themselves as usual, were now prepared to disregard the inconvenient fact that they were members of the same coalition. There was, however, speculation that the attempt to expand Kampi's ranks was also driven by the desire to snatch the speakership from Lakas's Jose de Venecia Jr., while another theory was that it was all about ensuring Malacañang control of both the majority and minority in the House, as the congressman with the second highest vote for Speaker would automatically become minority leader.

*

In April, columnist Conrado de Quiros estimated that, such was the unpopularity of Arroyo, even the bungling of the opposition would be unable to give her senatorial team the edge; this being so, the administration would "cheat massively."[25] We have already seen that there were suspicions that the administration was intervening in the party-list elections, but there were plenty of other signs.

Well before the campaign, a former Comelec director estimated that there were 200,000 "flying voters" (double or multiple registrants) in Metro Manila alone.[26] The Comelec would claim to have dealt with this, announcing in April that it had removed 1.3 million names from the voters' lists, but the opposition claimed there were still another five million to go, as a total of 45 million voters (over half the population) was a "preposterous number."[27] There were also suspicions that additional ballot papers would be deployed. In March, three men were found in the National Printing Office, allegedly copying serial numbers of ballot forms.[28] A few days before the election, *Newsbreak* magazine, basing its story on interviews with "operatives," said that the administration's "special operations" this time around would see the adoption of techniques proven successful in 2004, while those that had been uncovered would be ditched. Only "friendly cities" would be targeted, and these would witness "an unusually high voter turnout."[29] Shortly after this, Senator Pimentel revealed at a press conference that 396 ballot boxes containing prefabricated election returns favoring Team Unity had been discovered; furthermore, a pump boat intercepted by the authorities off the coast of Zamboanga del Norte was found to have been carrying millions in forged P500 bills.[30] At the same time, the number of registered voters in some towns in Cagayan and Lanao del Sur provinces had ballooned since 2004, the total in the latter province having risen to 395,488 from 276,980. (Others, however, showed a sharp decline, Santa Ana in Cagayan falling from 11,177 in 2004 to a current 2,466.[31] Was it possible that towns with dramatically fewer voters had seen the numbers artificially inflated in 2004?)

Promises of money were made. Governor Datu Andal Ampatuan was reported to have offered Maguindanao mayors P1 million each in return for a 12-0 Team Unity victory.[32] Justice secretary Raul Gonzalez admitted in an interview that he was prepared to give each barangay captain in his home province of Iloilo P10,000 for a similar result, seeming to believe this would be legal if he used his own resources. In Arroyo's home province of Pampanga, Lilia Pineda, the wife of her ally, alleged jueteng lord Rodolfo "Bong" Pineda, was running for governor against incumbent vice-governor Mark Lapid. According to Bishop Pablo Virgilio David, parishioners had sent countless text messages to the effect that Mrs. Pineda was crowding people into various venues to receive their cash gifts.[33] A third candidate, Fr. Ed Panlilio, claimed that "Bong" Pineda had met 2,000 jueteng area managers and collectors to enlist their help in his wife's campaign.[34] Needless to say, the Pinedas denied such accusations.

Philippine elections are expensive. This time around, for example, senatorial candidates were allowed to spend P120 million, and their parties could throw in a further P80 million. But that was just the legal expenditure. The *Inquirer* quoted political analyst Earl Parreño's estimate that to land in the top six a senatorial candidate would need between P500 million and P1 billion, with up to P250 million being spent on poll watchers. Another source told the same newspaper that some candidates purchased "their seats through a syndicate of corrupt retired and active election officials," and that votes were currently being ordered at P20 each for a minimum of between 10,000 and 50,000 votes.[35]

How could such sums be raised in a country like the Philippines? Well, some candidates had deep pockets, and there was always the possibility of business donations. But it was also reckoned that a third of the monthly jueteng take was used to buy the acquiescence of politicians at election time.[36] This was not a new development, for according to US historian Alfred W. McCoy in the second decade of the twentieth century, "ten years after the first local elections, gambling was integrated, top-to-bottom, into provincial politics." Following the full development of machine politics after the establishment of a Senate and House of Representatives in 1916, by the 1930s "this cash-hungry system had fostered a symbiosis among police corruption, political patronage, and illegal gambling, particularly that distinctively Filipino lottery called jueteng." The same account claims that it was not until the late 1980s, however, that government tapped into the system, as the administration of Corazon Aquino was "the first to forge a direct link with provincial gambling syndicates, appropriating a share of illicit profits from jueteng lotteries to finance election campaigns and covert operations…" McCoy says that the estimated gross from jueteng ballooned from P18 billion in 1988 to P37 billion in 2000.[37]

With its runners and sellers, the jueteng underground sometimes doubles up as a political campaigning machine, but incumbent politicians at municipal, city and provincial level can also be called upon to undertake partisan activity--and, if they can get away with it, expenditure. The consequences of refusing to do so was made clear in 2007 with a brazenness which in most liberal democracies would be considered appalling, as when executive secretary Eduardo Ermita noted that local officials "will enjoy more benefits if they show support to our candidates, that's the essence of party politics."[38] A week before the election, leaving a meeting where Arroyo had told local government officials to promote only TU candidates, senatorial candidate Luis "Chavit" Singson reinforced the message delivered earlier by Ermita. "Sanctions? Maybe after the elections. We will know who will comply." Supporters, he said, know "if they will vote for the opposition they won't get any projects."[39]

*

Every election, the Philippine National Police issues a tally of poll-related deaths, but the problem is that of knowing when to start counting. This time around, for example, Congressman Robert Jaworski, Jr.'s car was bombed in December 2006 (although he was not hurt), and a few days later Congressman Luis Bersamin, an Arroyo ally, was assassinated. When the police picked up the governor of Abra province for questioning regarding the latter event, they found a grenade and seven handguns in his vehicle.[40]

But the count could have been started far earlier, because for several years, and particularly since early 2005, left-wing activists, members of legal organizations, had been routinely murdered. Teodoro Casiño, congressional representative for Bayan Muna, was led to proclaim: "At the rate things are going, our party will have been wiped out by the next elections,"[41] and that may have been the aim. By April 2006, the human rights organization Karapatan, thought to be sympathetic to the CPP, estimated that 750 had been killed since Arroyo took office in 2001,[42] while the police figure in mid-2006 was 124,[43] and the tally kept by the *Philippine Daily Inquirer* had reached 272 (including 114 Bayan Muna members) by February

2007.[44] That month, United Nations' special rapporteur on extra-judicial, summary or arbitrary executions Philip Alston arrived for a nine-day investigation, following which he swiftly produced an interim report in which he laid a significant portion of the blame at the door of the armed forces, which he found to be in "a state of almost complete denial."[45] Thereafter, the pace of the killings slowed appreciably.

The police seemed at pains to convey the impression that this election would be more peaceful than previous ones (111 killed in 2001, 148 in 2004), but this was little more than a pious hope. Due to the Bersamin killing and the existence of private armies (police chief Oscar Calderon reckoned that by late April only 52 of the 90 known private armies nationwide had been put out of business), Abra province was placed under control of the Comelec for the duration of the election campaign period. Calderon was considering recommending that another nine provinces be handed over, and Nueva Ecija qualified when a shoot-out occurred between the security details of the former mayor of Jaen (one of those dismissed the previous year) and Congressman Rodolfo Antonino, leaving two dead and 12 wounded (including the former mayor's two sons). Nationally, there were over 2,000 arrests for illegal firearms possession,[46] and by mid-June the tally of election-related deaths would, by the *Inquirer's* count, be "around 140."[47] It is important to note that few of these death at this stage were the result of the military assassinating left-wing party-listers or the NPA bumping off "enemies of the people" (although Calderon claimed that some NPA members "actually double as private armies or armed goons for some candidates or political interest groups"[48]). In the main, this was normal electoral violence, with the camp of one candidate killing members of a rival camp. Why? Because the stakes were high.

The opinion of the Asian Network for Free Elections, which provided 21 of the 219 foreign observers on polling day, was that the elections were characterized by violence, threats and manipulation.[49] Certainly, the violence extended beyond the campaign itself. On polling day, a supporter of the re-electionist mayor in Marfil, Rosario, Agusan del Sur was killed in a gunfight with the rival camp. Six grenades were thrown at a civic center during a brownout in Tubod, Lanao del Norte, although no one was hurt. In Batangas, a school was consumed by flames after ballot boxes were set alight, leaving two dead, and a third would die later; two policemen were among those arrested for the crime. In Surigao del Norte, the Kampi congressional candidate, his wife and daughter, survived an ambush. One person was hurt following a grenade attack on a polling station in Maguindanao.

It would have been surprising if, even in the Muslim areas of this most Catholic of countries, election-day had passed without a miracle or two. Thus, in parts of the Autonomous Region in Muslim Mindanao (ARMM), the dead rose up and made their way to the polling stations, and it later transpired that voters' lists in the region, not having been "cleansed," contained 300,000 double and multiple registrants.[50] Volunteers in Cotabato claimed that 45,000 names on the voters' lists were false.[51] On the other hand, there were complaints, which the Comelec undertook to investigate, that 100,000 citizens had been disenfranchised.[52] The town of Hadj Mohammad Ajul in Basilan province staged its own version of the loaves and fishes tale, as its 9,115 registered voters cast 26,939 votes for six party-list organizations, five of which were allegedly palace fronts.[53] In Lantawan town, in the same province, the party-list poll was topped by Biyaheng Pinoy (the organization based in Mandaluyong, Metro Manila, claiming to represent the interest of motorized tricycle drivers), despite the fact that Anak Mindanao had a mass base in the province.[54] Administration-linked party-list groups also prospered in remote Tawi-Tawi, which saw an 89 percent voter turnout in the party-list section, and Zamboanga del Sur, where the total party-list votes increased by 219 percent over the 2004 figure.[55] Just as miraculous was the fact that while, according to opinion polls, almost half of the nation had no knowledge of the party-list system,[56] these enthusiastic voters came from Muslim areas where, hitherto, it had been thought that many had no affinity with the Philippine state.

Irregularities were also found elsewhere in the archipelago. In Zambales province, 100,000 votes were shaved from the totals of GO's Cayetano and Escudero before, following the discovery of what Comelec chief Benjamin Abalos called an "honest mistake," they were restored.[57] In Ilocos Sur, priests, supported by Archbishop Ernesto Salgado, condemned the "dirty conduct" of elections there (allegedly involving vote buying, "opponent buying"— whereby potential opponents were bought off, enabling an uncontested, or easily contested, election for the purchaser—and other forms of fraud), where a large number of elective positions were taken by the Singsons, their cousins and other relatives.[58] In Pampanga, a fabricated front page of the *Sun.Star* newspaper claimed that gubernatorial candidate Fr. Ed Panlilio had admitted to having a wife and children and that the Chamber of Commerce had withdrawn its support.[59] The day before the election, armed men erected streamers promoting the Bayan Muna, Gabriela and Anakpawis party-list organizations supposedly signed by the CPA-NPA-NDF; when approached by the local authorities, the men said they were "special operatives" from Camp Crame, the national police headquarters.[60]

In Tagbilaran City, Bohol, retailers reported a threefold increase in cell phone sales in the days following the elections as bought voters spent the proceeds. Those who took money from all three mayoral candidates in Panglao would have walked away with P3,200, while in Loay households were offered between P10,000 and P20,000, depending on the number of voters in the family.[61] A week or so after the elections, counterfeit P500 and P1000 notes were identified by four Bohol banks.[62]

It must be said, however, that not all complainants were members of the opposition bloc. National security adviser Norberto Gonzales protested, after his daughter lost her bid for the congressional seat in Bataan, that P300 million was spent on polling day, while his daughter's whole campaign had cost "only" P7 million.[63] As the senatorial results were canvassed, Sonia Roco and Nikki Coseteng queried the votes of their GO colleagues Legarda and Escudero, and it was suggested that the votes of poll laggards were being shaved to improve the tallies of more fortunately-situated members of the same team.[64] According to Daisy Avance-Fuentes, the newly reelected governor of South Cotabato, the votes of five TU senatorial candidates and one from GO (Legarda) had been padded by as much as (or, in the case of Mike Defensor, more than) 100,000 votes, and in reality Edgardo Angara was the only TU candidate to appear in the top twelve choices of the province's voters[65]; Legarda asked that the 43,000 votes added to her tally be deducted, her lawyer claiming that this had been an attempt to "mislead people about the real intended beneficiaries of the operation."[66]

There is little doubt that the worst forms of electoral fraud took place in the ARMM provinces of Lanao del Sur and Maguindanao. Poll-watchers would later tell the Comelec that the price of a vote in Lanao del Sur ranged from P1,000 to P7,000, although someone who turned out to be a foreign observer was offered a mere P300; another observer who queried the practice was threatened with death. In a Marawi City barangay, each TU candidate received 250 votes, despite the fact there were only 169 registered voters. In many places, the watchdogs were denied access to the canvassing, there was no use of indelible ink, and campaign materials were displayed in the polling areas.[67]

A failure of elections was declared in 18 towns in Mindanao. Most of these were in Lanao del Sur (where the number of registered voters had increased by 43.9 percent since 2004), and here polling officials had been threatened with bombs if they turned up at the precincts. In another town, a local incumbent sat on the ballot boxes.[68] Special elections were therefore set for May 26. As they went ahead, poll monitors reported vote-buying, minors voting, voter-substitution, flying voters and coaching.[69] Namfrel (under new management, with Eric Alvia as secretary-general and Edward Go as chairman) monitors claimed that these special elections were worse that the 2004 poll in the same province, and even then the job was not completed, as a further failure was declared in some areas, one case involving an armed attack on a convoy conveying election materials.

In Maguindanao, where the governor had promised mayors P1 million each for a 12-0 TU victory, that unlikely outcome was announced two days after polling day. There were a number of improbable factors involved here: for example, no less than nineteen senatorial candidates had not received a single vote in the 22 municipalities, and topping the poll was Luis "Chavit" Singson (then trailing in 23rd place nationally in the partial count) from the other end of the archipelago, despite the fact there was a Muslim candidate on his own team. According to the Moro Islamic Liberation Front, there had, in fact, been no elections in many parts of the province.[70] Namfrel, while believing that people had gone to the polls, complained that its workers had been barred from the capitol building where the canvassing had taken place, and thus it excluded Maguindanao from its count. Then the Legal Network for Truthful Elections claimed that the thumbprints and signatures of minors had been used, with ballots for Senate seats being completed on May 13, the day before the poll. A teacher went on radio to claim that police, military and Comelec officials had been in collusion, and that she and her colleagues had also been ordered to complete the ballots the evening before polling day.[71] A board of election inspectors' member related that on May 14 he and others had been taken to a banana field by armed men and forced to complete ballots in favor of the TU candidates.[72] When the provincial board of canvassers failed to appear in Manila to present the relevant documents to the national canvassers, the Comelec pronounced that the results were "statistically improbable" and ordered a re-canvass.[73] Significantly, the Makati Business Club and the Management

Association of the Philippines issued a joint statement calling for an investigation, and the Comelec assembled a task force.

While special elections in Maguindanao were tentatively set for June 20 (when such elections were also for set for Taysan, Batangas, where the school had been burned down, and 168 precincts in Lanao del Sur, Basilan, Shariff Kabunsuan and Tawi-Tawi), the Comelec then backtracked, saying it would first determine whether or not polls were held in the province on May 14. Lintang Bedol, the provincial election supervisor (whom Comelec chief Abalos had promoted even after his name had cropped up in the "Hello, Garci" tapes), was ordered to Manila by June 12 upon pain of arrest. When winning local candidates failed to attend on June 11, the Comelec reset the hearing for four days later. In the meantime, Musa Dimasidsing, a district schools supervisor who had exposed some of the fraud in the province, was shot dead. Then almost a month after the election, Bedol claimed that the municipal certificates of canvas had been stolen from his office. As he had failed to appear in Manila, the Comelec ordered his arrest, citing him in contempt for his failure to either appear or provide a written explanation for the theft. In August, he was fined P1,000 and sentenced to six months' imprisonment, leading to complaints from the opposition that there had been no investigation of his possible involvement in poll fraud. Bedol then disappeared. He would resurface in 2011, offering to tell all.

Comelec commissioners traveled south in order to check the election documents, although chairman Abalos had already stated that there could have been no failure of elections in Maguindanao because, as indicated in the evidence provided by Governor Ampatuan's lawyer, all elected officials at local level had been proclaimed. The documents were viewed in General Santos City, and whereas these should have been the fourth copies of the certificates of canvass, only the second copies were available; as this was the set used for public posting, there were complaints that they could easily have been doctored. Nevertheless, the Comelec officials took the view that they were authentic, and therefore ordered a new canvass. At this stage, a Puwersa ng Masa coordinator alleged that the votes in the second copies had been manufactured, and that there had been two sets of election documents in some parts of the province—one used by the teachers (polling precincts are staffed by teachers) who completed them to provide a 12-0 Team Unity victory, and the other used for the actual voting.[74]

*

If advocates of fair electoral practices expected the developed countries, particularly those which had provided observers, to condemn the conduct of this poll, they were disappointed. US Assistant Secretary of State for East Asia Christopher Hill said he knew there had been "some problems with violence. But I would say overall the elections have been very successful and a real sign that the Philippines has a very well developed democracy."[75] The UK Ambassador Peter Beckingham was also concerned by the violence, but pronounced that the elections were generally peaceful and fairly conducted, signifying that the country was willing to progress and receive more foreign investments.[76] On May 18, the stock exchange closed at an all-time high. As far as western governments and capital were concerned, this had been a normal Philippine election and, as things were under control, it would now be business as usual.

Despite all the outrages and the weakness of the opposition, there were some surprising results. This time, the voters tended to turn their backs on movie stars and sporting personalities, so screen heart-throbs Cesar Montano (TU) and Richard Gomez (independent) went down to defeat, and boxer Manny Pacquiao, having been assiduously courted by the Arroyo camp for some time, was knocked to the seat of his pants by incumbent (and oppositionist) congresswoman Darlene Antonino when he tried to displace her in South Cotabato. Having run as an "independent" for a House seat in Bukidnon, Virgilio Garcillano, of "Hello, Garci" notoriety, conceded defeat early on, ironically complaining that incumbents enjoyed an "undue advantage" in their access to public resources.[77] In Metro Manila, "Peewee" Trinidad, suspended as Pasay City mayor in 2006, was swept back into office, as was, after a spell as senator, Alfredo Lim in Manila, up against the son of incumbent Lito Atienza. In Makati City, Mayor Jejomar Binay thanked Mrs. Arroyo for, in the administration's attempts to suspend him, virtually acting as his election agent, as he defeated actor-senator Lito Lapid by a nine-to-one margin and saw his supporters snap up all twenty elective posts in the city. In the province of Pampanga, Fr. Ed Panlilio defeated Arroyo ally Lilia Pineda, albeit by a slim margin (a result which would later be successfully challenged by Pineda).

In the Senate, it seemed to go better than the GO camp could have dreamed.

The Visayas was thought to be solid Arroyo territory, and the fact that the administration had its hands on the levers of power and influence in the majority of areas had not augured well for the opposition. In practice, the strength of the administration "machine" proved to be largely mythical, powerless to prevent the expression of anti-Arroyo sentiment. Even in conservative Bohol, four members of the GO team landed in the top twelve. In Iloilo City (where, of course, justice secretary Raul Gonzalez had promised to reward barangay captains for a 12-0 TU victory), the opposition took six of the top twelve senatorial slots, in Oriental Mindoro eight. In Leyte, where the incumbent governor had initially been a member of the TU slate, the administration could only manage to get five of its candidates into the top twelve. In Eastern Samar, where Governor Ben Evardone was head of TU's media bureau, GO candidates took the top five slots, followed by the independent Pangilinan.

According to Manuel L. Quezon III, administration supporters at local level simply gave up in view of the strength of the tide of anti-Malacañang sentiment, took the palace's money and went through the motions; he was also of the view (shared by the unsuccessful "Chavit" Singson) that resources which might otherwise have been deployed against GO were diverted into the internecine contests between Lakas and Kampi.[78] The heightened vigilance and increased effectiveness (apart from in those few provinces where they were barred from witnessing the canvassing) of poll-watchers and watchdog bodies also played a role; at the suggestion of Panfilo Lacson, the GO camp, lacking adequate numbers of poll-watchers but with access to the official results, entered into an alliance with the left-wing party-listers in this regard. Conrado de Quiros thought that the absence from the scene of Mike Arroyo, who underwent heart surgery during the campaign, would have acted adversely on the TU campaign by rupturing lines of communication and giving rise to the crass nature of poll fraud in Maguindanao and Lanao del Sur.[79]

Due to the arthritic bureaucracy of the Philippine electoral system and the irregularities in Mindanao, it would be a long time before the full results were known. On June 6, the Comelec proclaimed the top ten: Legarda, Escudero, Villar, Lacson, Aquino and Cayetano for the opposition, Joker Arroyo and Angara for the administration, and the independents Pangilinan and Honasan. Nine days later, the military rebel Trillanes, who was still in a detention cell, was proclaimed as the eleventh. Throughout the count, the opposition's Pimentel had been leading Miguel Zubiri, but as the outstanding votes, including those from Maguindanao, were canvassed, the gap between Pimentel and Zubiri gradually narrowed, and finally the latter was in the lead by around 19,000 votes. On July 14, exactly two months after the election, the Comelec proclaimed Zubiri as the twelfth elected senator. Pimentel's only recourse now was to pursue his case at the Senate Electoral Tribunal, and it would be 2011 before this body ruled that he was the legitimate winner and he was able to occupy his seat for the remaining two years of his term.

Still, with a 7-3-2 victory, the opposition now had control of the Senate—or so it seemed.

*

Given the overwhelming nature of the opposition victory in the Senate, it might have been thought that the 2007 elections would constitute a landmark, following which principled politics would succeed in reining in the excesses of the Arroyo administration during the three years left to it. All too soon, however, it became apparent that some of the victors were busy focusing on what lay at the end of those three years—the next presidential election.

By the time the final election results were declared, members of both chambers had turned their thoughts to the leading positions that would need to be filled once the 14th Congress was convened. In the upper chamber, the elder Pimentel, having occupied the post during the Estrada regime, was thought to have a legitimate claim on the Senate presidency, but Manuel Villar who, due to a term-sharing agreement with Franklin Drilon, had filled the seat for the latter part of the 13th Congress, had other ideas, one of which concerned a more substantial presidential job in 2010. Panfilo Lacson, who was known to harbor thoughts of displacing Joker Arroyo from the chairmanship of the powerful Blue Ribbon Committee, warned that individual horse-trading could split the opposition, for it soon became clear that although the electorate had voted for an opposition-dominated Senate, some of those elected were going to set the will of the "sovereign people" aside.

During the third week of June, executive secretary Eduardo Ermita mentioned the possibility of amnesty for Trillanes and Honasan in return for reconciliation. The next day, the justice department, having increased the charges against Honasan after he was released on bail, now withdrew *all* charges relating to his involvement in the alleged military mutiny of 2003 on the basis of lack of evidence; as state prosecutors expressed dismay, a GO spokesman said this reinforced the perception that a deal had been done. As Trillanes gave every indication that reconciliation was the last thing on his mind, doggedly maintaining an anti-administration stance, justice department lawyers opposed his participation in Senate sessions. A secret ballot to determine the opposition candidate for Senate President did not take place as arranged, as several members were absent, and soon the Villar camp was claiming fourteen supporters, which could only mean that a substantial proportion of the opposition had linked up with the pro-administration senators.

In due course, it emerged that Villar was supported by the administration bloc, the independents Honasan, and Pangilinan, and "oppositionists" Cayetano, Escudero and Jinggoy Estrada. Pimentel had the support of Lacson, "Jamby" Madrigal (who wrote to the detained Estrada to accuse him of partially causing the disunity in order to mitigate the judgment in his plunder case), Aquino, Biazon, Legarda and Roxas. Cayetano was rewarded with the chairmanship of the Blue Ribbon committee coveted by Lacson.

Even greater disunity could be observed in the House. In a speech before that chamber to mark the centennial of the Philippine Assembly on June 7, Mrs. Arroyo pronounced: "We close the chapter of electoral battles and open the chapter of national solidarity."[80] And yet while, in the third week of May, Kampi chairman Ronaldo Puno had announced that his party would be supporting Lakas's Jose de Venecia Jr. in his bid to regain the post of House Speaker, less than a week later Kampi president Luis Villafuerte had retorted that the party would not only be challenging De Venecia, but in Pablo Garcia (the 81-year-old former governor of Cebu, and father of the incumbent in that position, Gwen Garcia) it had a contender. There were suspicions at this stage that this was, far from being a genuine power struggle, merely shadow-boxing, and that, as the current House rules provided that the candidate for Speaker with the second highest number of votes would automatically become House Minority Leader, the real aim was to secure total control of the chamber for the administration bloc, freezing out the opposition (one might even say, in this context, the "genuine opposition") from committees. But

165

the Garcia camp certainly began to behave as if it were in earnest.

On this occasion the conspiracy theorists were wrong, as after a period of acrimony both contenders eventually agreed that the minority leader should be elected by the opposition alone. And then De Venecia was elected Speaker unopposed, Garcia saying that he wanted no part of a "sham procedure."[81] Later, he would complain that 89 congressmen pledged to support him had made the same promise to De Venecia.[82] The Garcia-Villafuerte camp announced that it was leaving the administration coalition to form its own bloc, and while this new "middle force" promised to support Mrs. Arroyo, its members were said to be "crestfallen" over her failure to honor her commitment to remain neutral in the speakership race and, thus, they would no longer dismiss future impeachment complaints out of hand but would consider them on their merits.

Where, during all of this, was the "genuine" opposition in the House? To begin with, there was confusion as to how many (or few) opposition members there were. In the third week of May, Ernesto Maceda, complaining that administration candidates had received between P50 million and P150 million each in the last week of the campaign, reckoned that only around 30 oppositionists had been elected.[83] Still to be included, of course, were those party-list members who could be relied upon to side with the opposition. Here, the news was not good, as the Comelec announced that it would be applying a new formula,[84] which would reduce the number of left party-listers. In addition, Didagen Dilangalen, a former Estrada spokesman, joined the new Garcia bloc. By the time the dust had settled, it seemed that opposition members totaled a lowly 32.

Thus, well into the seventh year of her long crisis, after elections in which the voters had rejected all but two (or three if Zubiri were included) of her senatorial candidates, Gloria Macapagal Arroyo faced an upper chamber which looked suddenly friendlier than she could have hoped, and a House of Representatives in which her majority, subject to further shifts occasioned by personal or group interests, appeared unassailable.

*

Members of the Ampatuan family, the political rulers of Maguindanao who delivered a 12-0 victory for Mrs. Arroyo's senatorial slate in 2007, were involved in a far graver event in late 2009. In the following year's elections, the family was going to be challenged by Esmail Mangudadatu, who had announced that he would be running for the governor's seat, and the Ampatuans had apparently decided to do something about it.

On November 23, a convoy supporting Mangudadatu was traveling to the Comelec office to file his certificate of candidacy. Having the previous week noted movements by armed followers of the Ampatuan family, which had held sway in the province since 2001, he had decided that his certificate should be filed by women, accompanied by as many journalists as possible, thinking that this would deter attacks. Before it reached its destination, the convoy was halted at a checkpoint manned by 100 police, militia and "civilian volunteers" — essentially Ampatuan bodyguards. They were allegedly led by Andal Ampatuan Jr. Son of the family patriarch, he was mayor of Datu Unsay town and a prospective candidate for provincial governor.

All members of the convoy, including Mangudadatu's wife and two sisters, two women lawyers, and at least 30 media workers were killed. In all, fifty-seven people were slaughtered. Fifty-seven. A backhoe owned by the provincial government was used to bury some of the bodies. The graves were dug earlier with the apparent intention of interring all the corpses along with their vehicles, but the murderers were interrupted when troops, alerted by a helicopter, began to make their way to the area. In due course, members of the Ampatuan clan and many members of their private army (armed by the government purportedly to act as a paramilitary force against rebels) were arrested, and at the time of writing marathon trials are ongoing. These days, the case only hits the headlines when another witness is killed.

NOTES

1. *Daily Tribune*, January 21, 2007.

2. www.inquirer.net, March 1, 2007.

3. Dante C. Simbulan, *The Modern Principalia: The Historical Evolution of the*

Philippine Ruling Class (Quezon City, UP Press, 2005), 187.

4. Simbulan, 2005, 302.

5. Carlos H. Conde, "Family Dynasties Bind Politics in the Philippines," *International Herald Tribune*, May 11, 2007.

6. www.inquirer.net, February 9, 2007.

7. Ibid., April 27, 2007.

8. Team Unity, "Team Unity Spells Out Legislative Program to Create More Jobs, Sustain Growth," April 9, 2007.

9. Team Unity, "Team Unity to Press for LaborCom in Next Congress," April 30, 2007.

10. Genuine Opposition, "10 Point Program of the Genuine Opposition," undated, www.genuineopposition.com.

11. Genuine Opposition, "Osmen□a Bares Four-Point Program to Ease Poverty," April 30, 2007.

12. *Daily Tribune*, March 3, 2007.

13. *Malaya*, March 5, 2007.

14. *Malaya*, March 14, 2007.

15. *Philippine Daily Inquirer*, February 17, 2007.

16. *Philippine Daily Inquirer*, March 27, 2007.

17. Ibid., February 18, 2007.

18. See *Daily Tribune*, March 16, 2007 and April 27, 2007, www.inquirer.net, April 28, 2007, *Philippine Daily Inquirer*, April 12, 2007, *Philippine Star*, April 21, 2007. Allegations of palace-supported party-list groups had also been made in the 2004 Elections—see Bobby M. Tuazon (ed.), *Oligarchic Politics: Elections and the Party-List System in the Philippines* (Quezon City: Center for People Empowerment in Governance, 2007).

19. www.inquirer.net, March 22, 2007.

20. *Daily Tribune*, March 29, 2007,

21. *Daily Tribune*, April 19, 2007.

22. www.inquirer.net, May 1, 2007.

23. *Daily Tribune*, March 25, 2007, *Manila Times*, February 20, 2007 and www.inquirer.net, reprinted in *Asian Journal Online*, March 26, 2007.

24. www.inquirer.net, reprinted in *Asian Journal Online*, March 7, 2007.

25. Conrado de Quiros, "Writing on the Wall," *Philippine Daily Inquirer*, April 12, 2007.

26. GMA7, January 14, 2007.

27. *Malaya*, April 13, 2007.

28. *Philippine Daily Inquirer*, March 12, 2007.

29. Miriam Grace A. Go, "Cheats Adjust Style for Monday Polls," Newsbreak online at www.pubtrust.org/index.php, May 11, 2007.

30. *Daily Tribune*, May 12, 2007.

31. www.inquirer.net, May 11, 2007.

32. *Daily Tribune*, April 16, 2007.

33. www.inquirer.net, May 2, 2007.

34. *Philippine Daily Inquirer*, May 4, 2007.

35. *Philippine Daily Inquirer*, May 3, 2007.

36. www.inquirer.net, May 3, 2007.

37. Alfred W, McCoy, *Policing America's Empire: The United States, The Philippines, and the Rise of the Surveillance State* (Quezon City: Ateneo de Manila University Press, 2011), 156, 351, 434, 451. As the USA was responsible for both criminalizing jueteng (after pressure from missionaries), thus opening the way for the development of a vast underworld, and installing a political system vulnerable to corruption, this lamentable situation may reasonably be said to constitute yet another gift of colonialism.

38. *Daily Tribune*, April 19, 2007.

39. www.inquirer.net, May 7, 2007.

40. *Manila Times*, December 30, 2006.

41. www.inq7.net, March 15, 2005.

42. Ibid., April 22, 2006.

43. *BusinessWorld*, June 1, 2006.

44. *Philippine Daily Inquirer*, February 10, 2007.

45. Ibid., February 22, 2007.

46. www.inquirer.net, April 30, 2007.

47. The *Inquirer* provided this figure in July, when the police announced that 121 had died, and 176 had been injured, between January 14 and June 13 (www.inquirer.net, July 5, 2007). However, in his "As I See It" column in the *Inquirer* on May 18, Neal H. Cruz had already estimated the total of death as over 150.

48. www.inquirer.net, April 8, 2007.

49. *Philippine Daily Inquirer*, May 17, 2007.

50. *Daily Tribune*, May 22, 2007.

51. www.inquirer.net, May 14, 2007.

52. *Philippine Daily Inquirer*, May 16, 2007.

53. www.inquirer.net, May 22, 2007.

54. *Philippine Daily Inquirer*, May 25, 2007.

55. Ibid., May 26, 2007.

56. Elmer A. Ordoñez, "Forward," Tuazon, *Oligarchic Politics...*, 2007, iv.

57. www.inquirer.net, May 20, 2007.

58. *Daily Tribune*, May 23, 2007.

59. *Philippine Daily Inquirer*, May 15, 2007.

60. www.inquirer.net, May 20, 2007.

61. *Bohol Chronicle*, May 20, 2007.

62. www.inquirer.net, May 26, 2007.

63. *Philippine Daily Inquirer*, May 25, 2007.

64. *Manila Times*, May 30, 2007.

65. *Malaya*, May 30, 2007.

66. Ibid., May 31, 2007.

67. *Philippine Daily Inquirer*, May 24, 2007.

68. Ibid., May 15, 2007 and May 26, 2007.

69. www.inquirer.net, May 28, 2007.

70. *Philippine Daily Inquirer*, May 18, 2007.

71. Ibid., May 24, 2007.

72. Ibid., May 26, 2007.

73. *Manila Times*, May 31, 2007.

74. *Daily Tribune*, June 24, 2007.

75. *Daily Tribune*, May 26, 2007.

76. www.inquirer.net, May 31, 2007.

77. Ibid., May 14, 2007.

78. Manuel L. Quezon III, "Machinery Gives up the Ghost," *Philippine Daily Inquirer*, May 21, 2007.

79. Conrado de Quiros, "The Times They are A'Changin,'" *Philippine Daily Inquirer*, June 4, 2007,

80. *Philippine Daily Inquirer*, June 8, 2007.

81. www.inquirer.net, July 23, 2007.

82. Ibid., July 31, 2007.

83. *Daily Tribune*, May 24, 2007.

84. This was the "Panganiban formula" (used in a Supreme Court decision in the year 2000, but not applied by the Comelec in 2001 or 2004) whereby, instead of allotting a seat to a party for each two percent of the party-list vote it achieved, only the party topping the poll would receive the maximum three seats. Thereafter, having given one seat to each party achieving two percent of the vote, the number of any additional seats would calculated by dividing the votes of the party by those of the poll-topper, then multiplying the result by the number of additional seats received by the latter. As the Buhay party, linked to the El Shaddai evangelical Catholic sect, topped the poll, Bayan Muna received only two seats, even though it achieved more than six percent of the total vote.

9 "WE ARE OPEN TO OTHER ARRANGEMENTS"

In 1946, the USA granted independence to the Philippines from a position of strength, confident that its geopolitical and economic interests would continue to be served once the unhelpful "colonialist" tag had been shed. Had the departing colonizer been a waning European power lacking the energy and resources to compel continued obedience, there would have been rather more substance to Philippine independence than was actually the case; but the USA emerged from World War II as (although the word had not yet been coined) a superpower.

In 1960, leading nationalist Claro M. Recto offered this comparison of Spanish and American colonialism: "The only difference was that the first master did not take as much as the second. Ruthless in his ways, the first trampled upon all freedoms; the second sought our economic enslavement through subtle, legal and constitutional processes."[1] The pattern had been set in 1909 with the passage of the Payne-Aldrich Act, which purported to deliver to both nations the benefits of "free trade"; but while, as Recto observed, US products, mostly manufactured goods, were admitted into the Philippines without quantitative restrictions, "our exports to the U.S. were subjected to quota restrictions in order not to threaten American dairy and farm products, without any thought being given [Recto was perhaps too kind here] to the threat posed by American products on Philippine producers and the resulting nullification of our efforts to industrialize."[2]

While these arrangements continued, the Philippines would remain an agricultural country, relying upon US imports for its manufactured goods. The arrangements would, moreover, survive independence, being adopted as tariff law "through the influence of the late Ambassador McNutt..."[3] The Bell Trade Act, necessitating amendment of the Philippine Constitution (failing which, no claim for war damages in excess of $500 would be settled), granted American citizens and corporations "parity" with their Philippine counterparts in certain sectors of the economy, tied the peso to the dollar, and prohibited the Philippines from selling goods that might "come into substantial competition" with American products.[4]

Under the terms of the Quirino-Foster Agreement (which provided a five-year "aid" program, with US missions overseeing "reforms"), virtually all economic policy-areas became subject to US "advice," and in 1956 Recto would complain that the American advisors were "in all sectors of activity, both public, including practically all government offices and agencies, and private, including labor and peasant organizations, and in all fields—political, economic, military, social, and cultural..."[5] The government of the Philippines was obliged to provide Washington with detailed information regarding plans and operations under this agreement, along with information "regarding its economy and any other relevant information which the Government of the United States of America may need to determine the nature and scope of operations under this agreement and to evaluate the effectiveness of such operations."[6]

The Laurel-Langley Agreement of 1955, while providing for increased Philippine tariffs and lower American ones, also extended "parity" to new areas of the economy, enabling US firms, by setting up fully-owned subsidiaries, to move to the Philippine side of the tariff barrier. Observed a caustic Recto:

> With parity extended to business activities, packaging and assembly plants have mushroomed here as the latest American contribution—"new and necessary," in the convenient language of tax-exempting statutes—to the *industrialization* of the country and the solution of our unemployment problem.[7]

One of the effects of this process was to starve Philippine business of foreign exchange, Recto pointing out that in the fourth quarter of 1958 no less than 55 percent of this was cornered by US importers, while their Filipino counterparts had to make do with 18.88 percent.[8]

Neither was the emasculation of Philippine independence confined to the economic

174

sphere. The Military Bases Agreement granted the USA huge tracts of land, initially for 99 years, while the so-called Mutual Defense Treaty tied the Philippines into an arrangement that provided the latter with no guarantee of protection. And in his inaugural speech in July 1946, President Manuel Roxas had announced that in foreign policy the Philippines would follow the USA. Recto, having cast his eye over this situation, delivered a scathing verdict.

> For all practical purposes the Philippine Embassy in Washington is but the "Philippine desk" in the State Department, and the American Embassy in Manila is, rather than a diplomatic mission, a virtual extension of the State Department, assisted by Admirals and Generals commanding naval and military bases, and by JUSMAG [the Joint US Military Assistant Group], the Pentagon's general overseer of our military establishment, which has made its pressure felt even in the matter of promotion of top officers in our armed forces.[9]

This was, of course, the time of the Huk Rebellion, when US military advisers called the tune and CIA officer Col. Edward Lansdale moved his desk into the office of Defense Secretary Ramon Magsaysay, where he commenced to groom him for the presidency. The CIA's "propaganda workshop" churned out articles, which it then compiled as a digest for circulation to congressmen "and other opinion leaders in Manila,"[10] while (as noted by the National Security Council in Washington) "material is furnished daily to 122 newspapers and magazines, 18 radio stations, and 65 government officials,"[11] and the US Information Service had "contracts with Philippine motion picture companies to produce anti-Communist pictures which present positive democratic themes" and was a major source of programs for the fledgling television industry.[12] Such activity was part of the US's drive to ensure that the Philippines had an "effective government which will preserve and strengthen the pro-American and democratic orientation of the country, and serve as an example to the Far East of the application of Western ideas and institutions to Asian problems…"[13]

Recto found such aims laughable.

> Surely [the Americans] must realize that a spoon-fed capitalist democracy, unable to

survive outside the colonial incubator except through artificial respiration and periodic injections of borrowed dollars, will not strike the other peoples of Asia as a model to be followed.[14]

Even though US fortunes would fluctuate over the next fifty years, and the task of enforcing conformity on the economic front would be outsourced to the International Monetary Fund, the World Bank and, later, the World Trade Organization, the nationalism of Philippine presidents could be measured by their willingness (or, more frequently, their unwillingness) to incur the wrath of Washington in pursuit of Filipino goals.

*

Half a century of the Americanization of education, culture and politics had produced a situation in which, said Recto, "our foreign policy was conducted from the very beginning, and is being pursued, on the erroneous assumption of an identity of American and Filipino interests, or more correctly, of the desirability, and even the necessity, of subordinating our interests to those of America."[15] Four decades after Recto's death, little had changed.

In the wake of the attack on New York's World Trade Center on September 11, 2001, Gloria Macapagal Arroyo pledged "all-out support" for the US-led anti-terrorism coalition. This was not an entirely academic exercise, as the Philippines had its own problems in Mindanao, where the Moro Islamic Liberation Front (MILF) was waging an armed separatist struggle, and the Abu Sayyaf (said to have had its genesis in Afghanistan during the Soviet presence in that country) behaved, despite links to Jemaah Islamiya, like a bandit gang. Moreover, it was reported that 50 Filipinos, trained in Afghanistan, were manning one of Osama bin Laden's camps. In view of the alleged links between the Abu Sayyaf group and bin Laden's al Qaeda network, the USA volunteered military assistance in the form of training, intelligence, logistics and equipment.

Leaving for Washington in November 2001, Arroyo noted that her visit would coincide with the 50th anniversary of the Mutual Defense Treaty, "a pillar of our national security and defense and in our relationship with the United States."[16] In the US capital, she told the right-wing Heritage Foundation that while "there will be no more foreign bases...we are open to other arrangements short of permanent bases."[17] The "other arrangements" turned out to be a mutual logistics and support agreement (MLSA) that would allow the USA to construct roads, runways, helipads and barracks anywhere in the Philippines, and while these would have to be turned over to the Philippine government, US forces would be free to use them whenever they were in the country. Back home, nationalists in Congress accused Arroyo of using the tension concerning terrorism to strengthen the US presence in the country, but despite the controversy the agreement was signed.

When, in January 2002, it was announced that the annual Fil-Am Balikatan (Shoulder to Shoulder) war games would take place in Mindanao, with 160 special forces and 500 support and technical staff expected to arrive, opponents suspected that this might be a ploy to involve US troops directly in an internal conflict. Amazingly, foreign affairs secretary Teofisto Guingona Jr. (also vice-president, Guingona resigned the foreign affairs portfolio in July 2002 due mainly to his opposition to the use of US troops) was kept in the dark regarding this development, despite the fact that he, with US secretary of state Colin Powell, headed the body responsible for implementing the visiting forces agreement, under which the troops were deployed. But he had not been consulted over the MLSA, either.

Given the outcry, it was confirmed that the US troops would not be used for combat purposes, although they were authorized to return fire if attacked (something which became even more likely when the Pentagon approved a plan to send them on patrols with Filipino soldiers). On a second Washington trip in February 2002, Arroyo discussed the deployment of troops to Mindanao with Colin Powell, and he must have strengthened her resolve, as days later her language was decidedly intemperate. "You are not a Filipino," she declared, standing nationalism on its head, "if you are against the peace and progress being offered by the Balikatan 2002. You cannot be a Filipino if you are against the help being offered by a friend." Moreover, she added, indulging herself in the language of post-September 11, opponents of the US military presence were mere "terrorist lovers."[18] By the time the terms of reference for the exercises were signed in mid-February, the original formulation "Nothing shall infringe on the AFP [Armed Forces of the Philippines] Unit Commander's authority..." had been amended to

"AFP and US Unit Commanders will retain command of their respective forces under the overall authority of the Exercise Co-Directors."[19]

When an international peace mission arrived in March, Walden Bello, its Filipino member, said that he and his colleagues were "more and more worried that there is a strategic intent, and that is to establish and expand a military presence in the southern Philippines directed at Muslim revivalist movements there and in Southeast Asia."[20] This contention received support when, in April, the US intelligence company Stratfor opined: "Ultimately, US operations in the southern Philippines are directed less at defeating the Abu Sayyaf and more at establishing a forward operations base in Southeast Asia—with an eye on Indonesia as a likely first target."[21] Such suspicions seemed justified when, the following year, with the annual joint exercises due to be held in Jolo, the *New York Times* reported that 1,700 US troops were being dispatched to the Philippines to fight Muslim rebels. According to officials, both countries had been negotiating for months, and while the government was anxious to dismiss it as a mere exercise, an official said that this "mischaracterized" the operation.[22] The *Washington Post* then reported that the use of US troops to combat the Abu Sayyaf had been planned at the request of the Philippines.[23] Caught out, both countries then claimed that, while US troops would support AFP operations against the Abu Sayyaf, they would not participate in combat. As we will see, however, there is still some doubt as to whether that has been the case.

*

In the meantime, the USA was planning to go to war in Iraq. In late October 2002, Arroyo urged the UN Security Council to support the US motion calling on Saddam Hussein to declare all weapons of mass destruction within 30 days (a recipe for war because, as events would demonstrate, there were none to declare). It was obvious that the Arroyo government was going to be rewarded with a seat at the top table (albeit one routinely ignored by the USA) when, the very next day, the Asian caucus at the UN unanimously endorsed the Philippines' bid for a non-permanent seat on the Security Council for 2004-2005. As the situation came to the boil, Arroyo said that if war did break out it would be the fault of the country being invaded; it may not have been coincidental that US Army chief of staff Gen. Eric Shinseki had just arrived in Manila.

In May 2003, the Arroyo government received its second reward when George W. Bush designated the Philippines a "major non-NATO ally," putting it on the same footing as Australia, Egypt and Israel. Welcoming Arroyo on yet another trip to Washington, Bush revealed his ignorance of history by opening: "Just over a century ago, Americans and Filipinos worked side by side to liberate the Philippines."[24] During the trip, Arroyo signed an agreement for the mutual non-surrender of nationals to either a third country or to an international tribunal (or, putting it rather more honestly, granting US troops immunity from prosecution before the International Criminal Court: the US Patriot Act rules out military assistance to any country that is party to the court).

With war in Iraq imminent, Mrs. Arroyo cancelled trips to Europe and the USA, while a 10,000-strong demonstration called for her to be ousted due to her support for the impending invasion. In justifying the decision to join the "coalition of the willing" against Iraq, she followed a variant of the Bush-Blair line by expressing fear that weapons of mass destruction could fall into the hands of the Abu Sayyaf or the MILF, even though (leaving aside the fact that there was considerable doubt whether such weapons still existed in Iraq) there had never been any suggestion that the Saddam regime had been linked to either group. In March 2003, the US Embassy asked the governor of the Bangko Sentral to identify and freeze all Iraqi assets that might be used for postwar construction, and Iraqi diplomats and embassy staff were deported as "spies." Upon the collapse of the Saddam regime, Mrs. Arroyo rather prematurely (there was no government to which credentials might be presented) appointed a new ambassador and announced that police and humanitarian workers would be sent to Iraq. In assigning jobs in postwar Iraq, Arroyo said (with, as usual, no trace of irony) that priority would be given to Muslims from the war-torn areas of Mindanao as they would better appreciate the suffering and deprivation of Iraqis.[25]

Mrs. Arroyo received her third reward—one for which she had lobbied Colin Powell since the previous year—when George W. Bush paid a brief visit to Manila in October 2003.

A grateful administration gave Bush a grisly gift. When Fathur Rohman al-Ghozi (the top Jemaah Islamiya leader responsible for bomb outrages in Manila in December 2000) escaped from Camp Crame in July 2003, speculation was rife that he had been assisted by the police. On October 11, it was reported that there were hopes he would be recaptured before Bush arrived a week later. He was dead the next day, said by the military to have been killed in a shootout. Mrs. Arroyo flew to Zamboanga to view the body and proclaim a victory in the war against terrorism. It may have been essentially meaningless ritual, but it had its effect: the stock exchange closed 2.9 percent up (its highest since April 2002) and the peso hit a twelve-week high. Meanwhile, parts of Manila were given a P10 million makeover and fences were erected to ensure that no squatter colonies were glimpsed from the presidential limousine; 200 squatter families near the national assembly building, where Bush would address a joint session of Congress, were each given P10,000 when their homes were bulldozed.

Official society fawned on Bush as if he were royalty, paying him homage in much the same way as the richest and most "loyal" members of Britain's Indian empire must have done when welcoming their emperor, King George V, almost a century earlier. As state television cleared its schedules of all else, announcing its coverage of the visit with music of an appropriately regal and pompous tone, one suddenly appreciated the extent to which this archipelago had been damaged by colonialism, how ossified was its worldview, how weak its sense of self. But that was official society. Elsewhere in Metro Manila, thousands demonstrated and burned US flags.

In a private meeting with Arroyo, Bush said he wanted to remind the Filipino people what a great leader she was in fighting terrorism. "We want to continue to help you, and I want to thank you for your vision in fighting for freedom."[26] As he began his speech before Congress, seven party-list congressmen walked out. Bush began by repeating his earlier gaffe ("Together our soldiers liberated the country from colonial rule..."[27]) and went on to talk about terrorism, announcing that Mrs. Arroyo had that day committed the government to a five-year plan to reform the armed forces, for which the USA would provide technical assistance and expertise. In a tacit endorsement of Arroyo (the presidential election was just seven months away), he declared: "The world needs the Philippines to continue as a light to all of Asia and beyond."[28]

This was the high point of Mrs. Arroyo's relations with Washington. Soon, they would take an unexpected turn for the worse.

*

In mid-March 2004, terrorists claimed a new batch of civilian victims with the Madrid railway bombings, in an attack launched to protest the presence of Spanish troops in Iraq. The opposition in Manila warned after this it was clear that, by her continued support of the US role in Iraq, Arroyo was risking a major terrorist attack in the Philippines. At the end of the month, Mrs. Arroyo arrived at what the assembled media expected to be a routine news conference and announced that her government had, indeed, just averted a Madrid-style attack on Metro Manila, capturing 80 lbs of TNT intended for shopping malls and trains. One of those arrested was said to have been responsible for the beheading of US citizen and Abu Sayyaf kidnap victim Guillermo Sobero, while another had admitted involvement in the destruction of SuperFerry 14. This vessel had been destroyed by fire earlier in the year, with the loss of over 100 lives, and at the time the government had dismissed a claim by Abu Sayyaf leader Khaddafi Janjalani that his group had been responsible. Now, the government was no longer interested in dismissing Abu Sayyaf involvement in the tragedy.

While her claim to have thwarted a major attack would ordinarily have enhanced Mrs. Arroyo's anti-terrorist credentials, it emerged that she had recently attended a meeting with the US charge d'affaires (Ambassador Francis Ricciardone had been temporarily transferred to duties in, of all places, Iraq) at which, it was claimed, she had been criticized for not taking sufficiently seriously the warnings on terrorism issued by the USA, the United Kingdom and Australia. It was true that the government had declined the USA's offer of experts to help determine the cause of the SuperFerry 14 tragedy, and that Arroyo had recently blurted out an admission that the USA had been training Filipino troops to resist a Chinese assault on the Spratly islands. With regard to the latter, Mrs. Arroyo claimed that agreement was only reached to switch the focus to counter-terrorism after the events of September 11, 2001 and her strong support for Bush.[29] The implication was that, prior to the change of heart, the USA had been training Filipino troops for a purpose which did not have the support of the Philippine president, and that the country's independence was thus far more limited than even many nationalists would have believed.

The USA would not have been happy about either of these two incidents. So now it began to look as if the dramatic foiling of a Madrid-style attack had been stage-managed to both please Washington and notch up a few points just weeks before the 2004 election.

The meeting with the US charge d'affaires brought the first indication of US dissatisfaction with Mrs. Arroyo. There would be more after the flawed election of May 2004. Having headed the queue to pledge support for George W. Bush's "war against terrorism" in the wake of September 11, 2001, and having been equally enthusiastic in her support of the invasions of Afghanistan and Iraq, Mrs. Arroyo had sent a "humanitarian mission" of eight policemen and 43 soldiers to the latter country. In 2004, as attacks on "coalition" forces escalated and foreign civilians were kidnapped, calls were heard for the withdrawal of the Philippine contingent. Mrs. Arroyo, however, having first hinted that a withdrawal might be considered, said that the Philippines would stand by its commitment. A Philippine diplomat was quoted as saying: "Under American pressure, she will never order an evacuation".[30] Just days into her new administration, however, she was confronted with a dilemma of sizeable proportions.

Angelo de la Cruz, a truck driver employed by a Saudi company, was kidnapped as he drove into Iraq and threatened with beheading within 72 hours unless the Philippine government agreed to withdraw its troops. (Although the contingent would come to the end of its tour of duty on August 20, there had been discussion of an extension.) At this stage, the USA was full of praise for Mrs. Arroyo. "I see," intoned Ambassador Ricciardone, "a leader who has strength and compassion in a way that is truly inspirational."[31] But Arroyo's recent inauguration had taken place after an election dogged by allegations of fraud. Just as riot police had brutally dispersed protesters on that issue, they now clubbed those who took to the streets to demand a troop withdrawal. So far, the situation was under control, but if Angelo de la Cruz was beheaded the streets of Metro Manila might well see the long delayed explosion. Arroyo was faced with a choice between loyalty to Washington and self-preservation.

An offer of ransom was made, it was reported, but turned down by the kidnappers. Then it was announced that the contingent would return home ahead of schedule. Philippine policy was now assailed not by left-wing protesters but by the governments of the USA, Japan, Poland and Australia. Seeking to force a second u-turn, Ricciardone met Mrs. Arroyo. "In a time of crisis," he told the media, "an ally, a friend, helps a partner to be strong, and that's what we are trying to do."[32] He failed.

While some sections of the press criticized Arroyo for bowing to terrorists, most praised her (although some begrudgingly) for standing up to the USA, and this latter view was more in line with popular sentiment. The life of one Philippine citizen, ran the argument of the presidential palace (the political life of a Philippine president was, of course, not mentioned), was worth more than foreign commitments. This was Mrs. Arroyo repositioning herself. Although few expected her to say that the war in Iraq was unjustified in the first place, it was reported that she had told her advisers that her state of the nation speech due on July 26 would concentrate on domestic issues and on dispelling the view that she was a US puppet. On July 19, the day the last Philippine troops left Iraq, the opposition *Daily Tribune* reported that, far from the offer of ransom having been rejected, the kidnappers had accepted $6 million. Malaysia (said to have contributed $5 million), Landbank of the Philippines (allegedly the source of the other $1 million) and the presidential palace all denied the claim.

Ambassador Ricciardone initially attempted to get Mrs. Arroyo's decision reversed, even going to the office of defense secretary Eduardo Ermita to plead his case. Failing to get his way, on July 22 he left for Washington at the request of secretary of state Colin Powell for consultations to "reevaluate" relations with the Philippines. For those anxious to preserve the relationship, this was not a good sign. As Mrs. Arroyo now realized, the real test was not the hostage crisis but the management of diplomatic relations in its aftermath. Would the ship of state, launched from the colonial yards in 1946, finally make an independent voyage? After some defiant sounding of the ship's horn, at the end of July observers saw the vessel slowly turn and head back towards the comfort zone of traditional subservience.

By this time, presidential spokesman Ignacio Bunye was stressing the need to resume normal relations with the USA and Australia. The government, he said, was inhibiting itself from making any comment that might further inflame the situation. Even Senate minority leader Aquilino Pimentel Jr., whilst quite willing to give Australia a slap by switching the purchase of dairy products to New Zealand, warned that the Philippines could lose out if the "shattered" relationship with the USA did not improve. The traditionalists (contemptuously dubbed the "little brown brothers" by one opposition columnist[33]) were able to point to damage already sustained: a $20 million commodity loan (repayment spread over 30 years with an interest rate of 1 per cent) had fallen through; and, although the authorities in both countries were at pains to portray it as nothing out of the ordinary, 89 illegal Filipino immigrants were deported from the USA on July 26, raising fears that a punitive roundup of the remaining 200,000 might follow.

While the left urged Mrs. Arroyo to withdraw all support for the Iraq war, by now the presidential palace was even insisting that, despite evidence to the contrary, it was still a member of the "coalition." When Colin Powell hinted in an interview on Saudi radio that this was not the way things looked from Washington, presidential spokesman Ignacio Bunye was having none of it. The Philippines, he said, would continue to work with other allies and strategic partners, for the gains made on the anti-terrorism front were partly due to the Philippines' strategic partnership with the USA. Mrs. Arroyo emphasized the longevity and maturity of the relationship with the USA, which, she said, following the George W. Bush interpretation of history, was first forged "in the battlefield of freedom."

The assertion that the Philippines was still a member of the "coalition of the willing" defied belief. Officials initially claimed that the Philippines did not need to have troops in Iraq to assist in the rebuilding of that country. When they were reminded that the government had banned further deployments of OFWs, they raised the possibility of sending another military contingent, this time under UN auspices. It was pointed out that this was not the way the arrangement worked, whereupon it was suggested, apparently with a straight face, that Iraq could send people to Manila, where they could receive training in electoral processes, and the administration of justice, and governance. It was not until the US State Department clarified the matter that Manila finally conceded that it, having proved unwilling, was out of the coalition.

*

It took a trip to China in early September 2004 to restore Mrs. Arroyo's composure. According to Senate minority leader Aquilino Pimentel Jr., who accompanied her on the visit, this was originally envisaged as a mere speaking engagement, but was upgraded to a state visit after

Mrs. Arroyo finally waved goodbye to the US-led coalition. This was quite a step for both countries. It was Senator Gloria Arroyo, after all, who had visited Taiwan on its "national day" in 1994, triggering protests from Beijing. Now, she affirmed her support of the "one China" policy, which viewed Taiwan as a renegade province. In July 2004, a small group of Chinese had demonstrated outside the Philippine embassy in Beijing, protesting against the Philippines' stance on the Spratly Islands, and the fact that they were unhindered by the authorities led observers in Manila to conclude that the protest was officially sanctioned. Now, China and the Philippines (later joined by Vietnam, which also had a claim on the islands) agreed to jointly conduct a three-year seismic study of the South China Sea, including the area around the Spratlys, in search of gas and petroleum reserves.

The China trip led to the signing of a number of economic accords, but the really interesting agreement was that to increase bilateral trade to $20 billion within five years. As trade between the Philippines and the USA amounted to just $16 billion in 2002, sliding to $14.7 billion in 2003, there was a strong chance that China would become the Philippines' largest trading partner. That has yet to occur: by 2010, trade with China had reached just $10.35 billion, compared with the $13.44 billion trade with the USA.[34]

Washington maintained that it was not too bothered by the new relationship with China. It was natural, said charge d'affaires Joseph Mussomeli, for the Philippines to be on good terms with its powerful neighbor. But it would have been surprising if the USA had not been disturbed by the two countries' agreement to cooperate on defense, security matters and intelligence sharing. Defense secretary Avelino Cruz and armed forces chief Narciso Abaya were keen to discuss the possibilities of personnel training, joint exercises, and even the supply of arms. This development should be viewed in the context of the relationship between the Philippine military and its US counterpart, which had long been ambivalent. Officers often complained of the "junk" supplied by Washington, and the annual joint training exercises had also come in for criticism (see endnote 19). The former presence of huge US bases at Clark airfield and Subic Bay had given rise to further resentment, as for years Manila felt that it could afford to ignore the upgrading of its own military. As a result, the Philippine armed forces were now in a parlous condition. As recently as 1989, Japanese "Tora-Tora" aircraft, abandoned at the close of World War II, had been deployed against military rebels. Although an armed forces modernization act was passed in 1995, virtually no action had been taken due to the straitened circumstances in which the Philippines found itself. It still had nine of the 25 F-5 fighters delivered in 1965, but they had been grounded since structural defects were discovered following a fatal crash in 2002, and would later be decommissioned.

It was widely believed that Mrs. Arroyo was merely "playing the China card" in a poker game with Washington. This assumption rested upon the belief that what she really wanted was to be reinstated in the USA's good books. Whatever the truth, Mrs. Arroyo's new-found confidence seemed to indicate that she knew exactly what she was doing. Whether she was fully appreciative of the potential consequences of her actions, however, was another matter. Washington was, presumably, well aware that most of Philippine politics was deeply opportunist, and in the 1970s and early 1980s it had seen how President Ferdinand Marcos had played this same game, using the Soviet Union. Look what happened to him.

As Arroyo's domestic political problems deepened in 2005, there were clear indications that Washington was wondering whether to write off its investment in Arroyo immediately or sit it out until the end of her term in 2010. The Heritage Foundation, ideologically linked to the Bush administration, pondered whether the alliance with the Philippines could still be considered reliable, and on several occasions Washington expressed concern regarding the Arroyo government's handling of the Muslim "problem" in the south. As rumors of coup plots began to circulate, there were almost certainly, among the politicians and military men opposed to Arroyo, those willing to do Washington's bidding.

In September, the *Philippine Daily Inquirer* reported on a number of documents from various US Embassy officials in Manila, which were said to have been obtained from the FBI in Washington. These portrayed Arroyo as the president who had not come up to scratch, but they also warned that a Noli de Castro presidency would do more harm than good, as he was seen to be inept in most areas of policy. Other candidates were assessed—including Joseph Estrada, who was described as gaining in popularity. The reports also revealed that the embassy had received an account of a meeting of active military officers at which the possibility of a coup had been discussed, and that embassy officials received detailed accounts of cabinet meetings. If there were no expressions of outraged nationalism from the ranks of the opposition arising from such revelations, this may have been because, as was also apparent from the reports, the

Arroyo administration was not alone in seeking US support.

Quite apart from their unflattering content, the embassy reports demonstrated quite clearly that, while US interference and manipulation of Philippine political life was no longer at the levels it had reached in the 1950s, when CIA officer Edward Lansdale had a desk in Ramon Magsaysay's office, little had changed. Archbishop Ramon Arguelles put forward the view that, possibly as revenge for the withdrawal from Iraq, or because of the blossoming relationship with China, the political turmoil in the Philippines was at least partly due to American meddling. "The US," he said, "will use the leftists, the rightists [and, he might have added, the church], everything in order to achieve what they want to achieve in our country."[35] In late October 2005, newly-arrived charge d'affaires Paul Jones assured Arroyo that Washington supported both the country and her leadership of it, but coming after such explosive revelations this rang a little hollow.

Just when the Arroyo administration could have done without it, its relationship with the USA was further complicated in November, when, following completion of joint air and naval integration training with Philippine forces, a group of US Marines was accused of raping a 22-year-old Filipina in Subic. Government spokesmen seemed to alternate between playing to the nationalist gallery and striving to accommodate Washington, neatly illustrating the dilemma facing Malacañang: having to defend national dignity while, at the same time, avoiding a complete rupture with the USA. This was made more difficult when, two months after it was made, Washington denied the request for Philippine custody, saying that, in line with the provisions of the visiting forces agreement (VFA), the accused men would remain in US hands until the conclusion of all judicial proceedings. From this point on, the issue was less about what may have happened to one Filipina and more about the relationship between the Philippines and its former colonial master.

While demonstrators regularly assembled on Roxas Boulevard, opposite the US Embassy, to demand an end to the VFA and the expulsion of all US troops, advocacy groups claimed that not one of the many cases in which US service personnel had been accused of criminal acts had been successfully prosecuted, and in the Senate Miriam Defensor Santiago called for the revision of those VFA provisions unduly favoring the USA: exemption from passport and visa regulations on departure, compulsion on the Philippines to waive primary jurisdiction, the obligation to turn over American accused to US military custody if requested, and the waiver by the Philippines of claims of damage to property. Within days of the US rejection of Manila's request for custody, the bicameral legislative oversight committee on the VFA resolved that the treaty should be terminated and replaced with a status of forces agreement providing for local custody. Although the public stance by the foreign affairs department was that this would not adversely affect relations with Washington, an anonymous source said to have been privy to discussions with the US Embassy was of the view that military aid and other forms of support might be casualties.[36] After a meeting at the embassy, the oversight committee retreated, saying that it would suspend its resolution pending further discussions on custody.

*

As previously, the USA paid close attention to the Philippines' dealings with both its own Muslim population and the wider Muslim world. Although the embassy declined to comment on the matter, according to a US intelligence report Arroyo had ordered the release of an alleged financier of Abu Sayyaf and Jemaah Islamiya who had links with the Saudi royal family; it was further claimed that national security adviser Norberto Gonzales and immigration bureau chief Alipio Fernandez were negotiating with Saudi officials for the release and deportation of a suspected al-Qaeda operative. This presumably did little to increase US confidence in its ally.

The importance attached to Mindanao was underlined when Henry Crumpton, formerly with the CIA and now the department of state's anti-terrorism coordinator, said while visiting Australia in November 2005 that a peace agreement with the MILF was one of the key issues in the struggle against terrorism in Southeast Asia. "You look at the southern Philippines and the Sulawesi scene. That is a major issue—perhaps the major issue—right now in Southeast Asia, because there the enemy have [sic] the opportunity to gather and train and build cohesive groups and from there deploy outwards."[37] This was, of course, an accusation that Jemaah Islamiya (and therefore al-Qaeda) operatives were being trained in Mindanao. In the same

188

month, a local councilor alleged that a handful of US soldiers had joined an operation against the Abu Sayyaf in Sulu, although the US countered that the men were part of a humanitarian mission that would provide new classrooms and water systems.

Doubt was cast upon the humanitarian role of US troops in Mindanao when, in January 2007, a report by Focus on the Global South (FGS) reminded readers that a contingent of special operations forces (SOF) had been in the south for five years, and while both governments might claim that its role was to train Filipino troops and undertake humanitarian projects, the SOF itself defined special operations as those "conducted in hostile, denied, or politically sensitive environments" and requiring "covert, clandestine, or discreet capabilities." The SOF deployment had originally been dubbed "Operation Enduring Freedom—Philippines." The original Operation Enduring Freedom had been, of course, the invasion of Afghanistan; considered in this context, the warning in 2005 by US charge d'affaires Joseph Mussomeli that Mindanao could become the next Afghanistan appeared even more sinister.

The number of SOF troops deployed, said FGS, had never been disclosed, there was no exit date, and they had been spotted in combat zones, clearly distinguishing them from the US troops who took part in the annual joint military exercises. The original commander, Col. David Maxwell, had said that their mission was to "conduct unconventional warfare in the southern Philippines through, by and with the [Philippine armed forces]...to help the Philippine government separate the population and destroy the terrorist organization [a reference to Abu Sayyaf]." Maxwell maintained that combat operations by US troops were not prohibited by the Philippine Constitution, and described the activity of his troops as being "under the guise of an exercise." Members of the deployment who wrote an article for a US military magazine said the unit participated in "ongoing unconventional warfare operations..." Maxwell was reappointed as commander in October 2006. US defense secretary Donald Rumsfeld, it turned out, had authorized the troops to operate at company level and encouraged them to join patrols.[38]

Lending credence to the suspicions raised by FGS, in January 2007, after the reported deaths of two Abu Sayyaf leaders (see below), an armed forces commander was reported as saying: "The Americans have helped us a lot, not only in the combat operations but also in the medical and civic work in Sulu." The same newspaper quoted a source as saying that "Mindanao is crawling with CIA, FBI and even Australian federal agents" who, posing as tourists, businessmen or treasure hunters, were assisting in tracking down JI and AS fighters.[39]

There had been several indications that some US activity was concerned less with combating armed rebellion than with promoting it. In perhaps the most curious incident of all, in March 2002 Michael Terrence Meiring, said to be a US citizen of South African origin, was badly injured when explosives in his possession accidentally detonated in his hotel suite in Davao City. Three days later, he was taken from his hospital bed and flown to Manila by, allegedly, FBI and US national security agents. By the time a "hold-departure" order was issued, Meiring had been flown to the USA.[40] A *Philippine Star* report in July 2002 quoted "highly reliable sources" as saying that Meiring had been deployed by the CIA in the 1990s, since when he had provided his Mindanao acquaintances with explosives and had traded US federal reserve notes with the Abu Sayyaf, "a gang that provided the excuse for the new US-Philippine alliance."[41] The case against Meiring was shelved in 2003 and, although revived in 2005 when a Davao City judge issued certification for his extradition, does not seem to have prospered.

In Mindanao, things were not always as they appeared.

*

The two-month delay in responding to the Philippine request for custody of the accused in the Subic rape case was just one indication of Washington's displeasure. Another was the fact that after Ambassador Francis Ricciardone ended his tour of duty in May 2005, it was not until March the following year that his successor, Kristie Kenney, arrived. Then again, when foreign affairs secretary Alberto Romulo visited Washington in January 2006, he was met not by his counterpart (secretary of state Condaleeza Rice) but by a deputy assistant secretary of state. When Rice visited the region in March, the Philippines was not on her itinerary; released at the same time, her department's 2005 country report on human rights charged that the Philippine national police was the worst abuser of human rights in the country, citing extrajudicial killings by the security forces and political murders.

But while the USA evidently had a very low opinion of Arroyo, it continued to exert pressure on the administration when it felt it would yield results. In her address to the UN Security Council in September, 2005, Arroyo had praised the US role in the "campaign against terror," but Washington was looking for the passage of a tough anti-terrorism bill. When welcoming new charge d'affaires Paul Jones the following month, she had assured him that it was on the way, somewhat ominously vowing: "We will do anything to have it passed."[42] But the Philippine Senate was certainly in no hurry to do Arroyo's bidding on this issue, and so on December 6, when director of national intelligence John Negraponte arrived in Manila, the status of the bill was one of the items on his agenda. During the week-long state of emergency in 2006, as international unease regarding the government's threats to the media increased, and in the absence of any apparent danger of a coup, assistant secretary of state Christopher Hill, ostensibly in Manila for an ASEAN regional forum, met Arroyo. Two days later, she lifted the state of emergency.

It began to look as if Washington was, despite continuing dissatisfaction, prepared to sit it out until 2010. But then, in December 2006 things took a further turn for the worse when one of the Marines involved in the Subic case was convicted of rape and sentenced to up to 40 years' imprisonment. The Makati court ruled that the accused should be placed in the city jail until such time as custody arrangements had been agreed, pending appeal. A motion to return him to US custody immediately was denied, and just over a week later the US Embassy announced that the annual Balikatan exercises were off, a spokesman arguing that it "wouldn't be prudent to bring in US troops if the Philippines cannot assure their protection."[43]

A week later, at an hour before midnight, the convicted man was transferred to the US Embassy, but, although the department of foreign affairs had in the meantime concluded an agreement with the US ambassador, the legal nicety of seeking the Makati court's permission was foregone. Two days later, the Court of Appeals would uphold the transfer. The decision to move the prisoner was made, said interior secretary Ronaldo Puno, with Arroyo present, and was necessary in order to "forestall the further deterioration in our strategic relationship with the United States, which was being rapidly eroded by our non-compliance with the Visiting Forces Act."[44] Henceforth, there was never any doubt regarding whose interest the Arroyo government was representing in this matter. A grateful embassy indicated that the joint military exercises were back on. Amid renewed calls for a review of the VFA, an embassy spokesman said that this was premature before the current case had been appealed, somewhat ominously adding that even then the two countries would have to agree on a venue for detention.

In February 2009, the Supreme Court ruled that the convicted man should be confined in a Philippine government facility and ordered the appeal court to resolve any further petitions on the case without delay. The Arroyo government said that it would appeal the ruling, as the VFA gave custody to the USA. In March, however, it became known that the woman concerned had recanted and had gone to permanently reside in the USA, having been issued an immigrant visa. The following month, the Court of Appeal duly overturned the man's conviction and he was flown out of the country. A deal had been done as a result of which the injured party was, as usual, Philippine sovereignty and national pride.

*

Meanwhile in Sulu, thousands of Philippine troops with US support had been attempting to eliminate the Abu Sayyaf group and capture or kill two Indonesian operatives of Jemaah Islamiyah wanted in connection with the Bali bombings of 2002. It was not until January 2007, though, that the big names began to fall: second in command Abu Solaiman, thought to have masterminded the SuperFerry 14 operation, was killed, and then a DNA test confirmed that remains found the previous month had been those of Khaddafi Janjalani, the Abu Sayyaf leader. Suddenly, Arroyo was on a roll. US Ambassador Kristie Kenney pronounced US-Philippine relations stronger than ever, following which executive secretary Ermita went so far as to say that the Philippines would welcome US assistance in fighting the Maoist New People's Army. Clearly, a reward was appropriate in the circumstances, and thus it was that Arroyo, in Davos for a meeting of the World Economic Forum, received a telephone call from George W. Bush, thanking her for her support in the "global war on terror" after the victories in Sulu.

After the roller-coaster ride of the previous two-and-a-half years, Gloria Macapagal Arroyo was seemingly restored to grace.

*

Throughout the Arroyo years, Washington showed intense interest in the Muslim areas of Mindanao, and that interest went far beyond combating terrorism. Some posited the possibility that the USA regarded the Philippines as a virtually failed state and thus, seeing the need for an amenable Muslim regime in the region to act as a role model, it had an interest in an agreement between Manila and the MILF which would both end hostilities and usher in a much greater degree of Muslim autonomy than existed in the current Autonomous Region in Muslim Mindanao (ARMM).

A second theory, not necessarily contradicting the first, was that US interest in this dispute was, as in so many others, motivated by oil and gas. US diplomatic documents dated February 2006, released by Wikileaks in 2011, contain extensive references to the mineral wealth of Mindanao.[45] Five billion barrels of oil are said to lie beneath the waters of Sulu and Palawan alone.[46] Substantial oil and gas deposits are believed to lie beneath Liguasan Marsh, in the largely Muslim provinces of North Cotabato and Maguindano; in 2008, Nur Misuari, founder of the Moro National Liberation Front, from which the MILF split after the former's peace deal with the Ramos government, said that US experts had estimated that the natural gas alone was worth $580 billion. [47]

For several years, in negotiations brokered by Malaysia, the two parties haggled over the enlargement of the ARMM, to be ruled by a Bangsamoro Juridical Entity (BJE), which would enjoy new powers and rights, some pertaining to mineral wealth. While much of the opposition to the proposed agreement came from the descendents of Christian settlers and was hardly progressive in character, more anti-imperialist opponents questioned the US role, which it turn cast doubt on the true motives of the MILF.

In 2003, the nominally "independent" (but congressionally funded) US Institute for Peace (USIP) was engaged by the State Department to help expedite a peace agreement in Mindanao. Thus it was that the USIP's Philippine Facilitation Project, 2003-2007 oversaw the drafting of the agreement on the BJE. Many would consider it somewhat unusual that Washington, regardless of who occupied the White House or the seats in Congress, would assist an armed national liberation movement. But then the MILF is a fairly unusual national liberation movement. The State Department intervention was preceded by a January 2003 letter from then MILF leader Hashim Salamat who, frustrated by the lack of progress in negotiations with Manila, had requested assistance from, of all people, George W. Bush.

US-MILF relations became extremely close, even warm. Quite how close would be made clear by an editorial on the MILF Website[48] when, eleven months after the inauguration of President Barack Obama, it was announced that Kristie Kenney was to be replaced as US Ambassador. The editorial thanked Ms. Kenney for "being with us for three years and a half. Surely, we'll miss you!" and continued:

> Even as you said, your visit to the MILF administrative base in Darapanan, Sultan Kudarat, Maguindanao on February 19, 2008, was not carried out "in your official capacity as ambassador," it nevertheless carried so many positive implications. Besides, to the MILF, the line between personal and official when one is an official of government is truly blurred.

It was doubtful whether Ms. Kenney's employers shared the view that the "line between personal and official" was "truly blurred." They would be only too aware that such "personal" actions would be interpreted—as it obviously was by the MILF—as US support. The editorial went on:

> No matter what others say, the MILF views the above as part of the growing international understanding of the legitimacy of the MILF-led struggle for freedom and right to self-determination of the Bangsamoro people. It cannot be less.

It has been traditional for national liberation movements to make a sharp distinction between the government of the colonizing power and the people of the latter country. This, the editorial now made clear, was not the position of the MILF.

> Madame Ambassador, the Bangsamoro people have never considered the American people or even the United States Government as their enemy; they cried when America

departed from Mindanao in 1946.

They learned to love America despite the deaths of so many brave Moro warriors during the Moro-American War. But to this day, they bitterly opposed their turn-over to the Filipinos in the grant of so-called Philippine independence in 1946. We sent several petitions to the US Congress asking for the separation of our homeland, but the US ignored our pleas completely.

This we cannot forget until the US helps correct this "historic injustice" and give[s] them their right to govern themselves whether in the form of state or sub-state."

Such help, said the editorial, "can best be expressed or impacted outside of the formal peace process."

It would have been disturbing to many that the MILF believed, 63 years after Philippine independence, that the USA had the power to "give them their right to govern themselves." It was fascinating to speculate how this assistance "outside of the formal peace process" might be "expressed or impacted." It seemed that the MILF leaders, no matter how they might deny it, were afflicted with a typically Filipino malady in that their quest for so-called "self-determination" added up to little more than the choice of a new exploiter. They might care to ponder what happened to Aguinaldo—and, indeed, the Philippines—after he swallowed Commodore Dewey's promises of US assistance in throwing off Spanish rule.

There is another parallel with that earlier period. One of the roles of the Commission on National Integration established in the 1950s was the granting of scholarships to Muslims and other minorities. In an uncanny reflection of the emergence of Christian ilustrados in the 19th century, many of the young Muslims sent on such scholarships became politically aware at university and returned home as advocates of secession. The development of professional strata in the Muslim population meant that the cause of separatism now had a voice. The majority of the Christian ilustrados, having first demanded autonomy and then associating briefly with the anti-Spanish revolution, joined the camp of the US occupier—some even before the manufactured outbreak of the Philippine-American War. It seemed possible that there was now a similar migration by some of their Muslim counterparts.

Had it been established, the new homeland would have completely transformed large parts of the southern Philippines, for the draft agreement—or Memorandum on Ancestral Domain, as it was called—gave the BJE total control of natural resources within its borders and the right to enter into economic agreements with foreign countries.[49] Little surprise, then, that US Ambassador Kristie Kenny was one of those who traveled to Kuala Lumpur in August 2008 to witness the signing ceremony. At the eleventh hour, however, the Supreme Court intervened to grant critics of the agreement a temporary restraining order, and later ruled that the draft agreement was unconstitutional.

The new Obama administration seemed just as keen to offer encouragement to the MILF as its predecessor, US diplomats behaving like proconsuls and venturing into Mindanao with no apparent sanction from Manila. In October 2009, MILF chairman Murad Ebrahim (who had succeeded the deceased Hashim Salamat) was visited by the US charge d'affaires Leslie Bassett and her team.[50] On November 6, deputy assistant secretary of state Scott Marciel went to Maguindanao province to meet MILF chief negotiator Mohagher Iqbal, handing him a letter that, although signed by assistant secretary of state Kurt Campbell, was said to be Obama's reply to the letter Murad Ebrahim had written to him after his election. The contents of this correspondence were not revealed.[51]

The Supreme Court intervention was followed by numerous deaths as an MILF group commanded by Umbra Kato (this would evolve into the breakaway Bangsamoro Islamic Freedom Movement, with the Bangsmoro Islamic Freedom Fighters as its military arm) broke ranks and waged war, causing 160,000 people to be displaced within days. Despite this development, talks between the government and the MILF resumed the following year, the government explaining that the path was cleared by agreement on the composition of an "international contact group" to guarantee the results of the negotiating process. This group was composed of the UK, Turkey and Japan, along with some ostensible NGOs—including the Asia Foundation, formerly a CIA front and still funded by Washington, and the UK-based Conciliation Resources, which is funded by the Foreign and Commonwealth Office, the Department for International Development, several other European governments, the European Commission and various charities.

US pressure may also have played a role, for during her visit to Manila in November 2009 secretary of state Hillary Clinton urged Mrs. Arroyo to conclude a peace agreement, saying that in her experience it was far easier to take difficult decisions shortly before leaving office. In the Mindanao context, that sounded as if she were advising Arroyo to light the blue touch-paper before walking away, but when the latter left office on June 30, 2010 little progress had been made. At the time of writing, the government of Benigno Aquino III is expressing confidence that agreement with the MILF is close.

NOTES

1. Claro M. Recto, "Nationalism and Our Historic Past," in Renato Constantino (ed.), *Vintage Recto: Memorable Speeches and Writings* (Quezon City: Foundation for Nationalist Studies, 1986), 232.

2. Claro M. Recto, "The True Ultra-Nationalists," Renato Constantino (ed.), *Vintage Recto...*, 190.

3. Claro M. Recto, "Philippine-American Relations," Renato Constantino (ed.), *Vintage Recto...*, 124.

4. The real purpose of the Bell Act was, in the words of US Senator Millard Tydings, to "keep the Philippines economically though we lose them politically." Hernando J. Abaya claims that "the real author of the trade act was not its designated sponsor, Rep. Jasper Bell, but the American Chamber of Commerce in Manila. I know it because, as a researcher and political analyst on the US Embassy staff at the time, I was one of two members who read the galley proofs of the two measures which were rushed by air to Manila from Capitol Hill for fine-tooth combing for any possible error." See Hernando J. Abaya, "Will Cory Aquino Survive?", *Looking Back in Anger* (Quezon City: New Day Publishers, 1992), 222.

5. Claro M. Recto, in Renato Constantino (ed.), *The Recto Reader* (Quezon City: Karrel, Inc., 1965), 41.

6. From the implementing agreement signed by President Elpidio Quirino and US

Ambassador Myron Cowen, quoted in William Pomeroy, *An American-Made Tragedy* (New York: International Publishers, 1974), 25.

7. Claro M. Recto, "The True Ultra-Nationalists," in Renato Constantino (ed.), *Vintage Recto...*, 194.

8. Ibid., 191.

9. Claro M. Recto, "A Realistic Foreign Policy for the Philippines," in Renato Constantino (ed.), *Vintage Recto...*, 103.

10. Joseph B. Smith, *Portrait of a Cold Warrior* (Quezon City: Plaridel Books, 1976), 269.

11. US National Security Council, "Statement of US Policy Towards the Philippines," April 5, 1954, reproduced in Nick Culather (ed.), *Managing Nationalism: United States National Security Council Documents on the Philippines, 1953-1960* (Quezon City: New Day Publishers, 1992), 17.

12. Ibid., 25.

13. Ibid., 18.

14. Claro M. Recto, "Our Lingering Colonial Complex," in Renato Constantino (ed.), *Vintage Recto...*, 88.

15. Claro M. Recto, "Our Mendicant Foreign Policy," in Renato Constantino (ed.), *Vintage Recto...*, 72

16. *Asia Pulse*, November 12, 2001.

17. Reuters report, November 15, 2001.

18. *Manila Times*, February 9, 2002.

19. Ibid., February 14, 2002. The following year, the visiting forces commission submitted a report to Mrs. Arroyo that recommended the conclusion of similar agreements with other "friendly" countries, as the joint exercises with the USA "seem to follow the biases of the American planners for the kind of war that will confront their troops and for which their forces have been designated...It follows that the US forces gain more out of the training and exercises undertaken than their Filipino counterparts." See *Philippine Daily Inquirer*, November 3, 2003.

20. www.inq7.net, March 28, 2002.

21. Ibid., June 5, 2002.

22. *New York Times*, February 20, 2003.

23. Cited in *Daily Tribune*, February 25, 2003.

24. Office of the Press Secretary, White House, Washington, May 19, 2003.

25. *Manila Bulletin*, April 29, 2003.

26. *Philippine Daily Inquirer*, October 19, 2003.

27. NBN television, October 18, 2003.

28. Ibid.

29. *Malaya,* April 4, 2004.

30. www.inq7.net, April 17, 2004.

31. Ibid., July 12, 2004.

32. Ibid., July 16, 2004.

33. Rod Kapunan in *Daily Tribune.*

34. www.nscb.gov.ph, accessed September 26, 2012.

35. www.inq7.net, October 3, 2005.

36. *Daily Tribune*, January 26, 2006.

37. www.inq7.net, November 22, 2005.

38. Herbert Docena, "US troops 'unconventional' presence," *Malaya*, January 15, 2007, based on his report for Focus on the Global South.

39. *Philippine Star*, January 20, 2007.

40. The basic elements of the Meiring story were detailed in a series of three articles by Dorian Zumel-Sicat and Jeannette Andrade, in the *Manila Times*, May 29-31, 2002.

41. *Philippine Star*, July 9, 2002.

42. www.inq7.net, October 21, 2005.

43. Ibid., December 22, 2006.

44. Ibid., January 2, 2007.

45. *Daily Tribune*, August 24, 2011.

46. Zoilo P. Dejaresco III, "Mindanao's secret," *Manila Bulletin*, August 18, 2011.

47. *BusinessWorld*, August 19, 2005; Rommel Collena, "Liguasan Marsh holds billions of dollars in gas — Misuari," GMANews.TV, July 28, 2008.

48. "Good Bye! [*sic*] Madame Ambassador," www.luwaran.com, November 23, 2009.

49. "GRP-MILF draft pact on Bangsamoro homeland," *Philippine Daily Inquirer*, August 4, 2008.

50. *Philippine Daily Inquirer*, October 19, 2009.

51. Ibid., November 15, 2009.

10 "A STEP THAT CANNOT BE BYPASSED"

In the 1950s and 1960s, the Philippines, like many other "developing" countries, had embarked upon a path of import-substitution that had seen high growth-rates and the sprouting of a modest but significant group of Philippine industrialists. This process was assisted by the exchange controls that, in a situation of economic crisis, had been imposed in 1949. That this was possible without fierce opposition from the former colonial power was due to the fact that the US authorities were prepared to tolerate such a development as long as it was temporary, and as long as US capital was able to invest on the Philippine side of the tariff walls.[1] However, unlike those countries that would develop (the word is deliberately chosen) "tiger economies," graduating to the status of newly industrializing countries (NICs), the Philippines made no attempt (which would have met opposition from Washington), to create a strong, developmental state independent of the domestic elite and the USA, or a far-reaching industrial strategy. For this, it would pay dearly.

Exchange controls were removed with the conclusion of the first IMF agreement in 1962 (during the presidency of Mrs. Arroyo's father, Diosdado Macapagal) and domestic business was immediately under threat, while the exchange rate of the peso, originally two to the US dollar, was halved and thereafter spiraled downwards. All this, however, was part of a drive by foreign capital and the multilateral financial institutions to reorient the Philippine economy: because the TNCs wished to transfer labor-intensive parts of their operations to low-wage economies, import-substitution was out and "export-orientation" was in.

This was the situation confronting Marcos. Far from being the "puppet of US imperialism" he is often painted, he was at most an inconsistent and unreliable partner for Washington, for the simple reason that his interests and those of the economic grouping he represented were often contrary to those of foreign capital. During the martial law period, it was almost certainly not coincidental that the USA began to raise concerns about human rights violations (of which there were, of course, many) at around the same time that businessmen like Eduardo Cojuangco were making inroads at the expense of TNCs.

By 1980, the international division of labor was undergoing further revision, as the TNCs (some of them now based in the new "tiger economies," where labor costs were rising) wished to transfer certain processes of the new industries like electronics to low-wage countries. To countries agreeing to undergo the necessary "structural adjustment," the World Bank and IMF held out the glittering prospect of achieving NIC status. The IMF would normally have been assigned the task of selling this to Marcos, but because it was feared that he would have nothing to do with it, the job of persuading him to accept a "structural adjustment loan," and the program accompanying it, was given to the World Bank, which had a more benign image. The World Bank then conducted a very subtle campaign, ensuring that control of the Central Bank passed to pro-TNC "technocrats," many of them trained in Washington, and that Marcos was effectively isolated. In brief, the World Bank program required the Philippines to reduce tariffs, lift import restrictions, introduce further investment incentives for foreign capital and allow the further devaluation of the peso—all in order to sharpen the focus on export orientation, with light manufacturing at its core.[2] Over thirty years later, the Philippines has still not achieved NIC status because, of course, liberalization and "enclave development" are simply unable to deliver it: the "tigers" were not developed by agreeing to become minor subcontractors, but by building whole industries.

Marcos's successor, Corazon Aquino, had no qualms about swallowing Washington's medicine. The interests of her branch of the Cojuangco family (Eduardo was an estranged cousin) lay in agriculture, principally the 6,000-hectare Hacienda Luisita in Tarlac province. So it was full steam ahead for deregulation and privatization, and it would not be long before the proceeds from the latter would be seen as a vital means of plugging the revenue gap. The multilateral financial institutions were much more comfortable with the new president, confident that the "reforms" it prescribed would be implemented.

When Fidel Ramos was elected in 1992, he vowed to achieve NIC status in eight years with his "Philippines 2000" program, but while the economic indicators were mostly more positive during his six-year term, this was not because he was genuinely developing a "tiger" but because he was pursuing the orthodox prescriptions with greater consistency than either Aquino or Marcos and, therefore, attracting more investment. But this was bad news for much of domestic business, for it entailed membership of the World Trade Organization (the "globalization bill," as it was called, was sponsored by Senator Gloria Macapagal Arroyo) and the president appeared keen to lower tariffs at a faster rate than required by either the WTO or the Association of Southeast Asian Nations (ASEAN). While foreign capital was attracted, much of it took the form of portfolio investment, which by its "hot money" nature would contribute to the 1997 financial crisis in Southeast Asia. The legislation for the liberalization of retail trade was commenced during Ramos's term (although it was actually signed into law by Estrada), and foreign debt, upon which the "development" model was dependent, grew at Marcosian rates. After his election Estrada, despite his "pro-poor" stance, simply went along with the traditional formula.

*

Members of the Makati Business Club were surveyed twice in January 2001, and while in the first half of the month, before Estrada departed, 85 percent were pessimistic, in the later survey, with Gloria Macapagal Arroyo installed, two-thirds looked forward to brighter prospects.[3] In February, after a meeting with Arroyo, World Bank Group managing director Peter Woicke reported: "We are optimistic. I think we are very encouraged because the president is focusing on all things which from the private sector point of view are very important to the market."[4]

The country was still subject to the IMF's "post-program monitoring" (the last program had been curtailed during the Estrada years). It was expected that by November 2003 the Philippines' net debt to the IMF would have declined to a level allowing the termination of its "supervision." But in December that year IMF mission leader Masahiko Takeda put paid to that hope (if, indeed, hope it was), saying that the Philippines would be supervised indefinitely. Upon his return to Washington, he would recommend "continued observance." Although the "post-program monitoring" was initially intended to last for two years, Takeda said that there was "unfinished business," such as reforms in the fiscal sector.[5] But the IMF need not have worried: Mrs. Arroyo extended the monitoring period, a decision welcomed by the Washington institution, which said that "close consultation" was important until the government's fiscal position had strengthened. Without comprehensive reforms, said the IMF, the country's situation would worsen, and particular concern was expressed about the public sector deficit and international debt.[6] The Philippines' debt to the IMF was finally repaid in full at the end of 2006, thus allowing the country to rid itself of close supervision by that institution for the first time in 45 years. But the IMF ideology has remained—as have the annual Article IV consultations which the IMF is, under its articles of agreement, obliged to conduct with member-countries.

Under Mrs. Arroyo, there were government promises aplenty—for the most part meaningless slogans that no one can have seriously intended to implement. In July 2001, for example, Lakas chairman Jose de Venecia Jr. pledged to swing the entire "People Power Coalition" behind the president's "executive-legislative initiative" to commence the reconstruction of the economy in the next one or two months, launching "variations of US President Franklin Delano Roosevelt's 'New Deal'..."[7] Nothing of the kind was ever seen, but the promises kept coming: one million rural jobs would be created every year as the president wielded an "iron hand' against corruption, and the country was enjoined to embrace "free enterprise with a social conscience." And the hollowest claim of all: "We...see in our great revolutions a progressive advancement towards the ultimate goal to transfer power over the state from the traditional economic and political bosses to the people."[8]

Mrs. Arroyo may have had a master's degree and a doctorate in economics, but the economic record of her government was to be entirely undistinguished. She merely followed in the footsteps of those predecessors who had seemed to believe that docile adherence to the formulae of the prevailing World Bank-IMF-WTO orthodoxy was the same as having an economic strategy. This "export-oriented" regime was consistently unable to achieve a balance of trade surplus, and unemployment and poverty continued at high levels. Like Estrada (but unlike Ramos), Arroyo was unable to balance the budget without recourse to new taxes, and the high level of the deficit would cause concern to the Bretton Woods twins. It was no use blaming problems on a "slowdown in the USA and Japan" or a "global slump" (itself a wild exaggeration at the time), as happened early in the Arroyo period: an "export-oriented" economy was always going to be at the mercy of external forces, and the persistence of these problems was an early sign that the malaise was systemic.

*

Table 1 tells much of the economic story during the Arroyo regime. In due course, we will submit each of the headings in this table to closer scrutiny. Growth is, of course, not the same as development, and while post-2000 growth in GDP might look fairly respectable, it *was* merely growth. Moreover, it was highest in 2004, 2007 and 2010—election years, when politicians throw substantial sums at their constituents, artificially inflating the growth figures. There was no attempt to embark upon the development of basic industries, or to reorient the economy towards the satisfaction of Filipino needs.

TABLE 1: Philippines 2001-2010, Some Indicators

	2001	2002	2003	2004	2005	2006	2007	2008	2009	2010
GDP Growth (%)	1.8	4.4	4.5	6.0	5.1	5.3	7.1	3.7	1.1	7.3
Balance of Trade (US $m)	(6265)	(5530)	(5851)	(5864)	(7546)	(6732)	(8391)	(12,885)	(8842)	(10,384)
Current Account Balance (US $m)	(1762)	(351)	282	1626	2354	5341	7112	3627	9358	8465
Merchandise Exports, Annual Change (%)	(16.2)	9.9	2.7	9.8	3.7	15.6	6.4	(2.5)	(22.1)	34.8
Merchandise Imports Annual Change (%)	(13.3)	6.3	3.1	6.0	7.4	10.9	8.7	5.6	(24.0)	31.5
Debt Service Ratio	15.8	16.4	16.9	13.8	13.3	12.0	10.1	9.6	10.3	8.7
Interest payments (% of Budget)	25.95		27.44	31.51	33.24	-	-	-	-	-
Budget Deficit (% of GDP)	4.0	5.3	4.7	3.9	2.7	1.1	0.2	0.9	3.9	3.7
Employed (millions, July)	29.3	30.1	30.45	31.6	32.52	33.26	33.3	34.6	35.5	36.3
Unemployment Rate (%)	11.1	11.4	11.3	11.8	11.4	8.0	7.3	7.4	7.5	7.3

Sources: Asian Development Bank, *Asian Development Outlook, 2006* (for years 2001-2005) and *Asian Development Outlook 2011* (for years 2006-2010), with the exception of those regarding interest payments, which are taken from Leonor Magtolis Briones, "The cost of financing development," Social Watch Philippines, 2006, and the "Employed" figures, which are taken from the Labor Force Survey at www.census.gov.ph; in each case, the July figures have been used so that the final date roughly coincides with the end of the Arroyo administration.

TABLE 2: Structure of Demand (percentage of GDP at current prices)

	2001	2002	2003	2004	2005	2006	2007	2008	2009	2010
Private Consumption*	70.6	69.4	69.6	69.3	70.1					
Gross Domestic Investment	19.0	17.7	16.7	17.1	15.7	14.5	15.4	15.3	14.6	15.6

Source: Asian Development Bank, *Asian Development Outlook, 2006* (years 2001-2005), *Asian Development Outlook, 2011* (years 2006-2010).

* The ADB's *Asian Development Outlook* seems to have dispensed with this category in recent years.

The absence of real development is woefully apparent in the Table 2. It will be seen from this that by far the largest element in GDP is private consumption, the growth of which is, year after year, propelled by the growth in remittances from overseas Filipino workers (OFWs). On the other hand, we see that, as a percentage of GDP, gross domestic capital formation (more recently referred to as "gross domestic investment") had steadily declined over the same period. The latter is, of course, a key factor in national development, being the addition of new plant, equipment and buildings, land improvements, etc.

By comparison, we can see in Table 3 that, in some economies in the region which are genuinely developing, the structure of demand is somewhat different. Thus, the share of private consumption in the composition of GDP in the Philippines exceeds that of six of the seven other ASEAN countries for which Asian Development Bank data are available for 2005. In the one exception, Cambodia, this category has been steadily declining as a percentage, having stood at 96 percent in 1995. In the Philippines, on the other hand, we saw in Table 1 that it has remained fairly constant. Among the same seven countries, only in Myanmar do we find gross domestic investment playing a lesser role (while Malaysia's 14.5 percent for 2009 is lower that the

Philippines' 14.6 percent, the former's results for 2008 and 2010 were more characteristically 19.3 percent and 21.3 percent).

TABLE 3: Structure of Demand, ASEAN Countries, 2005 (% of GDP)

Country	Private Consumption 2005	Gross Investment	Domestic
		2005	2009
Brunei Darussalam	N/A	N/A	17.6
Cambodia (2003)	80.3	26.4	21.4
Indonesia (2003)	65.4	21.3	31.0
Laos	N/A	N/A	N/A
Malaysia	43.7	19.8	14.5
Myanmar (2002)	Private and government consumption: 89.5	10.4	N/A
Philippines	70.1	15.7	14.6
Singapore	41.9	18.6	26.4
Thailand	56.9	31.6	21.2
Vietnam	63.6	35.4	38.1

Source: Asian Development Bank, *Asian Development Outlook, 2006* (for 2005), *Asian Development Outlook 2011* (for 2009).

If Table 3 indicates that most other ASEAN countries have developed and/or are developing faster than the Philippines, this receives confirmation when we turn, in Table 4, to a comparison of the structure of output in the ten countries.

TABLE 4: ASEAN Countries, Structure of Output, 2005, 2009

Country	Agriculture (% of GDP)		Industry (% of GDP)		Services (% of GDP)	
	2005	2009	2005	2009	2005	2009
Brunei Darussalam	3.6	1.2	48.3	53.0	48.1	45.8
Cambodia (2004)	32.9	30.1	29.2	26.8	37.9	43.2
Indonesia	13.4	13.6	45.8	44.7	40.8	44.7
Laos	47.0	33.6	27.3	25.0	25.7	41.4
Malaysia	8.4	7.5	49.8	46.6	41.8	55.9
Myanmar (2002)	54.6	N/A	13.0	N/A	32.3	N/A
Philippines	14.4	18.1	32.6	32.1	53.0	49.8
Singapore	0.1	0.0	32.5	30.4	67.4	69.5
Thailand	9.9	9.2	44.1	46.6	46.0	44.3
Vietnam	20.9	17.1	41.0	40.6	38.1	44.4

Source: Asian Development Bank: *Asian Development Outlook, 2006* (for 2005), *Asian Development Outlook, 2011* (for 2009).

It is in this table that the lessons begin to become startlingly apparent. We see that the industrial share of the economy is higher in Vietnam, Thailand, Malaysia, Indonesia and Brunei than it is in the Philippines. The high figures for domestic capital growth formation in Cambodia and Viet Nam we saw in Table 3 obviously have a direct bearing on this. Moreover, our table is a snapshot in time, concealing the fact that the industrial share of the economy has been at much the same level in the Philippines for some time, whereas it some other countries it has been steadily growing. Table 5 reveals the process underway.

TABLE 5: Industry as % of GDP, ASEAN Countries, 1988-2005

Country	1988	1990	1995	2001	2002	2003	2004	2005	2006	2007	2008	2009	2010
Brunei	52.3	54.8	43.9	46.1	45.1	46.0	49.2	48.3	-	56.6	54.8	53.0	52.5
Cambodia	13.7	11.2	14.8	24.9	26.5	27.8	29.2	-	30.2	30.2	29.5	26.8	28.6
Indonesia	37.3	39.1	41.8	46.8	44.6	43.6	44.0	45.8	43.7	43.0	42.1	41.7	41.1
Laos	11.9	14.5	19.1	23.7	24.7	25.9	27.3	-	32.0	22.7	23.3	25.0	27.7
Malaysia	38.1	41.5	40.5	46.0	45.2	46.5	48.5	49.8	44.9	40.5	39.1	36.6	36.9
Myanmar	10.3 (1987)	10.5	9.9	10.6	13.0	-	-	-	16.5	19.8	-	-	-
Philippines	35.2	34.5	32.1	31.6	31.8	32.0	31.9	32.6	32.5	32.5	32.8	32.1	32.6
Singapore	35.0	32.5	32.9	30.6	30.6	30.3	32.4	32.5	32.1	31.8	30.2	30.4	32.9
Thailand	34.6	37.2	40.8	42.1	42.4	43.6	43.5	44.1	47.2	47.5	48.0	46.6	48.7
Viet Nam	24.0	22.7	28.8	38.1	38.5	39.5	40.2	41.0	41.0	41.8	41.6	41.6	41.9

Sources: Data for the years 1988-2005 are taken from Asian Development Bank, *Asian Development Outlook, 2006*, accessed in the year of publication; data for subsequent years are taken from the 2008, 2009, 2010, 2011 and 2012 editions of the same publication, accessed on April 14, 2012.

While industrial share of GDP in the Philippines has floated down from 35.2 percent, it has registered steady, and in some cases dramatic, progress almost everywhere else. True, it has fluctuated around the halfway mark in oil-rich Brunei, and in Singapore it occupies almost exactly the same share as in the Philippines, but one must bear in mind the small size of

Singapore and the consequent pressure on industrial land-use. Everywhere else, the industrial sector has been expanding for some years, and those countries that have yet to overtake the Philippines in this regard will obviously do so in the fairly near future. This development (in both senses of the word) did not occur by accident: state policy has played a crucial role. In the Philippines, unless a strategic change of direction is adopted by the government, state policy (or its absence) will succeed in ensuring that the country is the least developed in the region, with all which that implies for competitiveness, investment and living standards.

*

We saw in Table 1 that this "export-oriented" economy has a chronic inability to achieve a balance of trade surplus. This problem is systemic: with genuine development, a much greater proportion of inputs in the export sector would be manufactured locally, with the development of backward linkages and the construction of whole industries; as it is, a great many inputs are imported, contributing to successive balance of trade deficits.

To a limited extent, Mrs. Arroyo's record departed from those of her predecessors. At an early stage, the dangers of excessive "liberalization" had become so apparent that even the Makati Business Club, the corporate warrior of EDSA Dos, was reporting that local companies (but especially the small and medium enterprises which account for over 90 percent of Philippine business) were urging a "more careful approach" to liberalization due to factors such as cheap imports and (as in the case of the cement industry, which in Southeast Asia had excess capacity) dumping.[9] Mrs. Arroyo appeared to be listening, and in January 2003 she announced that "unbridled globalization is no longer in vogue" and that tariff liberalization would be slowed down to the minimum required by the World Trade Organization and the ASEAN Free Trade Agreement, taking "full advantage of all exemption windows allowed..."[10]

In October 2003, speaking in Bali after the collapse of the WTO talks in Cancun over the use of agricultural subsidies by developed countries, Mrs. Arroyo told a business audience that ASEAN nations should unite for their collective interest within the WTO for a "just and fair global trading system," and that Cancun had alerted "all nations to refocus on the stark relationship between world poverty and world trade."[11] That month, an executive order raised tariffs on almost 400 items. Trade secretary Roxas (who would enter the Senate in 2004) announced that as the review of finished goods was complete, a review of raw materials would now commence. In April 2004, the government advised the WTO that it would maintain high rice tariffs in order to protect the agricultural sector.

While this approach may have contributed to reducing the government's budget deficit, the revised tariffs had no noticeable impact on imports, which, after falling in 2001, accelerated in the following two years, so that while the high point reached by Estrada in 2000 had been $34.5 billion, by 2003 imports cost $37.5 billion.[12] After Mrs. Arroyo's January 2003 announcement, former senator Wigberto W. Tañada, now lead convenor of the Fair Trade Alliance, complained that

> it comes fairly late in the day. Late in the sense that more than 90 percent of our tariff lines are already under the 0-5 percent tariff regime. Late in the sense that many of our industries, including agriculture, have already suffered serious reverses and losses, with a large number irreparably shut down, permanently.[13]

There were further dangers on the horizon, for the government appeared to want to have its cake and eat it: while, on the one hand, it announced the end of full-blooded liberalization and increased some tariffs, on the other it was keen on concluding as many free trade agreements (FTAs) as possible. The Philippines was already committed to the FTA concluded between ASEAN and China, due to be implemented in full in 2010, but it was under no obligation to join the "early harvest" program, by means of which trade in an agreed range of products could be liberalized on a bilateral basis. "First," said the Fair Trade Alliance's Rene Ofreneo in 2005, "they said there would be no 'early harvest,' but then this was reversed and, as a result, our vegetable farmers in particular are under threat."

Next came negotiation of a Japan-Philippines Economic Partnership Agreement (JPEPA). "Up to now," Ofreneo complained in the same interview, "the responsible undersecretary has not complied with the request of Congress — and our demand — that he hand over a copy of the draft agreement. It's all cloaked in secrecy."[14] In May 2006, government lawyers, arguing "privileged information," asked the Supreme Court to reject a petition by some legislators to halt the negotiations until the draft provisions were made public. The secrecy remained until the agreement was signed by Mrs. Arroyo in Helsinki in September 2006.

It seemed that the Philippines had been holding out for a provision that would allow it, despite the damage already done to the Philippine health service by the exodus of medical staff (see below), to export nurses to Japan. While economic planning secretary Romulo Neri claimed that the agreement would provide over P350 billion in revenues for the Philippines over the following two or three years,[15] a representative of Migrante, the overseas workers' organization, charged that Japan was merely "aiming for a more liberalized entry of Japanese businesses in the Philippines under the guise of a bilateral free trade agreement."[16] It was then alleged that the agreement would allow Japan to export toxic and hazardous waste to the Philippines. This would certainly have explained the secrecy, although the charge was denied by the Japanese Embassy, which pointed out that Japan was bound by a legal framework in this regard. The JPEPA was supposed to take effect 30 days after it had been signed, but, curiously, it was over two months before Arroyo sent it to the Senate where, as the document had treaty status, it would need a two-thirds vote before it could be implemented. The Senate failed to act on it before the midterm elections of May 2007, which saw the opposition and independents take the vast majority of the twelve seats (half the chamber) up for election.

It may seem curious, in view of this, that a few days after she sent the JPEPA to the Senate, Arroyo said that she wanted an FTA with the United States by July 2007 (this was not achieved). It is possible that, fearing that the current Senate would reject the JPEPA, she was pinning her hopes (forlornly, as it turned out) on changing its composition in May. She certainly was not following the advice of Dr Joseph Yap, president of the Philippine Institute for Development Studies, who had argued in a report in May 2006 that most FTAs were knee-jerk reactions to initiatives proposed by other nations. He pointed out that East Asian countries with high growth-rates did not have FTAs, and argued that economic resources should be directed to more developmental tasks, such as addressing weak institutions and uneven wealth distribution, and modernizing agriculture.[17]

The 2003 Bali meeting referred to above had agreed that ASEAN would become a free-trade zone by 2020, the aim being to counter the giant Indian and Chinese economies that were attracting trade and investment that previously might have come to Southeast Asia. Whereas, according to the US-ASEAN Business Council, a decade earlier 75 percent of all US investment in East Asia had gone to the ASEAN countries, that proportion had been reduced to 10 percent, while 80 percent went to China.[18] But while it was true that, given the balance of economic and political forces in the world, countries like the Philippines would need to combine with others in order to strengthen their ability to withstand predators, membership of a free-trade zone might be distinctly counter-productive. The Philippine Chamber of Commerce and Industry (PCCI) revealed that assessments it had commissioned for 24 sectors had found that they were unprepared for liberalized trade. Citing a host of factors, PCCI president Donald G. Dee concluded: "The Philippines therefore cannot blindly pursue liberalization if it seeks to become an industrialized state."[19] Nevertheless, despite the fact that trade secretary Peter Favila had argued against the proposal, the target date for the ASEAN FTA was brought forward to 2015.

*

The annual averages for the rate of unemployment cited in Table 1 are somewhat misleading in that they conceal the wild swings caused by the temporary nature of many "jobs" and the regional and seasonal variations. Thus, while the annual average for 2002 was 11.4 percent, in April of that year it had been as high as 13.9 percent. While the rate fell to 10.2 percent in July the same year, twelve months later it was back up to 12.6 percent,[20] falling back thereafter. In January 2004, having hit 11 percent (3.9 million) again nationally, the rate in the national capital region was 16.9 percent.

In her inaugural speech on June 30, 2004, Mrs. Arroyo had pledged to create between 6 and 10 million new jobs by the end of her term in 2010. We saw in Table 1, however, that the number of "employed" increased by just 4.7 million in that period - although that might be viewed as something of an achievement, as it exceeded labor-market growth by 1.5 million, the size of the labor force, comparing the Labor Force Survey (LFS) for 2004 with that for 2010, having increased by only 3.2 million. But did it? Is an average annual labor-force increase of merely 533,333 credible? When one considers that the labor force grew by 6.4 million over the whole nine years July 2001-July 2010 (i.e. an average annual increase of 711, 111), the former figure seems anomalous — and even more so when we compare it with the 2001-2004 annual average of 1.066 million (3.2 million for the three-year period). Why would the rate slow to just over half of that in the following six years? One effect of this decline, of course, was to reduce the rate of unemployment from what it would have been had the previous rate of labor-force increase been maintained — and this, as we will see, explains the conundrum.

In June 2005, the government announced that in April that year unemployment had fallen to 8.3 percent (2.9 million), from the January figure of 11.3 percent (4.03 million).[21] Had this been true, it would have been cause for celebration, but the government had merely amended the method of calculation, leaving out those not seeking work. Using the previous formula, unemployment was 12.9 percent (4.786 million).[22] This largely explains the anomaly regarding the labor-force growth figures noted above: the growth-rate slowed, it is now apparent, for the simple reason that almost 2 million people (and rising) were no longer counted. Thus, in actual fact job-creation did *not* exceed labor-force growth. If the average annual rate of labor-force growth of 3.27 percent for the period July 2001-July 2004 is applied to the period July 2004-July 2010, we arrive at a labor force of 42.82 million as opposed to the officially-cited 39 million. Restoration of the hidden millions would mean that in the period July 2001-July 2010 the labor force would have grown by 10.2 million as opposed to the official 6.4 million, outstripping the additional number of "employed" of 7 million.

But what of the "jobs" that *were* created? As Rene Ofreneo has pointed out, many of these are temporary or casual, or are "precarious," i.e. subject to poor conditions.[23] This was almost certainly bound to be the case, due to the fact that Mrs. Arroyo lifted the prohibition of labor-only subcontracting, known by workers the world over as a recipe for worsened wages and conditions. In addition, it should be understood that under the LFS system a person need only have worked one hour in the reference week to qualify as employed. Mahar Mangahas of Social Weather Stations (SWS) believes that this innovation was introduced in 2005 (the same time, as we have seen, the method of counting the unemployed was changed), and "shows excessive intent in classifying persons surveyed as employed." SWS's own unemployment surveys, he says, did not differ greatly from the government's until that same year, and then the divergence became dramatic. By way of illustration, the SWS survey conducted in March 2012 produced an unemployment figure of 34.4 percent, compared to the government's January figure (the Aquino administration having declined to correct the sleight of hand introduced by its predecessor) of 7.2 percent.[24]

A consideration of the status of the "employed" brings home the underdeveloped state of the Philippine economy.

TABLE 6: Status of the "employed," July 2004 and July 2010 (%)

Year	Wage & Salary Workers	Own Account Workers	Unpaid Family Workers
2004	52.8	36.0	11.2
2010	53.2	34.8	12.0

Source: Labor Force Survey, July 2004, July 2010.

The next table gives the same analysis by numbers of workers.

TABLE 7: Status of the "employed," July 2004 and July 2010 (millions)

Year	Wage & Salary Workers	Own Account Workers	Unpaid Family Workers
2004	16.7	11.9	3.5
2010*	19.3	12.6	4.35

* By 2010, the LFS had ceased to express these classifications numerically. These figures are arrived at by multiplying the 36.3 million "employed" by the percentages in the survey.

We see, therefore, that in contrast to the six to ten million jobs promised by Mrs. Arroyo in 2004, that six-year term saw the creation of just 2.6 million waged and salaried positions, an increase of 700,000 own-account workers (who can be anything from employers of labor to street pedlars) and 850,000 extra unpaid family workers. (The total of 4.15 million, it will be noted, falls rather short of the 4.7 million derived from the "employed" figures.) Given the fact that 46.8 percent of "employed" in July 2010 were either own-account or unpaid family workers, it is apparent that even before the Arroyo government changed the LFS methodology in 2005, the unemployment rate had been grossly understated and that, excessive though they might seem at first glance, the rates calculated by Mangahas's SWS surveys might be much nearer the truth.

Moreover, according to the July 2010 LFS, no less than 35 percent of those "employed" worked less than 40 hours a week, indicating a significant underemployment problem. The same survey shows that in a country with a pressing need for the development of a manufacturing base, only 14.9 percent worked in industry (a mere 8.3 percent in manufacturing), while 33.9 percent were employed in agriculture and 51.2 percent in services.[25]

*

Filipinos continued to flock overseas. During the controversy surrounding the execution of overseas worker Flor Contemplacion in Singapore during the Ramos regime, it had been said that the creation of a million jobs a year was required to stem the flow, but we saw above that Mrs. Arroyo did not manage this and, in addition, many of the jobs created were of an inadequate or temporary nature, and so now the number of OFWs increased more dramatically than ever, in addition to which the government came to view them and their remittances as a component of economic policy.

Three weeks after entering Malacañang, Mrs. Arroyo said she hoped that Filipinos would no longer need to seek employment abroad, as she was determined to fight poverty, but by August labor secretary Patricia Sto. Tomas was announcing that, with 466,663 applications processed in the first six months, 2001 was going to be a bumper year.[26] And so, by the time she spoke to OFWs in Singapore that same month, Mrs. Arroyo's tune had changed, as she admitted: "The Philippine economy will be, for the foreseeable future, heavily dependent still on overseas workers' remittances."[27]

The mass exodus was having an alarming effect on the Philippine health service. In May 2002, presidential adviser on job creation Luis Lorenzo observed that many doctors were

217

retraining as nurses in the hope of achieving better-paid employment in the USA and UK. In December of that year, it was revealed that no less than 150,000 Filipino nurses were working abroad.[28] In a ten-year period, 3,500 doctors had retrained as nurses and left the country, while ten percent of Philippine hospitals closed between 2002 and 2005, by which time a further 5,500 doctors were enrolled in nursing schools.[29] Negros Oriental Provincial Hospital had a requirement for 75 doctors, but six had already left for the USA and only seven of the remaining 43 had not studied nursing.[30]

In a full-page advertisement on March 23, 2006, the Fair Trade Alliance (FTA), which brings together nationalist business groups and labor organizations, warned that overseas employment was turning into the country's "gravedigger." Although 5 million OFWs and 3 million emigrants "directly support the needs of one-fourth of the population," the outflow of skills "is threatening to decimate the few but vital industries that we still have."

Apart from medical staff, the exodus consisted of radio frequency engineers (text-messaging and communications), linemen (electricity), first mates (shipping), plant engineers (steel, petrochemicals, etc.), and pilots, aircraft mechanics (of the previous 14,684, only 1,500 remained) and air traffic controllers. The FTA demanded stricter regulation to restrict the export of "mission-critical personnel" and professionals, and the passage of legislation requiring such personnel to remain in post for a minimum period before being allowed to leave the country. Salaries, said the organization, should be upgraded, along with the formulation of an integrated human resources development program, a "reinvigorated and integrated agro-industrial development program," and a review of the economic policies promoted by the IMF and World Bank and the migration policy to which they had led.

Even the Asian Development Bank warned that as the Philippine diaspora contained a disproportionate number of 25-44 year-olds—the most productive—the continued brain drain could discourage foreign investment, as often happened when emigrants were disproportionately skilled and education expenditure became a subsidy for the destination countries.[31]

During her December 2002 trip to Japan,[32] it became apparent that Mrs. Arroyo now regarded Filipino labor as little different from any other export commodity, as she proposed a discussion on free trade with Japan that, with an eye to Japan's aging population, would encompass human resources. Similarly, in the initial stages of the war in Iraq, Foreign Affairs Secretary Blas Ople said that the Philippines expected to be "awarded" 100,000 jobs in the reconstruction of that country. A month later, the administration was making the more modest estimate that between 30,000 and 50,000 OFWs would be hired in the initial restructuring phase. This target would be abandoned when, after the election, the government banned deployments to Iraq after a Filipino worker was kidnapped; and yet still there were 6,000 Filipinos there, most of them working for contractors on US bases, having entered Iraq from third countries.

In March 2004, the Department of Labor and Employment (DOLE) expected OFW deployment to increase by 25-28 percent in the first half of the year. January's deployments had hit a phenomenal 111,879, a 23.3 percent increase on January 2003. Remittances in 2003 were $7.6 billion, and the government was now aiming for $8 billion in 2004. This target was exceeded, reaching $8.5 billion. This amount made a very substantial contribution to the economy, equaling 10.5 percent of GDP, or 20 percent of export earnings.[33] Having started by expressing the hope that Filipinos might soon not have to travel abroad for employment, the Arroyo government was now encouraging them to do so. Nor was that all: labor secretary Patricia Sto. Tomas suggested that OFWs be counted in the workforce, an innovation which would, without creating a single new job, have reduced the unemployment rate.

Targets were now set for annual deployments. The 2004 target of one million deployments was not reached as, after the early increases, figures for the whole year were flat. The target was reset for 2005, when the opening of new "markets" for hotel, restaurant and casino workers, healthcare staff and others gave government planners confidence that it would be reached—and, indeed, the half-million mark was reached in the first six months. Once again, the full-year figures fell short, but in 2006 the one million mark was passed by November.

When Israel mounted its assault on Lebanon in 2006, it became clear that some Filipinos were prepared to take considerable risks to avoid returning to a life of poverty in the Philippines. In early August, Mrs. Arroyo (while refusing to denounce the Israeli attack) ordered all OFWs in Lebanon to return home. This met with a less than enthusiastic response. It was true that there were a number of problems: perhaps more than half the Filipinos in the country were undocumented; initially, there was considerable confusion regarding the funding of the evacuation; and some Lebanese employers took steps to prevent their staff from leaving.

But many OFWs simply refused to leave, telling the Philippine officials that they had not been repatriated during their host country's long civil war and saw no reason to be driven home by mere air strikes.[34] Of the 30-40,000 OFWs in the country, only 6,287 had arrived home by mid-October.[35] It was estimated by DOLE that, during the same period, a further two to three thousand undocumented Filipino workers had entered Lebanon.[36] For those who were repatriated, there was a promise from Mrs. Arroyo that they would be offered retraining to include skills such as first aid and evacuation of high-rise buildings in the event of fire, transforming them into "supermaids."[37]

Table 8 traces the export of unemployment over the years. We see from this the perhaps surprising fact that the number of deployments really began to take off during the Aquino years (1986-1992), when, comparing her last full year (1991) with 1985, they registered a cumulative increase of 65 percent. Under Ramos and Estrada (1992-2000), there was a further increase of just 22.6 percent, whereas when we compare deployments in 2000 with those in 2010 we find an increase of 74.76 percent.

TABLE 8: Deployment of OFWs, 1984-2010*

Year	Landbased	Growth Rate (%)	Seabased	Growth Rate (%)	Total	Growth Rate (%)
1984	300,378	-	50,064	-	350,983	-
1985	320,494	6.7	52,290	3.33	372,784	6.21
1986	323,517	0.94	54,697	4.6	378,214	1.46
1987	382,229	18.15	67,042	22.57	449,271	18.79
1988	385,117	0.76	85,913	28.15	471,030	4.84
1989	355,346	-7.73	103,280	20.21	458,626	-2.63
1990	334,883	-5.76	111,212	7.68	446,095	-2.73
1991	489,260	46.1	125,759	13.08	615,019	37.87
1992	546,655	12.34	136,806	8.78	686,461	11.62
1993	550,872	0.22	145,758	6.54	696,630	1.48
1994	564,031	2.39	154,376	5.91	718,407	3.13
1995	488,173	-13.45	165,401	7.14	653,574	-9.02
1996	484,653	-0.72	175,469	6.09	660,122	1.0
1997	559,227	15.39	188,469	7.41	747,696	13.27
1998	638,343	14.15	193,300	2.56	831,643	11.23
1999	640,331	0.31	196,689	1.75	837,020	0.65
2000	643,304	0.46	198,324	0.83	841,628	0.55
2001	662,648	3.0	204,951	3.3	867,599	3.08
2002	682,315	3.0	209,595	2.3	891,908	2.80
2003	651,935	-4.45	216,031	3.07	867,969	-2.68
2004	704,586	8.01	229,002	6.0	933,588	7.56
2005	740,632	5.12	247,983	8.29	988,615	5.89
2006	788,070	6.41	274,497	10.7	1,062,567	7.5
2007	811,070	2.92	266,553	-2.89	1,077,623	1.42
2008	974,399	20.14	261,614	-1.85	1,236,013	14.7
2009	1,092,162	12.09	330,424	26.3	1,422,586	15.09
2010	1,123,676	2.86	347,150	5.06	1,470,826	3.39

Source: Philippine Overseas Employment Administration

*It must be stressed that the annual deployments are not all new hirings. Contracts are usually for three years, and thus it is possible for an individual to have appeared in the statistics several times. As of December 2009, the Philippine Overseas Employment Administration estimated that there were a total of 8,579,378 Filipinos abroad, including "irregulars."

Even more dramatic than the increase in deployments has been the increase in OFW remittances, as Table 9 clearly shows.

TABLE 9: OFW Remittances, 1997-2010 (US$ billions)

Year	Total	Landbased	Seabased
1997	5.742	5.484	0.258
1998	4.926	4.651	0.275
1999	6.795	5.948	0.846
2000	6.05	5.124	0.927
2001	6.031	4.938	1.093
2002	6.886	5.687	1.199
2003	7.578	6.280	1.298
2004	8.550	7.085	1.465
2005	10.689	9.020	1.669
2006	12.8	10.812	1.949
2007	14.45	12.214	2.236
2008	16.43	-	-
2009	17.35	-	-
2010	18.76	-	-

Source: Philippine Overseas Employment Administration

Although deployments may have increased by 74.76 percent since 2000, the amount of money these workers sent home each year had, by 2010, increased by 210 percent. Speaking in January 2008, labor secretary Arturo Brion explained that one reason for the recent dramatic increase in remittances lay in the fact that "we have more professional and skilled workers going overseas..." By 2006, 60 percent of all OFWs deployed were professionals.[38]

Had this increase in remittances not taken place, the amounts sent would have been insufficient to convert the trade deficits into balance of payments surpluses, and presumably for this reason the Arroyo government, more than any other, encouraged OFWs to send money home, persuading banks to reduce charges and taking a number of measures to facilitate the transactions. Table 9, however, refers to sums sent through official channels; in addition, it is estimated that a further $2 billion arrived through informal channels in 2005, and this was expected to increase to $2.8 billion in 2006.[39]

Of course, when these huge sums reach the Philippines, they do not lie idle, but feed through into a number of economic headings and activities. But precious little is used as development capital, most finding its way into private consumption. To a certain extent, this is perfectly understandable, as most OFWs tear themselves away from their families in order to house, feed and clothe them. But at the end of the day, that would be best accomplished by the creation of new economic capacity within the domestic sector. In this sense, a key opportunity is being missed.

In the long run, it must be recognized that increasing flows of OFW remittances, far from being an economic strength, are an indication of the weakness of the domestic economy — which may be further weakened by the fact that, as we have seen, over half the emigrants are professionals.

*

In August 2004, eleven economists at the University of the Philippines predicted that economic collapse was two or three years away unless both the debt and the budget deficit were brought under control. However, their suggested remedies differed little from those already proposed by Mrs. Arroyo and the IMF, and nationalist observers accused the UP professors of ideological bias, neglecting to mention the role which globalization had played in reducing customs revenues and destroying much of the business tax base, and of displaying a distinct reticence in discussing any remedy for the foreign debt which departed from full repayment. Mrs. Arroyo then announced there was a "fiscal crisis" and that the pain was "imminent." When both share prices and the peso then took a dive, ministers scrambled to clarify that the situation had not yet deteriorated to the extent of a crisis, and that Mrs. Arroyo (the economics expert) had used the term "rhetorically." Many observers believed she had been trying to frighten Congress into passing the tax laws recommended by the IMF.

The government attempted to overcome its budget deficit with the proceeds from privatization, but there were two major problems here: it was running out of enterprises to sell, and some of those offered were unattractive to prospective buyers.[40] In 2004, the target budget deficit was P197.8 billion, slightly less than in 2003 (in fact, the government would do better than anticipated, reducing it to P186.1 billion, for although the expenditure target was exceeded, revenue was higher than targeted). With little in the way of privatization proceeds, the plan was to simply borrow to plug the shortfall.

As of February 2004, however, the consolidated public debt was already P5.39 trillion (130 percent of GDP), almost half of it owed to foreign lenders. Total foreign debt (public and private) was $56.7 billion at the end of March,[41] by which time the international community was worried about a possible default. Senator Ralph Recto warned that the Philippines was caught in a trap, as inadequate revenues forced it to borrow more to service its debt, and that the "debt meter ticks like a time bomb."[42] Moreover, most borrowing was undertaken simply to repay and service previous debts. Thus, in 2005 the government planned to borrow P125 billion from the foreign market and P475 billion from domestic lenders, of which P385 billion would be used to repay maturing principal on previous loans. In the draft 2005 budget Mrs. Arroyo submitted to Congress, one third of the total would go on interest rates, overtaking public salaries for the first time. With maturing principal (an "off-budget" item) added, debt payments would equate to around two-thirds of the budget.

Even so, the total foreign debt declined somewhat in 2004, closing that year at $54.4 billion, although by March 2005 it had climbed back to $55.3 billion.[43] The decline was not really as healthy as it seemed, for while principal had been paid off, some debt papers had been sold to Philippine residents, simply transforming foreign debt into domestic debt. Walden Bello noted that, while the official story was that around 47 percent of total debt was foreign, some sources estimated that the true figure might be 80 percent, if debt owed to resident foreigners was included.[44] In April 2005, the IMF expressed concern regarding the extent of Philippine banks' exposure to government debt papers—as well it might, for the government's indebtedness had increased by 13.6 percent in the year December 2003 to December 2004.[45] Comparisons with Argentina began to be made.

In order to cope with this nightmare, Mrs. Arroyo put forward a whole raft of new taxes – most of them proposed by the IMF—along with reductions in national and local government expenditure and a review of tax perks granted to foreign investors (somewhat surprisingly, the IMF had also proposed the latter measure. In 2003, these perks amounted to P230 billion, more than enough to cover the budget deficit). Mrs. Arroyo faced resistance to any reduction of local government expenditure, and there were soon indications of a retreat on this front.

Arroyo proposed eight new revenue measures: a move to gross income tax; repeal of VAT and its replacement by a system easier to administer; a tax on windfall telecom income; increased "sin" (i.e. tobacco and alcohol) taxes; increased taxes on petroleum products; a "lateral attrition bill" that would provide a system of penalties and rewards for the revenue-collection agencies; the rationalization of investment incentives; and a general amnesty for current defaulters. By and large, of course, these were regressive taxes that would intensify the plight of the poor, who already shouldered a disproportionate share of the tax burden (Briones points out that in 2006 regressive or indirect taxes constituted 59 percent of total projected revenue[46]).

The very prospect of new taxes (no mention of which, pointed out Senator Joker Arroyo, had been made during Mrs. Arroyo's 2004 election campaign) caused real consternation among legislators, as they were now being asked to vote for measures that would impact negatively upon those who had just elected them to office. Many argued that existing tax laws should be implemented to the hilt before new ones were considered. Senate Minority Leader Aquilino Pimentel Jr. quoted a finance department study showing that each year the government failed to collect 72.7 percent of individual income tax, 39.8 percent of corporate income tax and 49.4 percent of VAT.[47] (Similarly, in 2006 the bureau of internal revenue found that, of the 49,225 business establishments it had checked as of July, 24,656 had committed at least one violation of the tax code.[48]) The government's case was not helped when it was revealed that courts dealing with 14 cases of corporate tax fraud had thrown them out due to "failure to prosecute" by the customs authorities.

Business had rather more success than the opposition. After Arroyo met tobacco companies, the proposals for sin taxes were watered down. The telecom proposal was dropped. Rather than being abolished and replaced, VAT would be increased from 10 percent to 12 percent and the exemptions removed; thus the proposal to increase taxes on petroleum products was withdrawn, as they would now be subject to VAT.

Although Arroyo had asked that all measures be passed by Christmas 2004, only the increase in sin taxes made it. The proposal to increase VAT faced the greatest difficulty, and it was several months before the deadlock was broken by a suggestion by Senator Ralph Recto: why not leave the rate at 10 percent, but grant Arroyo "standby authority" to impose the further 2 percent herself if it was found necessary? This clinched the matter, for legislators could now tell their constituents that their hands were clean, and that it was the president, not them, who had raised the rate to 12 percent. And this, of course, is precisely what she did. The drive to remove or rationalize fiscal incentives granted to investors made little progress.[49]

The results of the tax offensive were less cheering than anticipated. In April 2006, the take on excise taxes was down 19 percent on a year earlier, (decreases of 25 percent for alcohol, 7 percent for tobacco and 32 percent for petroleum products). The VAT increase was not implemented until February 2006, in which year the revenue bureau's collection fell P31 billion short of the target set for it; the customs bureau's collection came in at only slightly over target, but 29 percent up on the previous year.[50] We will see below that, while the budget deficit was substantially reduced, it was debatable whether the "sin taxes" and the increased VAT made the major contribution to this.

*

If the Arroyo administrations had achieved real economic success, the Philippines would have seen a dramatic reduction in poverty. According to official figures, poverty incidence declined from 27.5 percent of families (33 percent of the population) in 2000 to 24.4 percent of families (30.0 percent of the population) in 2003. The poor are defined as those with "income short of the minimum cost of satisfying the basic requirements." It was claimed that the improvement over the three years meant that 1.6 million people had been lifted out of poverty. But the national averages, which were themselves disputed (see below), were misleading, as in some areas poverty became more widespread. No less than seven of the ten poorest provinces were on the southern island of Mindanao, and in the poorest, Zamboanga del Norte, poverty incidence increased from 47 percent in 2000 to 64.6 percent in 2003.[51]

The claims of poverty reduction were challenged. Dr Ernesto M. Pernia, an economist at the University of the Philippines, pointed to the inconvenient fact that, according to the 2003 Family Income and Expenditure Survey, real total family incomes had declined by 2.9 percent. How did this square with the claim that poverty incidence had been reduced? In fact the average income of families fell 10 percent in real terms from 2000 to 2003.[52] According to Salil Shetty, UN Millennium Development Goals campaign director, lack of political will and financial resources were having an adverse effect on efforts to reduce poverty, and he expressed doubt regarding the official figures. The Asian Development Bank, meanwhile, held the view that poverty incidence had increased between 2000 and 2003.[53] Official figures for 2006 (released in March 2008) were more believable, indicating that 32.9 percent of the population (up from 30 percent in 2003) was now impoverished, and that 14.6 percent (up from 13.5 percent) were food-poor.[54]

It may be argued that the self-rated poverty surveys conducted every three months since the mid-1980s by Social Weather Stations (SWS) come up with highly subjective results. In that respondents are asked whether they *think* their family is poor (or "not poor," or "on the line"), this is of course true. But use of the results for comparative purposes can certainly provide an indication of popular perceptions regarding poverty. For example, an average of 56.5 percent of the respondents in the four surveys conducted in 2000 considered their families to be poor, while in 2003 this figure had increased to 59.5 percent. In 2004, the four-survey average declined to 51.25 percent (electoral largesse may have played a part in this), climbing back to 52.75 percent in 2005 and 54.25 percent in 2006.

The SWS survey in March 2006 showed that moderate hunger (where respondents claimed that their families had not had anything to eat "once or a few times" in the previous three months) affected 12.8 percent (the same as December 2005, the highest figure since this survey began in July 1998), while severe hunger (where respondents claimed that their families had experienced hunger "often or always" in the previous three months) affected 4.2 percent (a figure exceeded only twice—in March 2000, when it hit 5.4 percent, and November 1998, when it was 5.3 percent—since July 1998). The percentages claiming moderate or severe hunger in the following three 2006 surveys were, respectively: 10.1 and 3.4 (June); 12.3 and 4.6 (September); and 15.1 and 3.9 (November). Thus, in November 2006, overall hunger of 19 percent was the highest recorded since the surveys began in 1998, as was moderate hunger, while severe hunger of 3.9 percent compared to the July 1998-November 2006 average of 3.2 percent.[55]

If the SWS surveys were accurate, it was clear that Filipinos did not believe that they were appreciably less poor or hungry. When, in March 2007, the SWS survey had overall hunger stuck at 19 percent for the second quarter running, Mrs. Arroyo made two mistakes: first, she ordered appropriate departments to reduce poverty and hunger over the next six months (thus creating "anti-poverty" expenditure during a midterm election campaign) without addressing the fundamental and long-term problems; then, with what one editorial called "abysmal insensitivity," she quipped that, having skipped the odd meal, she had also experienced hunger during the previous three months.[56]

In 2005, the Department of Social Welfare and Development claimed that of the 17 million children aged between two and ten, 12 million were malnourished; 39 percent between three and six were short, 28.3 percent were underweight, and 3.5 percent were thin.[57] The same year, a survey by the Department of Science and Technology's food and nutrition research institute found that higher food prices had meant that, in the previous decade, the consumption of nutritious food was below the recommended amounts. The average Filipino diet was short of Vitamins A and C, riboflavin, iron and calcium, and over half of Filipinos were not receiving the recommended average daily intake of energy.[58]

*

In the debate on the export of unemployment, the Catholic Bishops Conference of the Philippines (CBCP), through its Episcopal Commission for the Pastoral Care of Migrants and Itinerant People, urged the government to cease its attempts to increase emigration and, instead, address its causes—poverty and unemployment. However, the persistence of high poverty-rates, continuing high unemployment and, therefore, increasing numbers of OFWs, is in part a result of the high birthrate. On this question, of course, the Catholic Church is dogmatic and inflexible, opposing all forms of artificial birth control, and thus it makes a major contribution to the immiseration of Filipinos.

Prior to 2005, Mrs. Arroyo did nothing to encourage birth control for, just as she looked to the World Bank and IMF for economic guidance and (apart from a violent hiccup in 2004) the White House for her foreign policy, on this matter she followed the lead, at least initially, of the Vatican.[59] During her first two weeks in office, she stated: "We will push for responsible parenthood and a population policy that is in keeping with our culture."[60] Even though the Commission on Population in March 2001 reported a slowing of population growth over the previous 20 years, it would need to slow further if economic growth was not to be compromised, for, according to the Asian Development Bank, if current trends continued the Philippines would have difficulty in feeding the 160 million-strong population it would have in 30 years' time. Although in late 2002 the executive director of the commission expressed the hope that the government would still be able to reduce the rate, there seemed to be little chance of this because the health department had allocated no funds for the purchase of contraceptives for the following year and USAID, which had provided 80 percent of the country's contraceptive needs for three decades, had said it would stop funding the pill, inter-uterine devices and condoms.

Mrs. Arroyo defended her population policy (based on "moral choice") and in her radio program argued that the answer was to fight poverty; but the US-based Human Rights Watch warned that in following the policy of the Catholic Church on birth control (to the extent that some local officials banned condoms from health centers), the government was risking a "possible explosion" of the AIDS virus.[61] As an interesting counterpoint to Mrs. Arroyo's ideological commitment to further pauperization by population growth, in March 2004 200 Muslim clerics meeting in Davao issued a fatwah which gave the green light to family planning, including contraceptive use, although it forbade vasectomy and ligation.

After the election of 2004, the profile of this issue was raised when Congressman Edcel Lagman and others authored a bill aimed at encouraging a two-child policy, and reproductive health by persuasion and the dissemination of information. Then in February 2005, in an unexpected change of tack, the government launched its Ligtas-Buntis (Safe Pregnancy) campaign, which saw 15,000 health workers distributing reproductive information and 1.6 million contraceptive devices. Health secretary Manuel Dayrit, who had previously maintained that it was not the job of his department to distribute condoms, now made the alarming claim that 30 percent of Filipino couples were unaware that sexual intercourse led to conception, with some believing that children were simply gifts from God.[62] Even so, Dayrit was not happy in his new role, and he resigned a few months later. The CBCP came out fighting, claiming that both the bill and the campaign were assaults upon the family, and a pastoral letter from CBCP president Archbishop Fernando Capalla attempted to sabotage the campaign by saying that Catholic health workers had "the right of conscientious objection" and that, indeed, it was their Christian duty to insist upon this right.[63]

Edcel Lagman complained that Capalla and other church leaders had been texting congressmen to persuade them to withdraw support for the legislation, but when he challenged the CBCP to publicly debate his bill, Archbishop Ramon Arguelles was loftily dismissive: "We do not accept a 'kanto boy' [street tough] challenge like that. When someone challenges the president, do you think the president will go down to that level?"[64] This was an indication of how the Catholic Church regarded its position in Philippine society, regardless of the constitutional separation of church and state.

A further argument deployed by prelates was that the Lagman bill encouraged abortion, which it patently did not. In fact, in this country where the procedure was illegal, there were already a staggering 400,000 abortions a year, accounting for one in six pregnancies, and abortion was the fourth leading cause of maternal deaths. Thus, with twelve women dying each day from birth- or pregnancy-related causes, the Legislators' Committee on Population and Development Foundation warned that the church was "endangering thousands of lives."[65]

But that did not stop the church, and soon there were reports that Catholic health workers involved in the Ligtas-Buntis campaign were being denied communion. Bishops in the island province of Bohol, where the claim first surfaced, denied this, but Monsignor Jesus Dosado of Ozamiz, Misamis Oriental, was quite unambiguous: health workers who admitted to participating in the campaign would, he said, be barred from taking communion.[66] Lagman's bill, meanwhile, was bogged down in Congress, and Manuel Dayrit's replacement as health secretary (president of the Philippine Health Insurance Corporation Francisco Duque, who had rendered Mrs. Arroyo valuable assistance in her 2004 election campaign) announced that Ligtas-Buntis would need to be reviewed before any decision on its continuation.

It is against this background that much of the Catholic Church's mounting opposition to Mrs. Arroyo later in 2005 must be viewed. Following this, little more was heard of the issue, and when Arroyo left office in June 2010 the legislation had still not been passed.

*

Despite the anxious murmurings at home and abroad in 2004 and 2005, the threatened fiscal crisis did not materialize. The budget deficit, which stood at P210.741 billion in 2002, was reduced to P146.778 billion by 2005, and P62.2 billion in 2006. The new taxes constituted just one of several reasons for this. As Congress could not agree on the budget for 2006, the previous year's budget was re-enacted, meaning that there was no programmed growth (a saving of P28.2 billion). Also, the huge surge in OFW remittances already noted contributed, along with the weakness of the dollar, to a significant improvement in the value of the peso, which ended 2006 at just above P49 to the dollar (a year later, it was P41 to the dollar). The stronger peso meant, in turn, that interest payments on the external debt were now, as they were made in dollars, lower (a saving of P29.9 billion[67]), and, due to the narrowing budget deficit, the level of new borrowings could be reduced. However, this virtuous cycle was dependent upon the substantial element of chance in the currency markets and the continuing growth in OFW remittances, which in turn depended upon increasing numbers of OFWs and the persistence of the conditions that drove them abroad.

In mid-2007, with revenue-collection flagging, Mrs. Arroyo sacked internal revenue commissioner Mario Buñag for failing to meet his targets. Buñag claimed that the targets had been met, but admitted having massaged the figures for 2006 by, urged on by finance secretary Margarito Teves, asking large tax-payers to make advance payments.[68] Mrs. Arroyo promised that there would be no new taxes and that revenue from the existing ones would be maximized. While the Bureau of Internal Revenue was reorganized, however, the government also announced its intention to privatize assets worth P105 billion by the end of the year in order to plug the revenue gap. The achievement of this latter goal hardly demonstrated that the chronic deficit had been tamed, as this was a step that could only be taken once.

The results for the first six months demonstrated just how serious the backsliding was: revenue collections were adrift by P51 billion and the deficit, despite the fact that the peso had continued to strengthen throughout the semester, had reached P41 billion (as opposed to the targeted P31.3 billion for the first half and P63 billion for the whole year).[69] By the end of the second semester, the deficit had been wrestled down to P9.4 billion (later adjusted to P12.4 billion), but without privatization proceeds of P90.6 billion it would have been precisely P100 billion (P103 billion, following the adjustment). On paper, this was something of an achievement, as we saw in Table 1 that the deficit now represented just 0.2 percent of GDP. But it was extremely fragile, and as the government increased social spending to offset the effects of the international economic crisis, the deficit would creep up to 0.9 percent of GDP in 2008, 3.9 percent in 2009 and 3.7 percent in 2010. As the government continued to borrow to plug the gap, by 2010 the foreign debt had crept back to $60 billion.

*

There were further "positive" positive results for 2007, but these too were unable to withstand too close an examination. Although GDP grew by 7.3 percent, personal consumption accounted for no less than 77.3 percent of the whole (a result, obviously, of the huge surge in OFW remittances noted above and in Table 9); while capital formation had increased to 17.5 percent of GDP, this was largely due to infrastructural expenditure (in the fourth quarter, construction grew by 17.6 percent, with public construction growing by a third); and, as was usually the case, the service sector contributed the lion's share of the growth with 4.4 percent, while industry and agriculture contributed merely 1.8 percent and 1.2 percent, respectively. Industry's share of GDP was stuck at 32.3 percent.[71] Similarly, behind 2007's balance of payments surplus (at constant 1985 prices) of P19.968 billion lay the uncomfortable fact that merchandise trade was, as usual, in the red, this time to the tune of (at, again, constant 1985 prices) P34.265 billion.[72]

And what enabled the transition from red to black? Of course and as usual, it was those OFW remittances of (at current prices) $14.45 billion.

While there might be no crisis, it was clear that the patient would require continued treatment—or, rather, a different course of treatment.

Any "export-oriented" economy that cannot achieve a balance of trade surplus, has an insufficient rate of capital formation and is, at the end of the day, heavily dependent on regressive indirect taxation, ever-increasing levels of remittances from overseas workers and the continuing weakness of the dollar, can only be described as vulnerable. This vulnerability is increased by the fact that most of the Philippines' export eggs are in one basket: electronics, which accounted for 66 percent in 2005.[73] Furthermore, we have seen that poverty and unemployment (made worse in the Philippines by an approach to population policy rooted in superstition) appear to be persistent features of this "model," giving rise to horrendous social problems that, having been created within the economy, appear again in the form of high crime- and corruption-rates and low educational standards, and then come back to make a further negative impact in the economic sphere. The Philippine economy is, as much as it ever was, susceptible to external shocks, with little domestic capacity to help it weather a heavy storm. This vulnerability is further heightened by the reckless pursuit of free trade agreements, as no attempt is made to build an economic base to compare with those of neighboring countries.

"Industrialization," Jesus Felipe, principal economist at the Asian Development Bank, has urged, "is a step that cannot be bypassed…"[74] At first glance, the example of the Philippines suggests that it can be, as, without an industrial strategy, the country has for several decades been pursuing "growth without development," and it is still around to tell the tale. It might be argued that, given the longevity of this non-strategy, it must be considered sustainable. While it cannot be disputed that it has—although at considerable cost to millions of its citizens—been sustained, it must be doubted that this can continue to be the case.

NOTES

1. Temario C. Rivera, *Landlords & Capitalists: Class, Family, and State in Philippine*

Manufacturing (Quezon City: UP Center for Integrative and Development Studies/UP Press, 1994), 114, citing Sylvia Maxfield and James H. Nolt, "Protectionism and the Internationalisation of Capital: US Sponsorship of Import-Substitution Industrialisation in the Philippines, Turkey and Argentina," *International Studies Quarterly*, No. 34, 1990, 49-81.

2. A detailed account of this operation is given in Robin Broad, *Unequal Alliance, 1979-1986: The World Bank, the International Monetary Fund, and the Philippines* (Quezon City: Ateneo de Manila University Press, 1988).

3. Makati Business Club, *Research Report No. 29*, January 2001.

4. *Asia Pulse*, February 20, 2001.

5. *Daily Tribune*, December 18, 2003.

6. *Philippine Daily Inquirer*, April 1, 2004.

7. *Manila Bulletin*, July 9, 2001.

8. Reuters and www.inq7.net, July 23, 2001.

9. Maricar T. Manuzon, "The Downside of Trade Liberalization," Makati Business Club, *Research Report No. 30*, March 2001.

10. www.inq7.net, January 11, 2003.

11. *Philippine Daily Inquirer*, October 7, 2003.

12. National Statistics Coordination Board.

13. Wigberto E. Tañada, "Nationalism and Unbridled Globalization," in Fair Trade Alliance, *A Nation In Crisis: Agenda For Survival* (Quezon City: FTA, 2004).

14. Rene Ofreneo, interviewed by current writer, August 2005.

15. www.inq7.net, September 12, 2006.

16. Ibid., September 11, 2006.

17. Dr Joseph Yap, "The boom in FTAs: let prudence reign," reported in *Daily Tribune*, May 6, 2006.

18. *Philippine Daily Inquirer*, October 8, 2003.

19. *BusinessWorld*, November 10-11, 2006.

20. National Statistics Coordination Board. In April 2004, the unemployment rate hit 13.7 percent.

21. www.inq7.net, June 16, 2005.

22. *Daily Tribune*, June 16, 2005.

23. Rene Ofreneo, "An Employment Strategy for the Next Administration," *Manila Times*, February 26, 2004.

24. Mahar Mangahas, "Is 1 hour a week a 'job?" *Philippine Daily Inquirer*, May 25, 2012.

25. Labor Force Survey data can be most readily obtained from the National Statistics Office site at www.census.gov.ph.

26. www.inq7.net, August 4, 2001.

27. Agence France Presse, August 26, 2001.

28. *Manila Times*, December 2, 2002.

29. Chit Estella, "Lack of nurses burdens ailing healthcare system," *BusinessWorld*, March 21, 2005.

30. www.inq7.net, May 29, 2005.

31. *Philippine Daily Inquirer*, November 6, 2006.

32. While on this trip, Mrs. Arroyo named her husband as a special envoy for overseas Filipinos in an unthinking move from which, following a torrent of criticism, she was forced to retreat.

33. www.inq7.net, February 16, 2005.

34. Ibid., August 11, 2006.

35. Ibid., October 13, 2006.

36. *Daily Tribune*, November 29, 2006.

37. www.inq7.net, August 4, 2006.

38. Department of Labor and Employment, press release, "Prospects for Filipinos seeking employment abroad remain bright," January 3, 2008.

39. www.inq7.net, June 28, 2006.

40. One project of long-term significance that came on-stream was the Malampaya Deep Water Gas to Power Project, which Mrs Arroyo inaugurated in October 2001. However, the government only had a minority interest (10 percent, held by the Philippine National Oil Corporation, while Texaco and Shell each had 45-percent

Shares), and even this was seen as a potential source of privatization income: in December 2003, it was announced that almost half of PNOC's share would be sold, although the proposal was later shelved.

41. *Daily Tribune*, June 25, 2004.

42. Ibid., December 4, 2003.

43. Ibid., March 22, 2005 and June 25, 2005.

44. Walden Bello, "Debt and denial…or ensuring RP will end up like Argentina," *BusinessWorld*, March 22, 2005.

45. www.inq7.net, March 2, 2005.

46. Leonor Magtolis Briones, "The cost of financing development," Social Watch Philippines, 2006.

47. www.inq7.net, July 29, 2004.

48. Ibid., October 6, 2006.

49. Briones gives a clear indication of the irrational nature of such incentives, citing a University of the Philippines study as demonstrating that those "granted by the Board of Investments in 2004 alone resulted in a negative economic benefit of PHP 55.72 billion (USD 1.1 billion) which means that the amount of foregone revenues due to tax- and duty-free privileges was higher than the amount of economic benefits resulting from the investments for which these perks were provided."[48] (Briones, "The cost of financing development.")

50. *Philippine Daily Inquirer*, January 5, 2007 and January 8, 2007.

51. National Statistical Coordination Board, "Seven of the country's poorest in 2000 out of the poorest list in 2003," posted on NSCB website June 6, 2006.

52. *BusinessWorld*, February 8, 2005.

53. www.inq7.net, May 22, 2005.

54. www.inquirer.net, March 6, 2008.

55. All survey results are available at www.sws.org.ph.

56. Editorial, "Gutom," *Malaya*, March 23, 2007.

57. www.inq7.net, June 17, 2005.

58. Ibid., February 23, 2005.

59. As with contraception, so with divorce: Mrs Arroyo stated her opposition to a proposed divorce bill as Cardinal Sin called divorce "immoral" and "un-Filipino". See www.inq7.net, July 6, 2001. In fact, divorce had been practised in the archipelago before the Spanish conquest, and so it might be argued that it is its prohibition that is "un-Filipino".

60. *Financial Times*, February 2, 2001.

61. www.jnq7.net, May 4, 2004.

62. *Daily Tribune*, March 1, 2005.

63. www.inq7.net, February 2, 2005.

64. Ibid., March 5, 2005.

65. Ibid., March 8, 2005.

66. Ibid., March 17, 2005.

67. *BusinessWorld*, February 2, 2007.

68. *Daily Tribune*, June 21, 2007.

69. Ibid., July 19, 2007.

70. *Manila Bulletin*, March 24, 2012.

71. NSCB press release, "Philippine economy soars to 7.4% GDP growth," January 31, 2008. Data in this paragraph not taken from this source are derived from the NSCB website, www.nscb.gov.ph. Felipe Medalla, NEDA chief under Estrada, took the view that the claimed 7.3 percent growth for 2007 was "in all likelihood, a statistical fiction," and that the true figure was probably 5.5 percent. His predecessor, Cielo Habito, pointed out that low job creation (only 150,000 jobs were created in 2007) was inconsistent with 7.3 percent growth. See Amando Doronila, "The fantasy of the 7.3% GDP growth," *Philippine Daily Inquirer*, March 31, 2008. A Pulse Asia survey, meanwhile, found that 66 percent of respondents believed that the economy had worsened over the previous three years. (*Manila Times*, April 1, 2008.)

72. www.nscb.gov.ph.

73. Asian Development Bank, *Asian Development Outlook, 2006*, 306 and 307.

74. *Daily Tribune*, March 28, 2007.

11 NATIONAL DEVELOPMENT, TRUTH AND

RECONCILIATION

In the approach to the 2010 presidential election campaign, it was feared that Mrs. Arroyo, constitutionally barred from serving a further term as president, planned to seek election as a congresswoman and then, should the post-election balance of forces be favorable, have her allies force through a constitutional change to a parliamentary system in which she might be elected prime minister by her peers, thus retaining her immunity to civil suit.

If plan it was, it came awry, for while Mrs. Arroyo was indeed elected to a congressional seat in her home province of Pampanga, her preferred successor Gilbert Teodoro paid the price of association with her, coming fourth in the presidential race. In first place was Benigno Aquino III, son of the late Corazon Aquino (whose death by cancer created a wave of sentiment leading to his adoption as the Liberal Party candidate) and Benigno "Ninoy" Aquino Jr., assassinated on his return from US exile in 1983. Most members of Congress who were not in the Aquino camp before the election now crossed over in order to ensure they received their share of patronage, thus ensuring that even in the unlikely event of a switch to a parliamentary system, Mrs. Arroyo would not be its beneficiary. Like any other citizen, she could now be sued.

Aquino made it known that he favored punishment for previous presidential wrongdoing, and after a few false starts Mrs. Arroyo found herself under arrest for having allegedly played a role in fixing the senatorial elections of 2007. Suffering from a neck complaint concerning which varying medical opinions were expressed, she was for several months confined in a government veterans' hospital. At the time of writing she is out on bail, but other charges have been leveled against her, her husband and some of her previous associates.

Does this mean, with Mrs. Arroyo off the scene, that the long crisis is over? It does not. The crisis of her presidency may be over, but the longer crisis, created by a combination of the Philippines' colonial history and the dysfunctional economic model dictated by the Bretton Woods twins on behalf of foreign capital, continues. And will continue, because Mr. Aquino has moved to strengthen the "alliance" with Washington and is pursuing an economic program based on "private-public partnerships" that will not take the Philippines a single step down the road of genuine development. By the end of 2011, the foreign debt had reached $61.7 billion.[1]

During Mrs. Arroyo's nine-and-a-half years' tenure, the energy of those who might otherwise have focused their attention to the question of nationalist industrialization was directed instead to the issues discussed in Chapters 3 to 8 of this book. As scandalous as these were, however, and as necessary as it was to engage with them, they were symptoms only; the deep sickness from which they sprang was virtually ignored during the Arroyo decade. It now seems as if Mr. Aquino's single six-year term (2010-2016) will be devoted to merely tackling one of the symptoms—corruption. But while there are individuals who still champion the cause of industrialization, and largely left-wing groups which pay lip-service to that cause, there are still no signs of a campaign being organized behind such a demand.

While reviewing and further developing some of the points made earlier, this chapter will also discuss what such a campaign might look like and what it might achieve.

*

In his *Philippine Daily Inquirer* column on November 20, 2005, sociologist and activist Randy David put forward the view that "the whole liberal framework of constitutionalism and rule of law...is now standing in the way of elite dominance, and that the existing order is unable to perpetuate itself without resorting to blatant violations of its own institutional processes." "From the railroading of Ms. Arroyo's proclamation in 2004," wrote David, "to the railroading of her impeachment a year after, everything else thereafter, including the ongoing effort to re-invent elite rule via Charter change, has been a blatant attempt to save a dying system. This is the heart of the crisis."

While David was correct when he said that "an enduring resolution to the crisis must go beyond the ouster of Ms. Arroyo, and begin to address the ills of the system itself,"[2] it is clear now that he somewhat mischaracterized the crisis. Had Mrs. Arroyo really been attempting to perpetuate elite rule? Was that really what the alleged electoral violations of 2004 and the cha-cha drive of 2006 were all about? Surely what Mrs. Arroyo and her supporters were attempting to perpetuate was her own period in office. And would her impeachment, or the election of Fernando Poe Jr., have signaled the end of elite rule? Such an outcome would have been highly unlikely. Was the system dying? It was certainly true that the economic and political culture was afflicted with a chronic sickness, but it can be argued that the "institutional processes" actually accommodated this, as when, following the 2007 senatorial elections, personal ambition and sectional interest saw to it that an outcome clearly expressing the will of the electorate was stood on its head. This was all perfectly legal and in conformity with the Constitution.

Facing no effective challenge, what David calls "elite dominance" showed little inclination to expire. Of course, when some, mainly on the left, challenged Arroyo, they would also issue calls for the end of elite rule. But in 2005 they—and some in the mainstream opposition, who only went as far as challenging the resident of Malacañang—acknowledged their own ineffectiveness by calling for (or letting it be known they would find acceptable) the intervention of military rebels. Ironically, then, rather than the elite (as opposed to one member of it) needing to resort to "blatant violations of its own institutional processes" in order to perpetuate its dominance, it was those seeking to end that dominance who felt driven to extra-constitutional methods.

And how do we explain the fact that in 2007 the "Genuine Opposition" could not even muster sufficient candidates to challenge the administration bloc's control of the House? This failure itself was not surprising, being merely the expression in electoral terms of the failure of anti-Arroyo forces to mobilize impressive numbers on the street over the previous six years. The last time big numbers were seen was May Day, 2001—EDSA Tres—but that event was largely spontaneous and leaderless, fueled by genuinely popular outrage at the manner of

Joseph Estrada's arrest. The treatment the demonstrators received at the hands of the security forces, despite earlier promises of protection and military defections, almost certainly led many to have second thoughts about future participation in street protests. While this reluctance may have played a part in the thin attendance at demonstrations in the intervening six years, however, it was only one factor. Yes, there was talk of "rally fatigue" or "people power fatigue" too, but it was also true that people were being asked to intervene in order to resolve differences within the elite. No one was offering workers, poor peasants or urban poor a stake in the future and so why, unless they were paid to do so, should any but the most committed or politically sophisticated make the effort?

Central to this problem is that there was—and is—no national vision around which opponents of the status quo might unite and blaze a trail of genuine national development. This absence of vision is a direct result of the sickness affecting the political and economic culture. Without such a vision, how could the opposition have possibly lined up candidates and constructed an organization to mobilize the electorate in 219 electoral districts without buying support? By the same token, how, once elected, is a politician to be disciplined unless he or she is a member of a party with a serious program of national development over which the members of that party have a sense of ownership, and around which the people have been mobilized? Unless, in other words, there is a national vision, a clear sense of direction and mission.

"The crisis" wrote Gramsci, "consists precisely in the fact that the old is dying, and the new cannot be born. In this interregnum a great variety of morbid symptoms appear."[3] The Philippines today is not Italy in 1930 (when, of course, Gramsci was referring to the rise of fascism), and "the old" is not exactly dying, but one suspects that, in the absence of a national vision capable of capturing the imagination and support of the majority of the people, morbid symptoms will continue to appear.

*

It is clear that, while Mrs. Arroyo's presidency may have exhibited the symptoms of the aforementioned sickness in a fairly virulent form, its roots must be sought elsewhere.

We have encountered various symptoms throughout this book. In a land saturated with formal religion, one manifestation of the sickness is an inability to subjugate the self to the benefit of the greater good. Individualism is rampant and, for the time being, uncontrollable. Rather than pressing for the genuine development of the national economy, local capitalists, somewhat like the ilustrados vis a vis Spain, approach government on single issues, and seek accommodations with each incoming regime. Yes, corruption is fuelled by poverty on the one hand and greed on the other, but it, too, is a form of individualism, springing from an urge to improve one's own circumstances regardless of the consequences for others or society as a whole; and, the sickness being of epidemic proportions, whatever peer pressure exists is ineffective, as the institutions that should play a part in curing the malady are themselves infected with it. Mainstream political parties exist only to deliver their leaders into high office, enjoying a long hibernation before each election, at which time the only question the electorate will be allowed to answer is who will be in charge of the mediocre status quo. And even then, as was seen in 2001, the result may be ignored if the winner is not to the liking of the elite, or, as in 2007, the successful candidates may decide that their longer-term advantage is served by bartering away the popular mandate. And even on the left, while some splits arise from genuine doctrinal differences it is difficult to believe that its serial schismatic activity is free from the influence of individualism.

The sickness is complicated in that alongside the symptoms of individualism we can identify those of colonial consciousness. Too often, Filipinos lack self-belief, the confidence that they are capable of resolving their own problems and charting their own destiny, and they therefore seek "protection" — often of God, or the USA, or both. Evidence of this can be found in some surprising places. It was Mrs. Arroyo's father, President Diosdado Macapagal, who switched Independence Day from July 4 (the date in 1946 when the country became nominally independent of the USA, and the date upon which Americans celebrate their own independence) to June 12, the day in 1898 when Emilio Aguinaldo declared the Philippines' independence from Spain. One wonders whether Macapagal realized that his nationalist gesture was compromised by the fact that the declaration, written not by Aguinaldo or the consistently anti-colonialist Apolinario Mabini, but by Ambrosio Bautista Rianzares, stated that the proclamation was made "under the protection of the Mighty and Humanitarian North American Nation." (Ilustrado authorship was also evident in the passage that identified Aguinaldo as "the instrument selected by God, *in spite of his humble origin*, to effect the redemption of this unfortunate people...")[4]

Even the Philippine flag ceremony, the purpose of which should surely be to emphasize the nation's uniqueness and, above all, its independence, is based on that of its former colonial master. In his *Little Brown Brother*, Leon Wolff points out that the US flag ceremony was only adopted in the 1890s, at the very time that the growing capitalist giant (or, at least, the dominant section of its ruling class) had concluded that foreign conquests were required in order to absorb the USA's surplus production. In 1898, six years after the US pledge of allegiance was adopted, Senator Beveridge told a well-heeled Boston audience: "American factories are making more than the American people can use; American soil is producing more than they can consume. Fate has written our policy for us; the trade of the world must and shall be ours...American law, American order, American civilization, and the American flag will plant themselves on shores hitherto bloody and benighted..." The Philippines, he said, was "logically our first target."[5]

How unutterably sad, then, that the Philippine flag ceremony, instituted in a further irony by Executive Order in 1996 on the 98th anniversary of Emilio Aguinaldo's declaration of independence, should be patterned on that established by the USA just shortly before it snuffed out that independence.

Writing of the Japanese occupation, Constantino discusses the complexities of collaboration as they were manifested in Claro M. Recto, who became foreign secretary in the puppet Republic, but who later became a leading nationalist in the post-war period. Furthermore, he points out that the resistance of many guerrilla groups, even that led by communists, was more complex than it appeared.

[Recto] was embittered by American abandonment yet he pinned his hopes on their return. These sentiments he shared with the people who by and large never doubted that the Americans would win the war. Their resistance was based on this certainty. For them, freedom meant that which they had under the Americans; so they fought for

American victory instead of seizing the opportunity to fight for their own freedom as their forebears had done at the turn of the century.

Not only Recto but also the guerrillas, including the Huks, committed this error. The long years of dependence on America affected the quality of our resistance to the Japanese, for this dependence developed in us a new consciousness which did not differentiate the interests of the two countries.

Thus, this "resistance was also a form of collaboration."[6] Probably most emblematic of this trait in the guerrilla resistance was Marcos V. Agustin, the founder of the Marking Guerrillas, who sported tattoos of the American eagle and the Stars and Stripes on his body.

With the benefit of hindsight, it is possible to see that, over the centuries, colonialism has unwittingly subjected the consciousness of Filipinos to the "bad cop, good cop" treatment: first the virtual theocracy of the long Spanish regime, followed by, after a brutal conquest, the relatively liberal American years; then, in December 1941, the entry of an even worse cop than the Spanish friarchy and, three years later, the return of the Americans on their "liberating" mission. It should, therefore, not surprise us that the USA was able to continue its control of Philippine economic and foreign policy long after formal "independence," or that, despite its horrendous consequences, "guidance" from the IMF and the World Bank has been welcomed by the latter-day ilustrados. Often, "nationalism" has consisted of little more than a choice between colonizers: on several occasions, Filipinos have asked the current writer whether the Philippines might have fared better if it had been colonized by the British!

Just as colonial consciousness was born of centuries of foreign domination, individualism and the failure to forge a national vision also have an objective basis (or, possibly, two). The archipelagic nature of the country has not assisted the cultivation of a national identity, and strong regional loyalties persist, despite the fact that well over four centuries have passed since the Spanish first brought the various language groups together as "Las Filipinas" — and, of course, the Moro separatists constitute a special problem.

But the nature of the economy has also retarded the development of a collective, truly *Filipino* mindset. In July 2006, according to the preliminary results of the Labor Force Survey for that month, the Philippines had a workforce of 36.2 million, of which 35.8 percent were own-account workers, 11.5 percent were "unpaid family workers," and 2.9 million (or 4.4 million using the previous criteria) were unemployed. Of those employed, 11.8 million worked less than 40 hours in the previous week, 8.2 million worked less than 30 hours, and 4.4 million worked less than 20 hours. Only 17.5 million, less than half the total workforce, were classified as "wage and salary workers."[7]

Just as the country is atomized into 7,100 islands, so the workforce is, to a very significant extent, atomized among a host of small and medium-sized workplaces (where it has a workplace at all) and largely solitary pursuits like fishing. Such circumstances are hardly conducive to collective thought and action. The Philippines' *real* long crisis is located in the economy, and while this is the result of colonialism and the remedies subsequently dispensed by the multilateral institutions, it is also true that the accommodation entered into by the ilustrados during and after the Philippine-American War ensured that the economy and institutions that would have been more conducive to the forging of a more collective, more *Filipino* world-view were simply not built.

The labor movement is one place where we might expect to observe a determined drive for collective solutions and, indeed, various trade union organizations have, over the years, issued calls for the adoption of a strategy of nationalist industrialization; currently, several labor organizations cooperate with nationalist businesspeople in the Fair Trade Alliance. But organized labor is itself a casualty of the underdeveloped economy, as the number of organizable workers is, relative to the size of the labor force, modest. Furthermore, it is also infected with individualism, at least at the leadership levels, as a host of rival labor organizations fight for the right to represent the relatively small pool of organizable labor. This rivalry, coupled with the objective economic conditions, leads to a situation in which the century-old movement is still the size of a stripling: in 2005, 2,793 collective bargaining agreements (CBAs) covered a mere 556,000 workers (although the labor department is not notified of all CBAs).[8]

Then, of course, there are anywhere between eight and ten million Filipinos living and/or working abroad, and while it is obviously the case that this huge exodus has been occasioned by poverty and the sense of hopelessness engendered by an economy geared to satisfy the requirements of foreign interests, it is also, judged in the harshest light, another example of individualism, the decision to search for individual solutions overseas rather than stay and work collectively to put things right. (This is not a new phenomenon, as Filipinos have been migrating for decades. In the early 1930s, the newly-formed Partido Komunista ng Pilipinas was besieged by requests from workers seeking to emigrate to the Soviet Union.[9]) But, as there is no national vision to unite and motivate them, who can blame them?

*

The absence of a national vision, a program of national development, explains not only why the masses refuse to be mobilized but also why various political forces attempt short-cuts, often going into "copycat mode."

The copycat syndrome is extremely common in Philippine politics. When opposition lawyers walked out of Congress in June 2004, despairing of securing a single favorable decision from the administration-dominated canvass committee, it is possible that they were harking back to 2001, when the prosecution team walked out of Estrada's impeachment trial—only this time the masses failed to turn up on the streets. In 2003, there were, as we have seen, allegations that the presidential spouse had stashed away ill-gotten wealth under the name "Jose Pidal." One could not say that this was merely an attempt by the opposition to replay the "Jose Velarde" drama with different characters (although there were astonishing similarities in the scripts), as there really was such a bank account. But was it not possible that Senator Lacson, when he produced his "Clarissa Ocampo" in the person of Eugenio Mahusay, was looking for something like the effect achieved by the original? Instead, Mahusay, for whatever reason, recanted.

The left is not immune from the copycat syndrome, although here one detects a penchant for strategic models, rather than the mere desire to reproduce the effects of a single event. In 1964, encouraged by President Diosdado Macapagal's professed desire to see the completion of the "Unfinished Revolution," the Partido Komunista ng Pilipinas, through its above-ground creation the Lapiang Manggagawa (Labor Party), concluded a tactical alliance with Macapagal. One gets the impression that Jose Maria Sison, then a PKP member and editor of the party-created *Progressive Review*, wanted to transform this relationship into the kind of alliance the Communist Party of Indonesia (PKI) enjoyed with President Sukarno. The Indonesian model became less attractive when, in 1965, the military annihilated the third largest communist party in the world, soaking the archipelago in blood. Then, of course, came the Chinese model, despite the huge differences in circumstances and topography between China and the Philippines. Given the National Democratic Front's insistence on belligerency status and a foreign venue for peace negotiations, it was evident that, at one stage, the Vietnamese diplomatic model was in vogue. On the political/military front, some of Sison's opponents within the CPP were said to favor the Nicaraguan model.

We have seen that, in declaring her state of emergency in February 2006, Mrs. Arroyo appeared to have used a 1972 template. And those praying (often literally) for Arroyo's downfall were also in copycat mode. Can we doubt that, as she hurried to Fort Bonifacio on the evening of Sunday, February 26, 2006, Mrs. Aquino was replaying the events of February 1986 in her mind? And inside the camp, was not Ariel Querubin, as he called first for "people power" and then church support, watching the same tape? The initial aim of the military dissidents had been, of course, to repeat the events of January 2001, with the withdrawal of military support leading to the toppling of the commander in chief.

Most of the time, of course, a switch to copycat mode is completely useless at producing positive results. There has been one exception, but this tends to prove the rule: EDSA Dos was able to reprise the downfall of a president because the same social forces that had participated in EDSA I—particularly the Catholic Church, now augmented by the CPP-influenced bloc— were once again on call. Where the ritual reproduction of one or two elements of a previously successful scenario fail to produce such results (i.e., most of the time), it is due to an insufficient grasp of the relationship between cause and effect, and a failure to analyze the situation and make an accurate estimation of the balance of forces.

In February 2006, that failure proved fatal. To a significant extent, those who supported the removal of Arroyo by military means were those who had complained that she had appointed so many military men to positions in her administration. What conclusion should have been drawn from the latter fact? Arroyo owed her ascendancy to the presidency in 2001 (and, some argued, her questionable electoral success in 2004) to the military. After EDSA Dos, she and the security forces had entered a symbiotic relationship (it matters little whether this is viewed as one in which she was their "prisoner" or one in which she had co-opted them). This was widely known. It should have been apparent, therefore, that in such circumstances the "copycat" model simply could not work. It was rather like a chess player seeking to deploy valuable pieces already taken by his opponent.

And, of course, only a thoroughgoing analysis of the national situation can provide the basis for a program of national development. Without such an analysis and program, any movement is without a compass, prone to adventurism, grasping at straws. Hence the copycat syndrome.

*

Quite apart from the presence of more questionable motives, we find the copycat syndrome, and a failure to distinguish cause from effect, at work in the desire for a parliament. "Charter change," said Mrs. Arroyo in 2004, "is our strategic hope of change."[10] The implication in this awkward formulation was, of course, that a change in the legislative system would automatically give rise to other transformations—a blossoming economy, greater prosperity, etc. As is so often the case in Philippine political life, there was some discussion about which foreign model to adopt, and the French received some mention. This was possibly the impulse of a class of people unused to *making* things for its own use, a philosophical reflection of the state of the economy. "As we don't have one of those, can't we just buy one off the shelf and import it?" Well, that is possible, of course. But the end result might be the same as that produced by importing a European or American DVD player: the local software may not play on it. The parliamentary system is, in any case, often a far from ideal solution for those interested in broadening democracy, even in countries where it has been in place for centuries. In the United Kingdom, for example, the House of Commons has for decades been routinely sidelined on all matters of strategic importance, with real decision-making power lying in the hands of the cabinet or, more recently, the prime minister.[11]

Is it appropriate for a people in Southeast Asia to adopt a legislative system that arose in

Western Europe (or, with regard to the current system, the USA) on the basis of very different economic and political histories? Is it not like expecting to be awarded the gold medal for the marathon without having run the race? (This is not to imply that the "race" run by the West European nations was "clean": their economic, and therefore political, development rested upon foreign conquest, exploitation and slavery.) Cause and effect: the Western European parliaments did not create the economic development of those nations but arose as a result of it.

During the cha-cha debate, most of the media chose to focus on the proposal to adopt a parliamentary system, but the plan to sweep away the nationalist economic safeguards in the Constitution surely merited equal attention. Most of the nationalist safeguards are to be found under Article XII, which is headed "National Economy and Patrimony." Section 2 provides that the state may only enter into arrangements to exploit the natural resources of the Philippines with "corporations or associations at least sixty per centum of whose capital is owned" by Filipino citizens. Section 10 allows Congress to reserve certain areas of investment to such companies and associations and concludes: "The State shall regulate and exercise authority over foreign investments within its national jurisdiction and in accordance with its national goals and priorities." Section 11 applies the same restriction to the granting of utility franchises.

These safeguards did not, of course, suddenly appear in 1986-87: they can be found in the charters of 1935 and 1973—and, in fact, the latter document, formulated by the Constitutional Commission of 1971 but introduced by Ferdinand Marcos after the declaration of martial law, went further, enabling the National Assembly (or Interim Batasang Pambansa, as it became after the amendments of 1976) to "reserve to citizens of the Philippines or to corporations or associations *wholly* owned by such citizens, certain traditional areas of investments when the national interest so dictates" (Article XIV, Section 3). It is clear, then, that these clauses represent rather more than a passing fancy of the commissioners appointed to draft the document adopted in 1987, and that they are not intended to constitute protectionism for its own sake. The key to understanding the safeguards is to be found, surely, in the words already quoted from Article XII, Section 10 of the current Constitution which, dealing with the national economy and patrimony, speaks of the "national goals and priorities" of the state. Those words need, in turn, to be read in conjunction with Article II, Section 19: "The State shall develop a self-reliant and independent national economy effectively controlled by Filipinos."

The safeguards, then, are part and parcel of the nationalist tradition of the Philippines, which developed as a result of, and in resistance to, the foreign domination holding the Philippines in its sway since the sixteenth century and persisting, using rather more subtle techniques, to this day.

It would appear, however, that the Philippine state currently has no "national goals and priorities" of a nationalist character. Those goals and priorities that do exist are, and have been for some time, dictated by the International Monetary Fund, the World Bank and the transnational capital represented by those institutions. Rather than developing a "self-reliant and independent economy," the main economic role of the Philippines (at least as far as intentions go) is to generate profits for transnational corporations (TNCs) in operations that are, for the most part, both geographically and economically unconnected with the domestic economy, i.e. with the needs of the Filipino people. It is *because* there is no attempt to *develop* the domestic economy that the nationalist safeguards in the Constitution are devalued, made to appear anachronistic, and become vulnerable to attack.

If the nationalist tradition is not to become a relic of former times, if it is to become less a tradition and more a vibrant reality, the Philippines *will* have to undertake its own marathon, developing the legislative forms most appropriate for running the race, not merely crossing the finish line. (Neighboring countries have, of course, demonstrated that the development marathon may now be completed in decades rather than centuries.)

To have any relevance to the political and economic needs of the Philippines, the only legislative system that would make sense would be one based on an analysis of concrete Philippine and international conditions. The only sensible requirement, surely, given the intention to develop, would be a legislative system based on the needs of a Third World country intent upon the construction of an integrated, industrialized economy, a system capable of involving the greatest possible number of the people in determining the destiny of the nation. Such a system is, though, hardly likely to see the light of day if left to the current party model, with its emphasis on individual advancement and prolonging terms of office.

There does, however, seem to be a certain degree of agreement on the need for electoral parties to have developed platforms (although there would be considerably less agreement on what those platforms should be), instead of being guided by personalities, and this might, therefore, be a logical first step in any reform worthy of the name.

*

Before proceeding to discuss the possibility of a development drive, it is necessary to counter an objection sometimes raised by what we might call development-doubters, those who, even though they may be sympathetic to the cause of nationalism, exhibit undue pessimism regarding the objective conditions necessary for the development of an economy geared to the satisfaction of Filipino needs.

For example, one columnist[12] has argued that the drafters of the 1935 Constitution were unwittingly responsible for "their nation's slow economic development decades later." Why? Because this document, like those that have followed it, insisted that participation in utilities and the development of natural resources should be restricted to enterprises with at least 60 percent Filipino ownership. The columnist thinks that this was a well-meaning but always doubtful venture, as "it was at best unlikely that Filipino investors could come up with the 60 percent domestic equity required to bring into being all the utility and natural resource-development projects needed to bring about the rapid development of this country's economy." As we saw in chapter 7, this argument was also advanced by charter change advocacy commission member Jarius Bondoc.

If true, this would probably send most nationalists into a bout of terminal depression, for without sufficient capital accumulation a society is unable to industrialize, exercise control of its own economy, and ensure that it is geared to the satisfaction of the needs of the people rather than the profit-margins of TNCs.

Our columnist has, however, overlooked a number of important facts.

For decades, TNCs that claim to be "investing" in the Philippines have raised much of their capital on the local market instead of bringing it in with them. In 1977, the Central Bank attempted to impose debt-to-equity ratios on foreign companies seeking peso loans. None other than William H. Sullivan, the US Ambassador, gave the game away when he protested with remarkable frankness that such a scheme "would work against multinationals [i.e. TNCs] who

252

come to the Philippines with nothing but a company name and a logo." Having raised its investment funds in the Philippines, of course, the TNC may "repatriate" the profits, or at least move them to a tax-friendly location.[13] In a development state, such funds would be devoted to development projects by the Filipino public or private sector, with any profits being ploughed back into the country.

Emilio Antonio, dean of the School of Economics at the University of Asia and the Pacific, has said that the private sector has excess funds and that its savings rate has dramatically increased, hence the fact that Treasury bond auctions are always over-subscribed. Furthermore, in early 2006 the Bangko Sentral ng Pilipinas said that $10.4 billion of the total $15.7 billion invested by Filipinos in Philippine banks was actually in foreign assets, via banks in foreign countries. This was equal to 10 percent of the local economy and, according to national treasurer Omar Cruz, did not include investments by those high rollers who do not usually go through banking channels.[14]

Potentially, therefore, it seems that there are more funds available than might be expected. In addition to those already mentioned, of course, the state itself could undertake many developments, were it not for the fact that the funds it might use are currently appropriated for debt servicing. Some adjustment is surely possible there. Furthermore, it is likely that, in a situation in which a vibrant national campaign for industrialization was putting down roots throughout the society, the proposition that some of the $20 billion per annum currently remitted by OFWs should make its way into development would receive a more responsive hearing. Finally, the Philippines probably has considerable mineral wealth, most of it unexplored; this will only become a source of development funding for the Philippines, however, if revenue going to foreign oil and gas companies is kept to a minimum.

There are, then, sufficient indications that there is not really a shortage of domestic capital. It is just that it is not being used for genuinely developmental purposes.

*

Currently, economic nationalism has no mainstream organizational expression. Instead, politicians who support the nationalist development of the economy are dispersed between several parties—which are, in essence, little more than electoral vehicles—where they inevitably find themselves outnumbered by office seekers or those who (possibly quite sincerely) believe that continued foreign domination of the economy provides the only road to salvation. It is surely a fact that the nationalist economic measures in the Constitution are vulnerable because they have no broad *organizational* support in the country, are not defended by a network committed to their full implementation. It is worth remembering in this regard that the Arroyo administration's cha-cha drive in 2006 was met not by a united people but by a *lack* of unity, by a host of uncoordinated campaign initiatives and ad hoc organizations and that, at the end of the day, the so-called "people's initiative" was defeated not by popular pressure but by the Supreme Court—and then only by the narrowest possible margin.

While the mainstream may not support the cause of economic nationalism organizationally, there are several left-wing parties who do so at a programmatic level. Since the splits in the CPP in the 1990s, however, they have never come together as a left bloc, campaigning for common objectives, and even those which have worked together have never done so with a view to promoting nationalist industrialization. Indeed, these are the forces which, more than any other, were sidetracked in the Arroyo decade, treading water with regard to their nationalist aims. And yet in the 2010 elections, almost four-and-a-half million people cast their single party-list vote for a left-wing party with a programmatic commitment (admittedly of varying strength) to economic nationalism. It is obvious that these parties could make a huge contribution to the nationalist cause if it became the main focus of their activity and their supporters were mobilized behind it.

There is, of course, nothing to stop nationalists forming their own party, campaign organization or alliance, bringing together all individuals and organizations whose first priority is the development of the domestic economy and its reorientation to the fulfilment of the needs of the Filipino people. To be truly democratic, such an organization would require a membership structure catering for both individuals and group affiliations (labor unions, the appropriate party-list organizations, etc.), and a constitution in which those members and affiliates would be assigned the major role in formulating the program and the strategy for achieving it.

The importance of this point cannot be stressed too much, for this would not be a case of merely mobilizing popular support for a single election but of transforming the popular consciousness to embrace a path of development leading to the building of a new Philippines. The promotion of such a vision and the construction of an organization to support it could only be achieved by those with a clear understanding of, and firm commitment to, the program. Such understanding and commitment most usually comes as a result of having participated in the formulation (at whatever level) and adoption of policy, resulting in a sense of ownership over both the agreed policies and strategies and the organization itself. This would have a further value in that when the successes of the development drive came under attack—as they undoubtedly would—such threats would be met by stout resistance. The broadest possible road rank-and-file participation would also act to check attempts by any single party or group to "capture" the organization.

With regard to program, a *Blueprint for a Viable Philippines* was, on the initiative of Francisco "Dodong" Nemenzo Jr., R.C. Constantino Jr., Roger Posadas and Randy David, developed by several organizations in 2005, addressing many of the problems discussed in this book and calling for a "strong developmentalist state."[15] This was supported by much of the left and the mainstream opposition, but the authors made it clear that any party was welcome to adopt the program, or parts of it. Such a document, which is still regarded as a work in progress, might, then, provide the basis for further discussion and the formation of a broad nationalist organization—be it a party or a mass movement coalition—devoted to achieving its aims.

It would almost certainly be a mistake, following exhaustive discussion and debate, to submit the proposed program to the public at the first available congressional election. The left party-list organizations have found that, if elected, they can only achieve tactical victories in Congress, in which they are vastly outnumbered by the district representatives. At the same time, they are conscious of the fact that it is all-but impossible in current circumstances to break the hold of the mainstream party machines on the districts.[16] Winning the Filipino people to a program of national development would be the work of years, not months, and electoral success would only be possible if preceded by a transformation of the popular consciousness. Such would be the task of the organization which formulated or adopted the development plan, establishing chapters throughout the archipelago for this very purpose.

And when the time was ripe, electoral activity would need to mark a decisive break with past practice, with personalities taking a back seat and candidates being adopted on the basis of their commitment to the development program and their past activity on its behalf. Indeed, it would be surprising if proselytizing and organizing activity—intensive and extensive—of the organization did not throw up new leaders at all levels of the society. As with the formulation of policy, the adoption of candidates should be the job not of a few top leaders but of the broad membership. If the organization was as democratic and participative as we have speculated here, the members would know better than anyone who was deserving of adoption.

At this stage, the network of chapters established as a result of previous activity would become the electoral machines for the organization or coalition. The nature of their activity would not change as, given that the whole point of electoral participation would be to win acceptance of the development program, their aim now would be explain its measures to an even wider audience, so the election campaign would merely see their proselytizing activity raised to the highest possible degree. Even in districts where such campaigns were unsuccessful, an extremely valuable by-product would be the educational, consciousness-raising effect on the communities in those districts and the further expansion of the pro-development organization.

If a coalition of forces organized around a detailed program of development were to be successful on the electoral front, then might be the time to consider constitutional reform, constructing a model designed to meets the needs of the developing Philippine nation and its people.

*

The left might provide many of the grassroots campaigners for a drive for genuine development, but the campaign would need to be as broad as possible, drawing in all with the interest and desire to develop their country, regardless of class, station, religion, or current political party. This is not as unlikely a prospect as it may sound, because a promising start has been made once before. In 1967, among the charter-members of the Movement for the Advancement of Nationalism (MAN) were 22 businessmen, 91 youth and students, 86 peasant leaders, 61 labor leaders, 21 women, 29 educators, 24 professionals, six scientists and technologists, 13 media workers, 17 writers, seven political leaders and eleven civic leaders.[17] MAN did not prosper, however, falling victim to the split in the communist movement as Jose Maria Sison (the MAN general secretary) broke from the Partido Komunista ng Pilipinas and formed the Communist Party of the Philippines (CPP), which adopted a strategy of Maoist "protracted people's war." Having declined, MAN's fate was finally sealed by the declaration of martial law in 1972.

The fact that there has never been an organization with a similar aim and breadth of membership since that time may be partly because the cause of nationalism has been confused in the minds of some with the armed left. In any case, the question of the armed rebel movements would have to be addressed if a development campaign were to gain both a broad membership and access to the whole archipelago.

In large part, the NPA and Muslim insurgencies exist due to the absence of a process of genuine national development. In Mindanao, there appear to be no easy solutions. For one thing, the process of Christian immigration that lies at the bottom of so much of the sense of grievance among the Muslim community has itself produced a major circumstance preventing easy resolution: in many parts of Mindanao, Muslims find themselves outnumbered. In addition, US meddling on the pretext of assisting the peace process further complicates the situation—doubly so in that its real motives are economic, having the mineral wealth of Mindanao in its sights, and geo-political.

It is abundantly clear that peace will not be achieved until the government adopts a fundamentally different approach, and (regardless of the form and extent of Muslim autonomy) the determined implementation of national development—with, this time, a double emphasis on the word "national." Hitherto, attempts to "integrate" the Muslim community into the Republic of the Philippines have all too often taken the form of co-opting leaders. And the "development" that has been proposed for Mindanao (often called the "last frontier") in recent years is the same debt-dependent process, dominated by foreign capital, that has singularly failed to develop a national economy and provide the people with livelihoods in the rest of the archipelago.

Unless the Philippines belatedly embarks upon the construction of an economy that is truly national, and of a nation in which injustices of the past are reconciled and the wounds healed, it is unlikely that the rebellion of the dispossessed in the south, given cultural cohesion by Islam, will abate. If, however, Muslims felt that they were equal partners in a truly national process of development that could deliver them benefits unavailable outside of that nation, things might be quite different. If this seems unlikely to some, it should be recalled that in 1967, before he formed the Moro National Liberation Front, Nur Misuari was a charter-member of MAN.

The same kind of process might attract the CPP also, although several hurdles would have to be crossed.

In 2006, the CPP-led National Democratic Front (NDF) urged the government to adopt a set of proposals it had put forward the previous year. This had included unity against foreign domination, the empowerment of workers and peasants, economic sovereignty, debt repudiation, the promotion of a scientific and pro-people culture, autonomy for national minorities, prosecution of those accused of treason, corruption and human rights violations, and an independent foreign policy.[18]

Many of these proposals could, of course, find their way into a program of national development such as that mentioned above. But for such a program to stand a chance of adoption, millions of people would have to be won to it (preferably having, directly or indirectly, played a part in its formulation) and be mobilized around it. There would also need to be, of course, a government in power willing to implement it, and one thing is absolutely certain: such a government would never arise in the absence of the kind of campaign discussed above.

The chances of the government of Mrs. Arroyo adopting such a program were, of course, practically nil, and the NDF would have seen in this rejection a justification for its continuation of the armed struggle. But over forty years of armed struggle have not produced a situation in which the population is mobilized behind the demand for genuine change. Indeed, the question must be asked: would it be possible to construct a national organization, mobilizing the broadest sections of the population behind proposals for national development while the armed struggle still affects many parts of the country and the security forces are able to find excuses to kill legal activists? Probably not. It is here, moreover, that one of the most difficult hurdles is to be found: the CPP committed itself to "protracted people's war" at its formation in 1968, since when there has not been a congress at which its program could be updated or amended.

Quite apart from the conditions that either side might attach to a peace agreement, both parties need to believe that "victory" cannot be achieved by military means. Even people like former mayor Rodrigo Duterte of Davao City have said this, giving rise to the hope that an attempt to persuade the government of the day of this truth may not be entirely hopeless. Government forces may win encounters, may overrun NPA camps or capture leaders, but while poverty and hunger remain, young men and women will be driven to the hills; equally, when people are persuaded of the futility of using the current legal system to seek justice, some will continue to seek alternative avenues. Poverty and injustice will not be substantially reduced overnight, but the perspective of national development, of helping to bring about an economy geared to the needs of Filipinos, would offer hope and a peaceful avenue. That will only be possible, however, if legal activists are allowed to campaign without fear of harassment, or worse.

Here, another challenging hurdle is encountered. The Melo Commission and the international community appeared to be in no doubt that the majority of activists murdered since 2001 had been victims of the armed forces, or units of it that, due to inaction by commanding officers and the civilian authority, had been able to act with relative impunity. However, once international concern was mobilized, the Arroyo government professed a willingness to accept the assistance of foreign experts. (In Mindanao, the ceasefire between the government and the MILF has for several years been monitored by an international team led by Malaysia.) Hitherto, the NDF has rejected the notion of a ceasefire prior to the successful completion of peace talks, arguing (pointing to the occasional clashes between government forces and the MILF) that the government would not abide by such an arrangement, or that Malacañang would have no reason to negotiate with a ceasefire already in place. An international monitoring force might address the first reservation, and the remit of such a body could even be broadened to encompass the monitoring of any violations of the right of legal activists to go about their business.

Regarding the second reservation, the CPP-NPA-NDF would have a political decision to make, balancing what it might hope to achieve by a continuation of its armed struggle against the progress towards some of its goals (particularly, but not exclusively, on the economic front) that might be made by campaigning legally, alongside other Filipinos who wish to see their country striding down the path of genuine development.

The extra-judicial killing of above-ground activists is, of course, a legal and moral question for the society as a whole. For the CPP, however, the phenomenon poses a further political question. Calls for the NPA to target "enemy" politicians and government officials, or instructions for the NPA to assassinate those guilty of extra-judicial killings, are provocative but might, in part, be explained by the fact that there is little hope that the guilty parties will be brought to book in any other way. But the more fundamental question is this: despite the fact that the CPP has, since the early 1990s, been a legal party, is it a reasonable expectation in a Third World country like the Philippines to be able to both operate legally via various mass organizations and party-list groups, while on the other hand directing an underground armed struggle?

There would, of course, be a "peace dividend" arising from settlements between the government and the armed political groups, allowing resources to be reallocated to social services, education, health and development. This dividend would be more than financial, for thousands of committed citizens would be free to work for the development of their country, quite possibly alongside those whom they had previously looked upon as "the enemy." It is a fact that some groups within the military have, at the programmatic level, more in common with the left and other nationalists than is generally realized. Rather than from time to time being deployed on "civic action" initiatives that are little more than temporary, and designed as counter-insurgency measures, would not the military prefer to be engaged, alongside or in partnership with civilians, in genuine development work?

But there is a further hurdle to be surmounted, as there are calls for punishment or revenge. Members of the military want those responsible for killing their comrades brought to book, while civilian activists demand punishment for those responsible for extrajudicial killings, disappearances and other forms of human rights violations. Since the 1970s, hundreds of thousands have died, and so this is rather more than a minor detail, for revanchism could derail the peace process and hamper the drive for development. It may, then, be worthwhile for all parties concerned to see how this question has been addressed in other countries—and South Africa, with its Truth and Reconciliation Commission (TRC), might offer the closest parallel. However, merely to import yet another "foreign model" might be inadequate. The South African TRC held hearings at which human rights violators from both the apartheid government and the liberation forces were invited to confess their guilt and seek amnesty. Although amnesty was not granted in all cases, some victims (or their relatives) still complained that there could be no reconciliation without justice, i.e., punishment of the guilty.

The process in the Philippines, therefore, might place rather more emphasis on the "truth"—not merely *what* happened and *which* acts were committed and by whom, but *why* these things occurred. If the country were at a point where genuine development was firmly on the agenda, would not all parties be concerned to tackle the questions "*Why* have we been doing these things to each other, *why* have we been divided and cast as antagonists by forces that do not have our real interests at heart?" If former antagonists, united by a shared understanding of the past, were now committed to working with each other to develop the country, would not the interest in meting out punishment for past transgressions wane? Who now remembers Claro M. Recto as a "traitor"? His record as a nationalist in the post-war years has erased his role as a member of the puppet government during the Japanese occupation from the national memory.

If truth and reconciliation came to be seen as indispensable elements in the very process of *genuine* national development (as opposed to the "development" prescribed by the IMF and the World Bank), would that not constitute their best chance of success?

*

There are at least two reasons why an author might feel somewhat reticent about rounding off a book concerning the affairs of a country in which he resides as a guest with anything approaching "conclusions." Firstly, of course, there is the danger of unintentionally offending one's hosts. Secondly, the country in question has for centuries suffered the disastrous consequences of foreign "advice" and "guidance." While some of the content of this final chapter might appear to verge on "advice," the author insists that the word "suggestions" is nearer the mark.

Any solutions must, at the end of the day, be Filipino ones.

NOTES

1. *Manila Bulletin*, March 24, 2012.

2. Randy David, "Public lives: the origins of the crisis," *Philippine Daily Inquirer*, November 20, 2005.

3. Antonio Gramsci. *Selections from the Prison Notebooks* (London: Lawrence & Wishart, 2005), 276.

4. Teodoro A. Agoncillo, *Malolos: The Crisis of the Republic* (Quezon City: University of the Philippines, 1960), 225, 226.

5. Leon Wolff, *Little Brown Brother: How the United States Purchased and Pacified the Philippine Islands at the Century's Turn* (New York: History Book Club, Francis Parkman Prize Edition, 2006), 13. 53.

6. Renato Constantino, *The Making of a Filipino* (Quezon City: Malaya Books, 1969), 117, 111.

7. www.census.gov.ph.

8. Department of Labor and Employment, "416 firms to renew CBAs", April 19, 2006.

9. Jim Richardson, *Komunista: The Genesis of the Philippine Communist Party, 1902-1935* (Quezon City: Ateneo de Manila University Press, 2011), 150-151.

10. www.inq7.net, July 6, 2004.

11. See, for example, Bruce P. Lenman, *The Eclipse of Parliament: Appearance and Reality in British Politics since 1914*, London, Edward Arnold, 1992.

12. Rudy Romero, "Zooming In", *Daily Tribune*, precise date unknown, but October or November, 2004.

13. See Ken Fuller, "Profit-shifting and transfer pricing," *Daily Tribune*, December 21, 2010.

14. Daxim L. Lucas, "$10.4 billion in Filipino funds invested overseas," *Philippine Daily Inquirer*, February 7, 2006.

15. See www.geocities.com/blueprint_bentonhall.

16. Satur Ocampo and Sonny Melencio, interviewed separately by the author, March 2011.

17. MAN, *Basic Documents and Speeches of Founding Congress* (Manila, 1967), cited in Ken Fuller, *A Movement Divided: Philippine Communism, 1957-1986* (Quezon City: University of the Philippines Press, 2011), 31.

18. www.inquirer.net, July 17, 2006.

BIBLIOGRAPHY

Books and Articles

Abaya, Hernando J. *Looking Back in Anger*, Quezon City: New Day Publishers, 1992.

----------. *The Untold Philippine Story*, Quezon City: Malaya Books, 1967.

Abuza, Zachary. "Balik-Terrorism: The Return of the Abu Sayyaf, Strategic Studies Institute, US Army War College, 2005.

Agoncillo, Teodoro. A. *Malolos: Crisis of the Republic*, Quezon City: University of the Philippines, 1960.

Angara, Edgardo. "Estrada's Final Hours Told," *Philippine Daily Inquirer*, February 4, 2001.

Baclagon, Uldarico S. *Lessons from the Huk Campaign in the Philippines*, Manila: M. Colcol & Company, 1960.

Bello, Walden, Herbert Docena, Marissa de Guzman and Marylou Malig. *The Anti-Development State: The Political Economy of Permanent Crisis in the Philippines*, Quezon City: Department of Sociology, College of Social Sciences and Philosophy, University of the Philippines and Focus on the Global South, 2004.

-----. "Debt and Denial... or Ensuring RP Will End up Like Argentina," *BusinessWorld*,

March 22, 2005.

Benigno, Teodoro C. "The Elite: An Anatomy/Why Our Crisis Today?", *Philippine Star*, December 8, 2000.

Briones, Leonor Magtolis. "The Cost of Financing Development," Social Watch Philippines, 2006.

Broad, Robin. *Unequal Alliance, 1979-1986: The World Bank, the International Monetary Fund, and the Philippines*, Quezon City: Ateneo de Manila University Press, 1988.

Chua, Yvonne T., Sheila Coronel and Vinia Datinguinoo. "The State of the President's Finances: Can Estrada Explain his Wealth?" Philippine Center for Investigative Journalism, at www.pcij.org., 2000.

Collena, Rommel. "Liguasan Marsh holds billions of dollars in gas – Misuari," GMANews.TV, July 28, 2008.

Conde, Carlos H. "Family Dynasties Bind Politics in the Philippines," *International Herald Tribune*, May 11, 2007.

Constantino, Renato. *The Making of a Filipino*, Quezon City: Malaya Books, 1969.

Cooperative Research History Commons. "Profile: Abu Sayyaf," Center for Grassroots Oversight, www.cooperativeresearch.org/entity.jsp?entity=abu_sayyaf.

Culather, Nick (ed.). *Managing Nationalism: United States National Security Council Documents on the Philippines, 1953-1960*, Quezon City: New Day Publishers, 1992.

David, Randy. "Public lives: the origins of the crisis," *Philippine Daily Inquirer*, November 20, 2005.

Dejaresco III, Zoilo P. "Mindanao's secret," *Manila Bulletin*, August 18, 2011.

Docena, Herbert. "Corruption and Poverty: Barking Up the Wrong Tree?" In Walden Bello, Herbert Docena, Marissa de Guzman and Marylou Malig, *The Anti-Development State: The Political Economy of Permanent Crisis in the Philippines*, Quezon City: Department of Sociology, University of the Philippines, 2004.

----------. "US Troops 'Unconventional' Presence," *Malaya*, January 15, 2007.

Doronila, Amando. "The fantasy of the 7.3% GDP growth," *Philippine Daily Inquirer*, March 31, 2008.

----------. "A Sinister Plan to Butcher Civilians," *Philippine Daily Inquirer*, June 21, 2006.

Editorial. "Auditing the auditors," *Philippine Star*, February 8, 2011.

----------. "Destructive Politics," *Philippine Daily Inquirer*, April 2, 2006.

----------. "Ending the NPA Insurgency," *Manila Times*, June 21, 2006.

----------. "Extermination," *Philippine Daily Inquirer*, March 22, 2006.

----------. "Force of Numbers," *Philippine Daily Inquirer*, March 31, 2006.

----------. "Good Bye! [*sic*] Madame Ambassador," www.luwaran.com, November 23, 2009.

----------. "Gutom," *Malaya*, March 23, 2007.

Estella, Chit. "Lack of Nurses Burdens Ailing Healthcare System," *BusinessWorld*, March 21, 2005.

Espinosa-Robles, Raissa. "As in 1973 the Ball is in the Supreme Court," *Manila Times*, May 3, 2006.

----------. "How They Copied from Marcos's Book," *Manila Times*, May 2, 2006.

----------. "President's Charter Campaign Copies FM's," *Manila Times*, May 1, 2006.

Fair Trade Alliance. *A Nation In Crisis: Agenda for Survival*, Quezon City: Free Trade Alliance, 2004.

Fast, Jonathan and Jim Richardson. *Roots of Dependency*, Quezon City: Foundation for Nationalist Studies, 1987.

Fortuna, Julius F. "China bashing in the upswing," *Manila Times*, September 27, 2007.

Fuller, Ken. *Forcing the Pace: The Partido Komunista ng Pilipinas, from Foundation to Armed Struggle*, Quezon City: UP Press, 2007.

----------. *A Movement Divided: Philippine Communism, 1957-1986*, Quezon City: University of the Philippines Press, 2011.

----------. "On the brink?" *Morning Star*, November 9, 2004.

----------. "Profit-shifting and transfer pricing," *Daily Tribune*, December 21, 2010.

Gatbonton, Juan T. "State's economic role abets corruption," *Manila Times*, February 18, 2008.

Gleeck, Lewis E. *The Third Philippine Republic, 1946-1972*, Quezon City: New Day,

1993.

Gloria, Glenda M. "More to Come," *Newsbreak* online edition, viewed on March 15, 2006.

Go, Miriam Grace A. "Madam Operator?" *Newsbreak* online edition, November 24, 2005.

----------. "In the Shadows," *Newsbreak* online edition, November 24, 2005.

----------. Aries Rufo, Carmela Fonbuena, "Romancing the Military," *Newsbreak* online edition, April 15, 2006.

----------. "Cheats Adjust Style for Monday Polls," *Newsbreak* online edition, May 11, 2007.

Gramsci, Antonio. *Selections from the Prison Notebooks*, London: Lawrence & Wishart, 2005.

Lenman, Bruce P. *The Eclipse of Parliament: Appearance and Reality in British Politics Since 1914*, London: Edward Arnold, 1992.

Lichauco, Alejandro. "The International Economic Order and the Philippine Experience." In Vivencio R. Jose, Vivencio, ed., *Mortgaging the Future: The World Bank and IMF in the Philippines*, Quezon City: Foundation for Nationalist Studies, 1982.

Lucas, Daxim M. "$10.4 billion in Filipino Funds Invested Overseas," *Philippine Daily Inquirer*, February 7, 2006.

McCoy, Alfred. *An Anarchy of Families*, Quezon City: Ateneo de Manila Press, 1995.

----------. *Policing America's Empire: The United States, the Philippines, and the Rise of the Surveillance State*, Quezon City: Ateneo de Manila University Press, 2011

McLintock, Michael. *Instruments of Statecraft: US Guerrilla Warfare, Counterinsurgency and Counterterrorism, 1940-1990*, New York: Pantheon Books, 1992.

Madlos, Jorge. "FPJ Won but Lost in Mindanao," *Daily Tribune*, June 21, 2004.

Majul, Cesar Adib. *The Contemporary Muslim Movement in the Philippines*, Berkeley: Mizan Press, 1985.

Makati Business Club. *Research Report No. 29*, January 2001.

Mangahas, Mahar. "Is 1 hour a week a 'job?" *Philippine Daily Inquirer*, May 25, 2012.

Manuzon, Maricar T., "The Downside of Trade Liberalization," Makati Business Club, *Research Report No. 30*, March 2001.

Marcos, Ferdinand E. *Today's Revolution: Democracy*, Manila: n.p., 1971.

Maxfield, Sylvia and James H. Nolt. "Protectionism and the Internationalization of Capital: US Sponsorship of Import-Substitution Industrialization in the Philippines, Turkey and Argentina," *International Studies Quarterly*, No. 34, 1990.

Moro National Liberation Front. "MILF: 2007 Make or Break for Peace Talks," www.luwaran.com, January 1, 2007.

----------. "MILF Confirms Receiving Gov't Proposal on Territory," www.luwaran.com, November 12, 2006.

----------. "MILF Meets EU, US Embassy Officials," www.luwaran.com, November 17, 2006.

Ofreneo, Rene. "An Employment Strategy for the Next Administration," *Manila Times*, February 26, 2004.

Ordoñez, Elmer A. "Forward." In Tuazon, *Oligarchic Politics...* (see below).

Pomeroy, William. *American Neo-colonialism: Its Emergence in the Philippines and Asia*, New York: International Publishers, 1970.

----------. *An American-Made Tragedy*, New York: International Publishers, 1974).

Quezon, Manuel L. III. "The destruction of the presidency," *Philippine Daily Inquirer*, April 3, 2008.

----------. "Machinery Gave up the Ghost," *Philippine Daily Inquirer*, May 21, 2007.

----------. "A State of Panic," *Philippine Daily Inquirer*, February 26, 2006.

Carlos Quirino. *Apo Lakay*, Makati: Total Book World, 1987.

Quiros, Conrado de. "The Times they are A'Changin'," *Philippine Daily Inquirer*, June 4, 2007.

----------. "Writing on the Wall," *Philippine Daily Inquirer*, April 12, 2007.

Recto, Claro M. *The Recto Reader*, edited by Renato Constantino, Quezon City: Karrel, Inc., 1965.

----------. *Vintage Recto: Memorable Speeches and Writings*, edited by Renato Constantino, Quezon City: Foundation for Nationalist Studies, 1986.

Richardson, Jim. *Komunista: The Genesis of the Philippine Communist Party, 1902-1935*, Quezon City: Ateneo de Manila University Press, 2011.

Rivera, Temario C. *Landlords and Capitalists: Class, Family, and State in Philippine Manufacturing*, Quezon City: UP Center for Integrative and Development Studies and UP Press, in cooperation with Philippine Center for Policy Studies, 1994.

Sarmiento, Edmundo. "Abu Sayyaf: CIA Monster Gone Berserk," *Manila Times*, June 6, 2001.

Schirmer, Daniel B., and Stephen Rosskamm Shalom. *The Philippines Reader*, Quezon City: KEN, Inc., 1987.

Sheehan, D. "More Power to the Powerful," *Far Eastern Economic Review*, February 1, 2001.

Simbulan, Dante C. *The Modern Principalia: The Historical Evolution of the Philippine Ruling Class*, Quezon City: UP Press, 2005.

Smith, Joseph B. *Cold Warrior*, Quezon City: Plaridel Books, 1976.

Strategic Forecasting. "Impeachment May Spark US-Philippine Alliance," Stratfor Global Update, October 17, 2000.

Tatad, Francisco. "Remembering Adrian Cristobal (February 20, 1932-December 22, 2007)," franciscotatd.blogspot.com, December 28, 2007.

Tuazon, Bobby M. *Oligarchic Politics: Elections and the Party-List System in the Philippines*. Quezon City: Center for People Empowerment in Governance, 2007.

Vitug, Marites Danguilan and Glenda M. Gloria. "Failed Enterprise," *Newsbreak* online edition, April 15, 2006.

----------. "Sunday Standoff," *Newsbreak* online edition, April 15, 2006.

Walsh, Bryan. "Dinner with Coup Plotters," *Time*, February 26, 2006.

Wolff, Leon. *Little Brown Brother: How the United States Purchased and Pacified the Philippine Islands at the Century's Turn*, New York: History Book Club, Francis Parkman Prize Edition, 2006.

Yap, Emmanuel Q. "The Ideology of Joint Resolution No. 2,"

www.sundalo.bravehost.com.

Yap, Dr. Joseph. "The boom in FTAs: let prudence reign," reported in *Daily Tribune*, May 6, 2006.

Statements, documents

Asian Development Bank. *Asian Development Outlook*, Manila: ADB, 2006, 2008, 2009, 2010, 2011, 2012.

Department of Labor and Employment, "416 Firms to Renew CBAs," April 19, 2006.

----------. Labor Force Survey, July 2001-July 2011 and January 2004. These data are, however, more accessible at www.census.gov.ph.

----------. "Prospects for Filipinos seeking employment abroad remain bright," January 3, 2008.

Genuine Opposition: "10 Point Program of the Genuine Opposition," 2007.

----------. "Osmena Bares Four-Point Program to Ease Poverty," April 30, 2007.

Government of the Republic of the Philippines. "GRP-MILF draft pact on Bangsamoro homeland," *Philippine Daily Inquirer*, August 4, 2008.

Movement for the Advancement of Nationalism. *Basic Documents and Speeches of Founding Congress*, Manila: MAN, 1967.

National Statistical Coordination Board. "Philippine economy soars to 7.4% GDP growth," January 31, 2008.

----------. "Seven of the country's poorest in 2000 out of the poorest list in 2003," posted on NSCB website June 6, 2006.

Partido ng Manggagawa, "Resign All for Transitional Revolutionary Government," 2005.

Philippine Congress. "Joint Resolution No. 2: The Magna Carta of Social Justice and Economic Freedom, www.sundalo.bravehost.com/Magna Carta of Social Justice and Economic Freedom.htm.

Senate Committee on Government Corporations and Public Enterprises. "Committee

Report on P.S. Res. No. 455," 2007.

Sison, Jose Maria. "A Call for a Broad United Front Against the Estrada Regime," NDF press statement, August 7, 1999.

----------. "Congratulations to the Filipino People, Carry the Struggle Through to the End," NDF press statement, January 20, 2001.

Team Unity. "GO Bets Bribing TU Leaders to Include Them on Sample Ballots," April 30, 2007.

----------. "Team Unity Bets Back Measures Against Global Warming," April 22, 2007.

----------. "Team Unity to Press for LaborCom in Next Congress," April 30, 2007.

----------. "Team Unity Spells out Legislative Program to Create More Jobs, Sustain Growth," April 9, 2007.

Interviews

Pedro Baguisa. Antipolo, Rizal, August 1998 and January 2001.

Renato Constantino Jr.. Manila, August 1998.

Gina de la Cruz. August 2005.

Sonny Melencio. March 2011.

Francisco Nemenzo Jr. January 2008.

Satur Ocampo. March 2011.

Rene Ofreneo. Manila, August 2005.

Columnists

Teodoro Bacani, "Bishop's Move," *Today*.

Ninez Cacho-Olivares, "Frontline," *Daily Tribune*.

Neal Cruz, "As I See It," *Philippine Daily Inquirer*.

Randy David, "Public Lives," *Philippine Daily Inquirer*.

Amando Doronila, "Analysis," *Philippine Daily Inquirer*.

Rod Kapunan, "Backbencher," *Daily Tribune*.

Herman Tiu Laurel, "Die Hard III," *Daily Tribune*.

Alejandro Lichauco, "Analysis," *Daily Tribune*.

Ernesto Maceda, "Mr. Expose," *Daily Tribune*.

Sylvia L. Mayuga, "Mixed Media," *Philippine Daily Inquirer*.

Ducky Paredes, *Malaya*.

Manuel L. Quezon III, "The Long View," *Philippine Daily Inquirer*.

Conrado de Quiros, "There's the Rub," *Philippine Daily Inquirer*.

Demaree J.B. Raval, "Enquiry," *Daily Tribune*.

Rudy Romero, "Zooming In," *Daily Tribune*.

Beth D. Romulo, *Manila Bulletin*.

Ramon Tulfo, "On Target," *Philippine Daily Inquirer*.

News Sources

ABS-CBN News

Agence France Presse

Associated Press

BBC News

Bohol Chronicle

BusinessWorld

Daily Tribune

Far Eastern Economic Review

Financial Times

GMA7

Liberation

Malaya

Manila Bulletin

Manila Times

Newsbreak

New York Times

NBN Television

Office of the Press Secretary, White House, Washington D.C.

Philippine Daily Inquirer

Philippines Free Press

Philippine Star

Reuters

Time

San Francisco Chronicle

Today

Washington Post

Websites

ABS-CBN News: www.abs-cbnnews.com

Asian Development Bank: www.adb.org

Asian Journal Online: www.asianjournal.com

Asia Pulse: www.asiapulse.com

Blueprint for a Viable Philippines: www.geocities.com/blueprint_bentonhall

BusinessWorld: www.bworld.com.ph

Daily Tribune: www.tribune.net.ph

Department of Labor and Employment: www.dole.gov.ph

Francisco Tatad: franciscotatd.blogspot.com

Genuine Opposition: www.genuineopposition.com.

GMA7: www.gmanews.tv, www.gmanetwork.com.

Malaya: www.malaya.com.ph

Manila Bulletin: www.mb.com.ph

Manila Times: www.manilatimes.net

Moro Islamic Liberation Front: www.luwaran.com

National Statistical Coordination Board: www.nscb.gov.ph

Newsbreak: www.pubtrust.org

Philippine census: www.census.gov.ph

Philippine Center for Investigative Journalism: www.pcij.org

Philippine Daily Inquirer: www.inquirer.net

Philippine Headline News Online: www.newsflash.org

Philippine Overseas Employment Administration: www.poea.gov.ph

Philippine Star: www.philstar.com

Social Weather Stations: www.sws.org.ph

Strategic Forecasting: www.stratfor.com

Team Unity: www.teamunity.ph

ABOUT THE AUTHOR

Ken Fuller is a former labor union official from London. He has been resident in the Philippines since 2003, having first visited the country in 1989. His *Radical Aristocrats*, a labor history of London bus workers, was published in London by Lawrence & Wishart in 1985. In 2007 University of the Philippines Press published his *Forcing the Pace: the Partido Komunista ng Pilipinas, from Foundation to Armed Struggle*, a finalist for the National Book Award (Manila Critics' Circle) the following year. This, the first installment of a three-volume history of the Philippine left, was followed by *A Movement Divided: Philippine Communism, 1957-1986* (University of the Philippines Press, 2011) and *The Lost Vision: the Philippine Left, 1986-2010* (University of the Philippines Press, 2015, a finalist for a Manila Critics' Circle National Book Award in 2016).

The Long Crisis: Gloria Macapagal Arroyo and Philippine Underdevelopment was first published as an e-book in April 2013 by Flipside Publishing.

In 2017, Praxis Press (Glasgow) published *Hardboiled Activist: The Work and Politics of Dashiell Hammett*.

Foreigners: A Philippine Satire, Fuller's first novel, was published as an e-book and paperback in 2019.

For several years, Fuller contributed commentaries to *BusinessWorld* and wrote a weekly column for the *Daily Tribune* (both based in Manila), while writing occasional features for progressive publications in London.

www.ingramcontent.com/pod-product-compliance
Lightning Source LLC
Chambersburg PA
CBHW080407290526
45791CB00008BA/2182